PORSCHE
LEGENDS

Inside History of the Epic Cars

Randy Leffingwell
Foreword by Vic Elford
Technical Editor Kerry Morse

Motorbooks International
Publishers & Wholesalers

*This book is dedicated to
the memory of Klaus Reichert*

First published in 1993 by Motorbooks International Publishers & Wholesalers, PO Box 2, 729 Prospect Avenue, Osceola, WI 54020 USA

© Randy Leffingwell, 1993

Motorbooks International books are also available at discounts in bulk quantity for industrial or sales-promotional use. For details write to Special Sales Manager at the Publisher's address

Library of Congress Cataloging-in-Publication Data
Leffingwell, Randy
    Porsche legends: inside history of the epic cars/Randy Leffingwell.
        p.   cm.
    Includes index.
    ISBN 0-87938-710-6
    1. Porsche automobile—History.
I. Title.
TL215.P75L44   1993   92-35443
629.222'2—dc20

On the front cover: Three Legendary Porsches owned by Otis Chandler of Oxnard, California: 1956 1600 Speedster; 1969 917K; and 1988 959 US Sport.

Printed and bound in Hong Kong

Contents

Prologue

**"There is strong shadow
where there is much light."**

*—Fritz Sittig Huschke Baron von Hanstein,
quoting Johann Wolfgang von Goethe,
1773*

Baron von Hanstein quoted Goethe to describe the company and the man, Ferdinand Porsche, for whom he worked for nearly three decades. Interpretation could cover many levels. This book deals with only one.

Porsche the man is Porsche the car. No other automobile firm in business today bears the direct imprint of the family whose name is on the wall. The light that is Porsche has for decades cast strong shadows across the brilliant engineers, designers, and drivers who have been attracted to the light. Technical interests have long overshadowed questions about those who performed the technical accomplishments.

This book will not be a complete history of Porsche. Rather, it will bring to light many of the contributors in the context of their contributions.

Throughout the conversations, these individuals have consistently spoken with mod-esty about their achievements. Individual accomplishment was always submerged within the team. After all respect is paid to Ferry Porsche, if one gives him nothing else, one must further credit him with assembling exceptional teams.

Illuminating individual shadows does not diminish the bright light. It makes it easier for the eyes to see the brilliance.

This book exists only with the total cooperation of Dr. Ing. h.c.F. Porsche Aktiengesellschaft, Stuttgart-Zuffenhausen. Klaus Parr, Peter Schneider, and the late Klaus Reichert encouraged and helped me immeasurably in accomplishing my goals.

At Weissach, Jürgen Barth, Dipl. Ing. Peter Falk, Dipl. Ing. Helmut Flegl, Manfred Jantke, Dipl. Ing. Hans Mezger, and Dipl. Ing. Norbert Singer generously accorded me many hours of their time.

Ferdinand A. Porsche, Porsche Design, Zell am See, Austria; Prof. Ernst Fuhrmann, Teufenbach, Austria; Dipl. Ing. Prof. Helmuth Bott, Pforzheim, Germany; Anatole Lapine, Baden-Baden, Germany; and Rico Steinemann, Russikon, Switzerland, graciously and cautiously reexamined history.

At Zuffenhausen, Christoph Bauer, Norbert Grabotin, Yvonne Keller, Rolf Koch, Olaf Lang, Katrin Müller, Bernd Oergel, Jürgen Pippig, Ina Schlegl, and Rolf Sprenger kindly bent their busy schedules to fit my requests. And at Porsche Cars North America, Ed Triolo and Bob Carlson started this project on its way.

In addition, I warmly thank Nuccio Bertone, Carrozzeria Bertone, Grugliasco, Italy, for the fascinating history of a beautiful Porsche; Ernst and Roland Beutler, Tacchino, Switzerland, who clarified the history of their family firm and Porsche's first production cabriolets; Bernhard Blank, Zurich, for opening his personal records to clear up long-standing mysteries; Fred Hampton, London, who often awoke to find faxes from me and whose enthusiasm and generosity seemed without bounds; Marco Marinello, Zurich, who offered an intense education, orderly direction, profound perspective, and great friendship throughout; David Mills, Tetbury, Gloucestershire, for providing me the English perspective; Mike Smith, Billericay, England, who reminded me of the necessity of chasing details out to the last mile, with numerous stops along the way to ask, ask, and ask again; Paul Ernst Strähle, Schorndorf, Germany, for offering his cars, archives, and his most enlightening films; Kurt Sauter, Gempen, Switzerland, for clarifying a most vexing confusion and creating a most startling little car.

I give special thanks to Helmut Pfeifhofer, Porsche Museum, Gmünd/Karnten, Austria, for his generous cooperation and his willingness to experiment, to open doors and move models.

I give sincere thanks to Ernst Freiberger, owner of the EFA-Automobil-Museum, Amerang, Germany, and to his general manager Jakob Maier for their extraordinary last-minute cooperation.

Porsche owners in America offered never ending enthusiasm for their cars and for this project; to Lynne Bentsen, Denver, Colorado; Otis Chandler, Oxnard, California; Michael Duffey, Emeryville, California; Warren Eads, Novato, California; Ray Fulcher, San Juan Capistrano, California; Frank Gallogly, Englewood, New Jersey; Tim Goodrich, Eugene, Oregon; Victor Ingram, Chatham, New Jersey; William Jackson, Denver, Colorado; Dirk Layer, Vail, Colorado; Jeffrey Lewis, Los Angeles, California; Brenda (Nicki) Morse, Irvine, California; Kent Morgan, Arcadia, California; Bryan Morse, Irvine, California; Dave Morse, Campbell, California; Jim Newton, Canton, Connecticut; John and Ray Paterek, Chatham, New Jersey; Jerry and Liz Reilly, Hardwick, Massachusetts; Richard Roth, Long Island City, New York; Marv Tonkin, Portland, Oregon; Bruce Trenery, Emeryville, California; Roy Walzer, Litchfield, Connecticut; and Joe Wong, Redding, California. Very sincere thanks!

Bo Beringer, General Manager of Laguna Seca Raceway, Monterey, California, gently flexed rules to allow me best light for photography.

Bonnie Summers, Director of Marketing Services, Sears Point International Raceway, Sonoma, California, kept her sense of humor and let us stay late.

To the many drivers, engineers, designers, and journalists who were there, and who willingly reminisced, and introduced me to others, I owe thanks. This book is your story: Jesse Alexander, Santa Barbara, California; Dick Barbour, San Diego, California; Derek Bell, Ft. Lauderdale, Florida; Tony Dron, London; Ted Field, Los Angeles, California; George Follmer, Fallbrook, California; Paul Frère, Vence, France; Bob Garretson, Lancaster, England; Dan and Evi Butz Gurney, Santa Ana, California; Matt Harrington, Los Angeles, California; Jo Hoppen, Detroit, Michigan; John Horseman, Tucson, Arizona; Ghislane Kaes, Zurich, Switzerland; Jean-Pierre Kunstle, Geneva, Switzerland; Jack McAfee, Seal Beach, California; Stirling Moss, London, England; John von Neumann, Palm Springs, California; Bill Oursler, Miami, Florida; Vasek Polak, Hermosa Beach, California; Kurt Sauter, Gempen; Rico Steinemann, Russikon; Paul Ernst Strähle, Schorndorf; Carl Thompson, Hermosa Beach, California; Bob Tronolone, Burbank, California; Dale von Trebra, Santa Paula, California; Betty Jo Turner, Atlanta, Georgia; and Heini Walter, Zurich, Switzerland.

Thanks also to John Clinard, Ford Motor Company, and Helen Hutchings, Buick Motor Division, General Motors, for their generous help with transportation throughout Europe.

My special friends Jim and Jilla Mollitt, London, opened their hearts, homes, and private phone books. They will never know how great was their contribution.

Vic Elford won my admiration from the first endurance race I watched in France in 1968. His historical contribution is only exceeded by his wonderful Foreword. I am honored.

To Kerry Morse, Tustin, California. "People like you are an influence to people like me."

Randy Leffingwell
Los Angeles, California

Foreword

By Vic Elford

In 1965, a plump, balding hotel owner from Stuttgart drove what in those days looked like a racing car to an astounding 2nd place finish in the Monte Carlo Rally.

Eugene Böhringer and the 904GTS had launched Porsche into a new era of motor sports.

By the middle of the following year, disillusioned by the cars I was driving, I approached Huschke von Hanstein about the possibility of a rally program with the new 911. We had a delightful lunch beside the pool of the Hotel Martinez in Cannes after the Coupe des Alpes and yet another failure in my Ford. He told me that Porsche did not really have a rally program as rallying was considered rather a poor relation to circuit racing in Stuttgart. But he'd see what he could do.

A few weeks later, he called me and said that he had approval for me to drive a 911 in the Tour de Corse. One car. One rally. No practice car, I would have to practice in a rental car (a Simca Aronde as it turned out). And no guarantees for the future.

The mechanics arrived in Corsica with a van and the rally car on a trailer behind. When I looked in the van I found only spare wheels and tires. Asking Huschke when the spare parts would arrive elicited the reply that "there are no spares. Porsches don't break!"

I spent the rally learning to drive a Porsche—very different from the front-engined cars I was used to—and was rewarded with 3rd place overall. Huschke was over the moon, and immediately got Stuttgart to agree to a full scale effort for the Monte Carlo Rally two months later. Still no contract, just one rally at a time if I was prepared to take the risk.

For me there was no risk. I had at last found the fastest rally car in the world and he was right—it didn't break. In fact, no production-based 911 that I drove ever broke!

The rest is history. We led the Monte all the way till the last special stage when I got caught with the wrong tires and finished 3rd. But we went on to win three other rallies and the European championship. Huschke incorporated me into the circuit racing team and arranged for the British importer to run a car for me in the British Touring Car championship, which I also won.

That first year with Porsche cemented a bond with Huschke that is still as strong today. At the same time was born a trust and respect for the engineers under the leadership of Ferdinand Piëch and an absolute and total faith in every Porsche I ever drove. From my first trip down the Mulsanne straight at about 175mph in a 906 in 1967 to the 225mph in the first 917 in 1969. From that almost undrivable monster to the fabulous 917 Langheck the following year that I could drive flat out through the Mulsanne kink, at night, in the rain, at almost 245mph!

In 1968 we went back to Monte Carlo and the Porsche juggernaut was about to make itself felt worldwide. We won the rally with a one-two finish to start an era which would see a 911 win virtually every important rally in the world. A week later I led two other 907s across the finish line at Daytona to herald what would be almost two decades of Porsche domination of sports car racing.

CHAPTER 1

1949 Gmünd Coupe

From Humble Beginnings

Coupes were built from mid-1948 through 1951, first in Gmünd, Austria, and then in Zuffenhausen after the firm returned to Germany. Total production seems to be uncertain. Chassis numbers as high as 58 have been found. This car, number 17, was built in 1949.

In the middle of the village, on the northwest side of the commercial square, there used to be a public scale. It existed for the farmers to weigh their cattle before auctions. But on certain week days, it was a magnet for the young boys in the Hauptschule, barely 50 meters away.

Once in a while, the engineers working for the sports car company outside town came calling. Their arrival worked the same effect as the Pied Piper of Hamlyn. Wilhelm Hild, the chief engineer, or Erwin Komenda, the chief designer, were Pied Pipers of Gmünd, and what they drove was a bare chassis, straight from its birthplace, an old sawmill. They snarled into the village, through the narrow archway beneath the clock tower of the Gasthof Prunner, heading to the scale to weigh their work. They came from the Northwest, along the narrow road that led through fields from Porsche Konstruktionen Ges.m.b.H. School classes simply stopped.

About 2km due north of the scale (or about 160km due south of Salzburg), was the birthplace of Porsche cars. The village of Gmünd is located in the Austrian state of Karnten, Carinthia in English.

Encircling the Gasthof Prunner at the southwest end and the Hauptschule—now a regional high school but formerly the *neue schloss Lodrun*, Lodrun Castle, on the northeast end—is the interrupted remnant of a walled city. Gates could be closed in either structure. It was only due to village expansion in more peaceful times that the wall that embraced the Pfarrkirche—the parish church, erected and consecrated in 1339 barely 500 meters from the old scales—no longer continues far enough around to include the Pension Prunner, erected and opened sometime in the 1940s, not quite 200 meters in the other direction.

Between the Gasthof and the Hauptschule, there are now eight cafes, six clothing stores, four hotels, three banks, two antiques stores, two book stores, two pharmacies, and one grocery. This is a town where the houses have names: Villa Sonnfried, Arien Ein.

In this village, the buildings have religious art on their facades. The Virgin Mary cradling the baby Jesus, borne on a sliver of the moon and attended by three wingedbaby cherubim, used to look out over dairy cows or engineer Karl Rabe and founder's son Ferdinand Porsche as they weighed their work on the public scales in Gmünd.

The Virgin Mary is still there; the scale is long gone. And so is Porsche.

But by 1944, the design firm had come back home to Austria.

In an effort to save something in the chaos of the war's end, the company had divided its operation into three parts. The headquarters stayed in Stuttgart, Germany, where it had been located since December 1, 1930, when Professor Ferdinand Porsche established his own engineering firm. Success and prosperity led to a move to nearby Zuffenhausen, Germany, in June 1938 and expansion to 176 employees dedicated to the activities of designing, testing, and assembling automobiles.

The Volkswagen had been designed there. Several other projects commissioned by the government, including tanks and armored weapons, had grown out of the facilities as well. But the German military

At the Geneva Auto Show in 1949, Porsche first showed its Gmünd coupe—with a sunroof—at right, and the Beutler-built cabriolet. Posed for the picture, from left to right, were: G. Dufaux, a Geneva Salon official, Heinrich Kunz, Porsche's first salesman, Ferry Porsche, Bernhard Blank, the sole distributor, Louise Piëch, and Ernst Schoch, director of Blank's various companies. Marco Marinello archives. Right, the replica holzmodel for the Gmünd coupe was constructed in ash, as was the original. Helmut Pfeifhofer commissioned the wood form for display in his museum in Gmünd. An unrestored Gmünd coupe shows the results of original panelbeater Friedrich Weber's labors.

command could not ensure the safety of Porsche during Allied bombing raids in 1943 and early 1944. And after bombs struck its factory that April, the family relocated to Austria. Storage was located in a former flying school in the family's hometown of Zell am See, Austria. Production was set up in a sawmill in Gmünd. When the war ended, Gmünd was held by British troops. Ferdinand Porsche's son, Ferry, moved to Gmünd.

Engineering and development work done for the German government before the war came back to haunt Ferdinand Porsche and his family after the peace. All the men in the family were arrested in late July 1945, and questioned about their wartime activities. Eventually it became clear the Porsche family were engineers, not warriors, and they were released. In early November, they all returned to Zell am See.

Two weeks later, the nightmare returned too. Ferry Porsche went to meet with French officials in Baden-Baden, Germany, to discuss establishing Volkswagen in France. The French insisted on speaking directly with the Professor. After nearly a month of discussions to work out the details for the meeting, the French arrested him as a war criminal. His work on tanks and jeeps for Hitler, and his development of the People's Car had little to do with the arrest. Instead, he was accused of acts of sabotage against Peugeot, and he was also accused—by Peugeot—of using French workers as forced laborers at his factory in Stuttgart.

Ironically, the French Communist Party was sincerely interested in producing the Volkswagen in France, and Marcel Paul, France's Minister for Industry was a Party member. Despite this, Porsche was forced to perform some development work on a new Renault 4CV. Then he was taken to Dijon and imprisoned.

Soon, political changes in France accompanied changes at Peugeot and new management, more familiar with the work and philosophy of Ferdinand Porsche, testified in his behalf. In mid-1947, Porsche was ordered to pay 1 million French francs bail for himself and his brother-in-law, lawyer Anton Piëch, to ensure their release.

All questions about young Ferry Porsche had been satisfied and after several false starts, the Professor's son returned to Austria in 1946. Other bits of life were returning to normal throughout Europe and among them was an interest in motor racing. An Italian industrialist, Piero Dusio, approached Ferry Porsche to commission the design of a new Formula 1 Grand Prix car. Dusio's own interests included a car company, Cisitalia, which had begun to produce small sports cars. But Dusio knew the reputation of the Porsche's engineering from before the war through his friendship with Karl Abarth (who changed his name to Carlo when he moved to Italy from Austria), and Tazio Nuvolari, who had driven Porsche-designed Mercedes-Benz racers.

Ferry Porsche's sister, Louise Piëch, had continued operating the Gmünd plant while her father, husband, and brother were in various internments. By late summer 1946, her successful operation employed nearly 200 workers. With Gmünd still under British supervision, Karl Rabe had been appointed Porsche manager.

After the war, travel was difficult, with French, English, or American forces supervising regions of each of the formerly unified nations. Business meetings and contract agreements and transfers of funds were extremely cumbersome. But one contract was signed. Porsche would design and produce a race car for Dusio. Other projects would follow, a sports car, a farm tractor. A payment schedule was arranged and Porsche's first order of business was to transfer funds from Dusio to Gmünd to Dijon.

The fifteen-month imprisonment had been hard on the 70-year-old professor. There had been no heat and little human contact in prison and when Ferdinand Porsche returned to Gmünd, he was no longer the same forceful, dynamic innovator he had been in Stuttgart before the war.

Ferry Porsche, now actively in charge of the firm sharing his and his father's name, set out soon after the Dusio contract to fulfill the ambitions he shared with his father as well: a Porsche sports car. A design from before the war called for mostly Volkswagen parts but with a much lower, wider, open body. With a large supply of the VW Kübelwagen in the British zone, parts were not difficult to locate. And with the large staff, it was not long before the Porsche Typ 356 was roadworthy.

As word spread that the Porsche family was in business in Gmünd, the extended "family" of engineers and designers and managers found their way to the Carinthian village. Body designer Erwin Komenda, "minister of finance" Hans Kern, Ferdinand Porsche's personal secretary Ghislane Kaes, engine designer Franz Reimspiess, aerodynamicist and human-computer Josef Mickl—they all drifted back to Porsche and picked up nearly where their work in Stuttgart had been interrupted.

Another talent was drawn to Gmünd, back to Porsche. Friedrich Weber had apprenticed at Austro-Daimler in 1922 when Ferdinand Porsche was chief of engineering. Porsche had advised Weber to learn coachbuilding, advice that Weber fol-

lowed. Arriving in Gmünd as a master craftsman, he was hired to pound the aluminum panels of the first 356 into Komenda's distinctive shape.

While Weber hammered, Ferry Porsche and one or another of his engineers ran the bare chassis up the old route 331, north from Gmünd to the Katschberg. The 10km run, from Rennweg up to Katschberg Höhe, the summit, and down to St. Michael in Lungau, provided an excellent hillclimb and descent test for chassis, drivetrain, and brakes. The south face, these days flattened out to merely a 17 percent grade, used to be nearly 30 percent in 1948. A round trip from Gmünd to St. Michael, 52km, would tell the engineers a great deal.

Stopping at Gmünd's municipal scale after a run might have also indicated the weight lost from driver and passenger sweat!

At the same time that the roadster was being completed, plans were progressing for the coupe versions. The first car, open, with its mid-engine, was impractical in several ways as a production-based automobile. Interior storage was severely limited by the tubular frame configuration. For the coupe, the basic Volkswagen formula—a floorpan with the engine located behind the rear axle—was resurrected. Friedrich Weber was put to work again hammering closed coupe bodies. After his prototype development experience, he began to produce a coupe body each week. But unfortunately, after a week of shaping aluminum

Porsche's first power was Volkswagen power, above left. The engine of preference was the 1131cc that produced 40hp at 4200rpm. The engine allowed Porsches to race in the popular 1.1 liter classes. Above, a test run with the 356/2 chassis occassionally ended up at the Gmünd municipal scale to check the weight of the engineers' work— and brought the villagers out to see. Porsche Werke

13

over a wooden form, Weber went out on a bender himself; the completion of each body was followed like clockwork by a brief binge. Still, his workmanship was generally good and even his eccentricity was reliable.

The basic VW engine, 1131cc, was installed, along with the VW suspension, gearbox, brakes, and running gear. While the roadster had weighed barely 609kg (1,340lb), the coupes were closer to 718kg (1,580lb), and the need for better brakes was obvious. But obtaining parts—even raw materials—had become difficult. And not only because Gmünd was 13km away from the nearest railway.

Europe was still under the control of postwar organization. The import and export of any industrial manufacturing pieces raised eyebrows between one sector and the next. While Ferry Porsche was free to travel in pursuit of work contracts and distributors, his father was still limited to living in Kitzbühl in the French zone, although he could visit Gmünd.

The Swiss, neutral through the war, were free to travel anywhere. And shortly after Ferry Porsche arrived in Gmünd, a Zurich man with lofty ambitions contacted Porsche in 1946 about building a car. Richard Von Senger was a licensed architect who had interests in other things as well, among them an advertising agency bearing his name. von Senger had a client for several of his services, Bernhard Blank, owner of Zurich's Hotel Europe. Blank was also an auto enthusiast and was Switzerland's agent for Preston Tucker's automobiles.

Von Senger convinced Blank to loan him

50,000 Swiss francs, slightly more than $16,000 at the time, without divulging its intended use. Then von Senger turned around and gave it to Dr. Anton Piëch as an investment. He sought to establish himself as the exclusive Porsche distributor and preferred to keep the proceeds of any success for himself.

With that money, Piëch transferred an order for ten coupes to Gmünd on behalf of the architect. Von Senger even orchestrated the sale of the first roadster, 356-001, to a Swiss, which provided a much-needed infusion of some 7,000 Swiss francs into the Gmünd accounts. But fate was not on von Senger's side.

In Zurich, the Bahnhofstrasse was the main financial street, and one day late in the summer of 1948, Blank ran into von Senger and a stranger, dressed unmistakably in the characteristic clothing of the Austrians—a medium green suit with knickers pants and a military-style jacket with a single epaulet. Blank greeted von Senger who did not introduce the stranger, Dr. Anton Piëch.

Within minutes, Piëch understood that von Senger's money had come from Blank. And within minutes more, von Senger's involvement ended. While the first ten cars were ordered by Richard von Senger, they were imported by Bernhard Blank.

Toward autumn, Blank arranged for Ernst and Fritz Beutler to produce a prototype and then five production cabriolets. Beutler, among more than a half dozen custom carrosseries in Switzerland, were well regarded and were the first to express interest in the assignment.

When Blank reserved space at the Geneva Auto Show to be held in March 1949, he registered as the sole distributor. And the Porsche stand inside featured a Beutler-bodied cabriolet as well as a Gmünd coupe with a sunroof. Outside, another Gmünd coupe, in green, stood by as a demonstrator. Blank's philosophy matched Porsche's: first comes the open car, then offer a hardtop, and finally, produce a closed car. And for countries like Switzerland and Germany, that consideration was essential. For the "sports" drivers, the open car was appealing. But winter brought other realities.

Bernhard Blank, now 89, recalled that "I didn't like to drive the bloody things, but they were interesting. And we could make some money!" One car was sold from the show, to a woman. "We got a lot of attention," he recalled, but apparently little else. Even when Blank hired a salesman, Heinrich Künz, the most effective sales technique was to send Künz with the cars to call upon all of Blank's wealthy friends.

Although Blank was enthusiastic, he was still practical. Production at Gmünd was insufficient and quality standards were inconsistent. When Blank received one of his Geneva show cars, he was quite concerned over the rippled aluminum and uneven paint. He had Künz drive the car direct to an aircraft manufacturer experienced with aluminum. Pilatus, near Lucerne, completely refinished the green coupe. Künz arrived outside the Geneva Salon the morning the show opened.

Pilatus declined to do more cars due to its own production requirements, but this did point out to Porsche the need to line up other facilities.

When Ernst Beutler was asked to produce additional cabriolets after his first six, he too excused himself. He was not interested in expanding his business so much for such an uncertain venture. Yet Beutler recalled that when Ferry Porsche and Ghislane Kaes came to see his prototype, he put them on a train bound for Lucerne, not one returning to Austria.

Kaes himself explained that they were not looking to have the cars produced in Switzerland...exclusively. It was simply that with so much of the raw material originating in Switzerland—instruments, lights, wiring, and even the raw aluminum for Friedrich Weber's hammer, Kaes said it would be short sighted not to examine the possibilities near to the resources.

From the first to the last Gmünd coupe was a period of nearly three and a half years. Bernhard Blank had not enough customers. And Porsche had neither enough money or capacity to build faster. Yet the foundation was set.

A new sports car name was introduced. Interest was piqued.

CHAPTER 2

1951 356 Cabriolet RHD

Porsche Crosses the Channel

Quarter windows gone and twin trim pieces no longer marking the nose, this was a Reutter Karosserie cabriolet, the first right-hand-drive model imported to England.

On September 17, 1948, even before Porsche cars from Austria first were shown in Geneva, Porsche went to work for Volkswagen in Wolfsburg, Germany. Again.

Currency in Germany had stabilized and Ferdinand Porsche's largest design and engineering client before the War had contracted with the firm for the same services afterwards. This began a gradual return to Germany. Several Porsche staff engineers were installed in Wolfsburg to work with VW and much of the Gmünd operation relocated into Salzburg.

The Salzburg operation quickly expanded. Porsche-Salzburg, under the guidance of Anton and Louise Piëch, included the distribution of VW cars in late spring 1949. But sales of Porsche cars—approximately forty-three Gmünd coupes and eight cabriolets in 1949 and 1950—most all of which were sold in Austria and Switzerland—had not yet generated any profit to the sports car company.

Klagenfurth, Austria, was controlled by the American forces. There, they hoarded War materiel taken from northern Italy, Yugoslavia, and Germany. It was a challenge for Porsche in Gmünd to get away from the GIs each of the VW Kübelwagen engines and gearboxes it needed to build its coupes and cabriolets.

Professor Porsche was freed to resume active life and regained his freedom of travel about the same time his daughter and son-in-law opened the Salzburg operation in 1949. The company's real goal was to return to its shops and studios in suburban Stuttgart. The space there, and the larger resource of trained workers, could only benefit the ailing firm. Encouraged by negotiations with Stuttgart's Lord Mayor Arnulf Klett and Ferry Porsche's childhood friend, Albert Prinzing, the firm moved another small group of engineers back to Stuttgart in fall 1949.

Planning to relocate car production as well, local Stuttgart firms were asked to submit bids. Reutter Karosserie, having continued to produce trolley cars and repair bodywork on private cars during the war, still had most of its skilled employees. In addition, its shops in Zuffenhausen were nearly adjacent to Porsche's own. Full of confidence in the future, Porsche ordered 500 car bodies from Reutter in November 1949. Thus burdened, Albert Prinzing and a colleague then set off from Stuttgart with a Gmünd coupe and a Beutler cabriolet to sell more like them to the largest VW dealers in Germany. They received many orders, with each dealer paying in advance for one. With that revenue and the income from VW, Porsche was back in business.

Original arrangements for Porsche to return to its own shops—still occupied by the US Army as a motor pool—were thwarted with the outbreak of the Korean War in June 1950. It was to be another two years that Porsche's designers worked out of the family's nearby villa and a cramped temporary bunker building. But the first Zuffenhausen car, a pale gray coupe, was completed in the spring 1950. The following October, the Professor drove with Ghislane Kaes to Paris in the gray coupe to display it at the motor show.

Bernhard Blank in Zurich had become sole distributor for the world. In March 1950, he tried international promotion again with the Geneva Show. Having so few sales,

At the 1951 Earl's Court Auto Show in London, Porsche premiered its first export cabriolet. David Mills archives. Below, The first importer saw something in the sporty German cars and, despite English feelings after the war, brought in several additional cars after this one premiered the marque at Earl's Court Motor Show in 1951. Far top, by 1951, instrumentation included a tachometer. As the first UK-export car, the cabriolet featured a speedometer in miles per hour, and a push-button radio manufactured by Telefunken. Far left, interior lighting was modest; power came from a 6 volt system. The rearview mirror was adjustable and could be swung around to provide a clear view over the folded top. Far right, Volkswagen power was still Porsche's propulsion. This, the Typ 506, still rated 40hp even with slightly larger, model 32 PBI Solex carburetors than the Gmünd coupes used.

however, he chose not to make the investment a third time. Soon after Blank decided against the Geneva expenses, in November 1950, Professor Ferdinand Porsche suffered a stroke at age 75. He died in January 1951.

On March 5, barely two months after Porsche's death and only a few days before the 1951 Geneva Salon was to open, French racer Auguste Veuillet took his own Gmünd coupe to the Monthléry circuit and ran several timed laps at 143.84km/h (89.9mph). The speed generated publicity. Blank, not part of the official show, hurriedly leased a vacant showroom just across the street. He hired people to plaster the area with signs, and he displayed the coupes and cabriolets in their own exclusive showroom.

The Porsche firm was not happy. But as Blank explained years later, "Until the record run, we didn't have much success and so I didn't think it worth the time and money to sign up for March 1951, in September 1950. Now, at least, we had something!"

Yet this may have been too late for Blank. The Geneva Show catalogs for 1949 and 1950 reported the significant data: Konstruktion GmB Porsche/Gmünd; Sales

B.Blank/Zurich. Without space in the 1951 show, there was no Porsche entry in the book. Yet Veuillet's firm, SonAuto, showed Porsches in Paris. Cars were displayed in Brussels and Turin. Max Hoffman, a Viennese living in New York City, with a love of European cars and a clear sense of America's growing appetites, had Porsches in his Park Avenue showroom by late 1950. He had already begun to set up distributors in the West. And Charles Meisl, a perceptive sales manager with Connaught Engineering in England, showed Porsche's first right-hand-drive coupe and cabriolet at the Earl's Court Motor Show.

By March 1952, when Porsche once again displayed at Geneva, the firm had been back in Stuttgart more than two years. Reutter in Zuffenhausen was doing Porsche's coachwork. The first Stuttgart-built Porsche was nearly two years old.

Nineteen months after Professor Ferdinand Porsche died, his son-in-law and friend, Dr. Anton Piëch, died of a heart attack, in August 1952. But by this time, the firm was well on its way.

Porsche cars were distributed throughout Europe and the United Kingdom. New cars were even delivered to South Africa, and a solid enthusiast market was well established in the United States. Racing and international rallying had returned the enthusiast world to normal. And the superior—if initially challenging—handling, as well as their quality and durability of construction, had become well known. Porsche listened to its customers and as a result, new customers from near and far began to seek out the firm.

Its Swiss importer, registered since mid-1951—now no longer the worldwide distributor but simply one of many throughout the world—was Auto und Motore AG, AMAG. Bernhard Blank was out.

Just as it was all finally beginning, as distribution networks were finally setting up throughout the world hungry for—and interested in—sports cars, the man who helped it all begin and who funded the first days of Porsche could no longer sell a Porsche. There was now no shortage of people waiting to become involved.

CHAPTER 3

1952 America Roadster

America's Marketing Power

Across the Atlantic Ocean, a hungry market developed, and Max Hoffman in New York understood the appetite. The hungriest was John von Neumann, a West Coast enthusiast who wanted a lightweight roadster to race—and sell—in America.

In Stuttgart, a young businessman named Heinrich Sauter commissioned Hans Klenk Karosserie to build a steel-bodied open car during the winter of 1950. Sauter was an enthusiastic rally participant, and asked Klenk to fit the car with front-opening—"suicide"—doors to give his navigator a running advantage at the rally check points.

The Klenk-built Sauter roadster weighed 590kg (1,298lb). It used a 1500cc engine, bored-out and tuned by another firm. Sauter not only rallied with the car but also raced it at Nürburgring's Eifelrennen shortly after he picked it up. Its most ambitious contest was the Liège-Rome-Liège rally in August, a 6,000km 100-hour event. But Sauter did not finish.

In 1952, the car was bought by the Porsche factory and was used as a kind of development mule for a short time. It ran the new Typ 528 engine, the 1500 Super. This was the first engine to use a new cam design by a recent hire, the young Viennese engineer named Ernst Fuhrmann. Front brake development work was done on the Sauter car as well.

François Picard, who had won his class in the 1951 Tour de France in an 1100cc coupe, bought the Sauter car and named it *le petit tank* but the tank did no better for the Frenchman than it had for the German. It went back to Stuttgart and languished in the shadow of Frankfurt VW dealer and racer Walter Glöckler's more successful Porsche-based racers.

In time for the 1953 racing season, the Sauter found its way to California and into the hands of Stan Mullin. By the time Mullin acquired the car, although it clearly resembled the brand new America Roadsters that others were racing, it was two years old—two years obsolete—and never finishing with any distinguished results.

In late 1950, Karl Rabe and Erwin Komenda had completed designs for a low-window-sill cabriolet, design Typ 540, a roadster destined for a growing market in America, a market created and encouraged by Max Hoffman. This design continued the natural evolution from Porsche's first Gmünd cars and from the subsequent six roadsters built by Beutler Karosserie; it also bore more than a passing resemblance to the Sauter car.

It is likely Hoffman saw the Sauter during one of his visits to Stuttgart to lobby for a roadster. Hoffman liked the car but he wanted changes: rear-opening doors were safer (and less of an embarrassment for women in skirts), and an aluminum body was lighter. His revisions led to the America Roadster.

With Porsche located in Stuttgart by that time, and all of Reutter Karosserie's capacity utilized with regular production, outside help was needed to complete Hoffman's special request. Porsche was drawn to Gläser Karosserie.

Heinrich Gläser Karosserie had been founded in Dresden in 1864 as a true coachbuilding firm. When Gläser died in 1898, his son-in-law, Emil Heuer, assumed control. Later, Emil's son, Erich, was business manager until World War II. Just before the end of the war—before Soviet formation of East Germany—Heuer moved a small portion of the firm to what would become West Germany, finally settling in Wieden-Ullersricht, near Nürnberg. By 1950, the company was back in business.

Gläser's specialty had been cabriolets

The America Roadster was built in two series, with bodies first by Glaser and then by Drauz. The traditional Komenda shape from Gmünd was surely influenced by Jaguar's XK120 and Ferrari's Barchetta. Below, for Max Hoffman, the America Roadster was imported with full interior appointments, now including a clock on the instrument panel. The price was luxurious too, $4,600 in 1952.

starting just after the turn of the century when it did its first automobiles. And it was with this expertise that Heuer approached Porsche, looking for work. Porsche contracted with Heuer's firm to build 250 standard cabriolets as well as sixteen special roadster bodies. But production ended there. While Gläser-Heuer made money off its auto repair business and other interests, coach-building was its loss-leader.

It could only have been a labor of love for Erich Heuer as it bankrupted him in December 1952. Transportation costs—of raw materials to Nürnberg and finished bodies back to Zuffenhausen—as well as the larger staff needed to accommodate Porsche's seasonal orders, were the reasons said to have finished the firm. When the wolves came to Heuer's doors in November, several cabriolets and two Roadsters were incomplete. Production time, bid by Heuer at 500 hours per car, had taken 640. Cars were late and Heuer was reportedly losing almost 1,600 DM on each Roadster.

Three series of the America Roadster were built, the first most visibly significant due to its single grille on the rear deck; later versions had twin grilles. Hoffman and his West Coast agent John von Neumann were interested in racing cars, so the first single-

grille cars were stripped of all luxury.

But von Neumann, racing one of the cars himself, discovered a flaw.

"There was one big problem with those cars," von Neumann recalled. "The aerodynamics!

"As Mr. Porsche once said to me about the air-cooled engine, 'The problem is not getting cool air to the engine, it's getting the hot air *away*....'

"Huschke von Hanstein, Porsche's baronnial jack of all trades, came to California for a visit. Von Hanstein had raced himself but at that point he was sort of Ferry Porsche's racing director, salesman, public relations man. And he, Jack McAfee, and I went up to Willow Springs. Trying the first Roadsters out. We found that after a few laps they lost power.

"Think about the interpretation: getting the hot air away," von Neumann explained. "And those Roadsters had a different shape in the back from the 356s. So they were recirculating the hot air from the engine. After so many laps, they were overheating so much they didn't have any power.

"We would have to change the back end. So we just made street cars out of them. That's why *my* other cars came upholstered. But my Roadster was fine."

Von Neumann's own car came outside

In early tests, the back end of the Glaser cars adversely affected engine cooling. By the time von Neumann's Drauz-bodied roadsters got into the hands of Jack McAfee, the stubbier back end improved cooling. Left, Jack McAfee in John von Neumann's competition roadster, the America Roadster, leads a Porsche 356 around the haybales at Palm Springs in early 1953. Warren Eads archives

Cars shipped to von Neumann were stripped down. But he removed front and rear bumpers and also cut the vents that fed air to the hard-working front brakes, funneled to the drums by backing plates made of old California license plates. Below, the Typ 528 engine, a 1498cc engine with Solex 40mm carburetors, produced 70hp at 5000rpm.

the number sequence, the seventeenth of sixteen cars built, with a body by Drauz. Von Neumann described it: "A prototype, unpainted, shipped to me. I said, 'Don't paint it. I'm going to modify it anyway. Ship it to me in primer. Don't put upholstery in because I going to rip it out. I want a car to race to win.'

"Jack McAfee was my dealer," von Neumann said. "I got him the car. To race."

Jack McAfee, the sprint car driver? In a Porsche?

"Right after the war," McAfee explained, filling in a little bit of history, "professional 'roadster' racing started out in a big way! I had a real famous race car, a three-quarter sprint car, raced by Babe Stapp. It was a stretched midget, with an 85 inches wheelbase. And I had some friends who offered to put together an engine. We ran every weekend somewhere. At Oakland, they had a five-eighths mile, banked. We ran the mile dirt at Sacramento."

McAfee, an extremely modest and self-effacing man, attributed much of his early success to luck and the hard work of others.

"I was real fortunate. I was always a reasonable driver, but this transition into professional driving...I was lucky that this car handled perfectly. I just learned to charge into the corners, toss the back end out and corner it on the gas. I just fell into it, because with that little car, I could do the number and run with the guys in front."

McAfee laughed self-consciously as he talked about regularly finishing in front of "the guys in front." At the time, he was working for Ernie McAfee—a friend, not a relative—who had a sports car shop on Cahuenga Boulevard in Hollywood. Jack's ambition was Indianapolis. Cars that turned left were his love even as he worked on cars that could turn right too.

A wealthy customer, John Edgar, was importing superchargers and had built a supercharged MG TC, which his regular driver consistently blew up. One weekend Ernie asked Jack to fill in. Jack said he would only do it "to finish." He admired and respected Edgar and felt the man deserved a race finish rather than another glorious attempt and another broken engine.

Edgar also imported Siatas and owned a Jaguar, so the next weekend at Palm Springs, Jack McAfee drove Edgar's Siata, Jaguar, and MG to finish in each race.

In 1st place.

"This really meant very little to me," McAfee laughed about it decades later. "I was a sprinter. I was looking at Indy. At Babe Stapp and myself and this whole crew." McAfee finished the races with his eye still over his shoulder on Indianapolis. He left Palm Springs to head home to Hollywood long before the victory banquet.

The next day, Ernie arrived, his arms full of Edgar's trophies. He carried something else as well: an offer. Edgar wanted McAfee to drive full time for him. He was buying a Ferrari, and Edgar's friend, Tony Parravano, was also getting one and wanted a driver for the Mexican Carrera.

John von Neumann and his wife Eleanor had opened their own shop on Cahuenga Boulevard, just a couple blocks from Ernie McAfee. Von Neumann imported Porsches from far off New York City, picking them up at Hoffman's Park Avenue showroom, disconnecting the speedometers, and driving them across country. These cars intrigued Edgar, Parravano, and most of all, Jack McAfee.

"That America Roadster," said McAfee, as he reappraised the car, "it was the beginning of the competition car for Porsche. All aluminum. Thing only weighed about 1,300 pounds (590kg). And it had the first set of real brakes on a car that I ever drove!

"Drum brakes....I don't care what size they were. Nothing worked. Initially all the stuff running around was English," McAfee explained. "It had been developed years before. Small drums. Couldn't get any air into them or out. You had no brakes on anything. The Ferrari was bad, they had aluminum. But I think their metallurgy was bad because they just expanded like crazy.

"No brakes on anything until this Porsche came along. And with the minimum weight of that roadster, you had brakes. You could out-brake anything on the road with that car. And out-handle!"

Out-handle? The early Porsches? With swing axles?

"I adapted to it. Because I ran the sprinters so long and throwing the car—using the car to scrape off the speed," McAfee grinned broadly. "I got right into this Porsche thing real easy where everybody else had a problem.

"The thing that upset everybody was the swinging axle suspension in the rear. When you came off the gas, the rear just got light in back. It was very scary. 'Jeez! I lost it!' That's what you'd think. 'I lost it!'

"And a lot of guys didn't know what to do. But boy, you could just drive the hell out of it....

"You could dive into a corner and at the right moment, come off the gas. Just a little flick with the wheel and you set it up so the back end is doing the steering. You're on the line out of the corner before everybody. Just lift quick, the back moves over and it's back down on the gas. It takes some courage but you don't even use the brakes....

"Vasek Polak used to get all over me because I never used the brakes." McAfee laughed at the memory of his former mechanic scolding him. "I'd run through

As shipped: no clock, no ashtray or lighter, no glovebox cover. Not even carpets. Door handles, rear reflecters, and license-plate lights were eliminated. John von Neumann told Hoffman he'd strip those things out anyway to lighten the car for racing.

the whole season. He'd tear off the wheels looking at the brakes and there's nothing wrong with them. We ran a whole season on the same shoes."

McAfee grinned like a young school boy finally confessing how he'd gotten away with something for all these years. He quit racing in the early 1960s to raise his family and run his businesses, Jack McAfee Volkswagen-Porsche. He got out of that years ago as well. His race driving abilities had nothing on his marketing and business sense.

McAfee reflected on the car a moment. "I think, years later now, that the Roadster America, this little Johnny von Neumann special, was a prototype really for the Speedster. Von Neumann, through Hoffman, complained that they needed something for a price for the American market. I think these last America Roadsters were a mockup for the Speedster.

"And it was great. Two things came out of it," McAfee explained. "One: they decided they could produce the Speedster, with its steel body and windshield wipers and the whole thing. And two: they recognized that winning races was a good way to advertise its cars."

While he had referred to other types of cars, he had summed it all up earlier in an unintended play on words: "Right after the war, professional 'Roadster' racing started out in a big way."

Jack McAfee was right out in front, running ahead of the guys out in front. But Porsche understood that to remain in front, in races and sales, in Europe and now in America, more power was needed.

Jack McAfee:
"I think, years later now, that the Roadster America, this little Johnny von Neumann special, was a prototype really for the Speedster."

CHAPTER 4

1955 Carrera GS 1959 GS-GT

"Years Ahead In Engineering; Miles Ahead On The Road"

The engine came out of the Spyder, the name came out of Mexico. Throughout the last half of the 1950s, the Carrera coupe came out of Stuttgart, and taught racers and spectators that, on banked turns or flat, in any language, Porsche meant winner. Purchased new by Richard Steed, an amateur racer, he reportedly only acquired the car to race against his friend, Stirling Moss. Competing against Moss in the mid-1950s, Steed's finishing results can only be guessed.

"Look," Ernst Fuhrmann said, turning in his chair, "that was the first engine I ever designed. I had no other experience at all!"

He leaned forward, laughing quietly. For nearly 40 years, his engine, the Carrera four-cam, had been a legend.

Ernst Fuhrmann was 28 when he joined Porsche in Gmünd in 1947. At Vienna Technical Academy he earned a doctorate in engineering and his first jobs in Gmünd involved work on Piero Dusio's Cisitalia and work with Josef Mickl, the theoretical engineer Porsche relied on for aerodynamics and computations for new designs.

When Porsche moved back to Zuffenhausen, Fuhrmann was assigned to engine development. He was asked first to create the new camshaft of a new pushrod Typ 528 engine. With Fuhrmann's cam, the Typ 528 revved as high as 7000rpm. In the summer of 1952, he began to design his next work, the new Typ 547 engine.

Fuhrmann is a man with a quick sense of humor. He takes pleasure in irony. The reverential status accorded to his engine does not escape the engineer.

"The reason that some things were new," he continued, "was because I didn't know what was done before. So if you go fresh into a situation....I had no teacher, no adviser.

"The problem was that we had an engine that was too slow. Because of the camshafts in their position."

At the time, in early 1952, Porsche still used the Volkswagen-derived opposed four-cylinder engine. In its highest tune, on alcohol, 87hp had been stretched out of it, for purely racing applications. In coupe and cabriolet forms, this 1500 Super engine produced 78hp, and competed in sports car road races and international rallies.

But the time had come within Porsche to consider and conceive a true racing car with a true racing engine. Ferry Porsche approved the engine design project first, and it received project number 547. The new race car, an open sports car, was given number 550.

"I had the order to design an engine for a racing spyder," Fuhrmann said. "High speed, short stroke? The main question was the movement of the valves. The second question was the movement of the pistons.

"If you have more diameter and shorter stroke, you have...." Fuhrmann stopped, interrupting his lecture himself.

"This was the decision for the movement of the camshafts, the shaft through the middle: so the engine could become shorter. If I put it at the end of the engine, it makes it longer.

"There was another reason: If the engine becomes warm or cold, it was a symmetric heating or cooling. This was why the engine was really stable against overheating.

"And the size, the physical dimensions, of that engine was without any interest. So I designed that engine so it fit into the normal Porsche 356. My interest was always to have that engine in my personal car." He laughed again.

"We had some small trouble to overcome," he said, referring to the first running of the engine. "But there was no problem really that forced us to make a change in the design. It was very quickly done. I think it ran the first time in August (1953) and its first race was in September in Freiberg.

"But it was much more simple in that

While the Typ 547 engine was first raced in 550 Spyders, it was in the 356 coupes that the public later came to know the engine and the name "Carrera."

time to design an engine. It was...."

In that time. That was the key: in that time. Designs were made, precedents were set that moved Porsche further along in a single, unwavering direction, one from which deviation would not be easy. Not welcome. Not well received. Porsche was still air-cooled. Still with the engine behind

the rear axle.

"Today, you must combine the exhaust and think of poisoning of the air, take into account the electrics and so on. It was very simple in that time.

"Another thing I remember now was that the distributors in the first engines were connected directly to the camshafts. And after two years or so we changed this and drove them from the crankshaft. The reason was that because of play in the gear drive before it reaches the distributors; it was too big and unequal for both sides. There you got imprecise timing. So it was very rough.

"The connection was a nail through the shaft. And the nail broke the first times. We improved it several times, made a little bit of rubber in the shaft. And then finally we changed the location and the problem was over.

"We had a foaming of the oil which came out of the housing. These were minor things. But very important." Fuhrmann sat back.

"You know," he began again, "sometime in 1955...we had been using Weber carburetors. I think they were a little ahead at the time in racing carburetors. But the owner of Solex was a personal friend. And he complained to me because we didn't use his carburetors on our cars. So, he designed a special carburetor for that engine so that the business went back to him...."

The Carrera engine not only improved Porsche. It gently forced those doing business with the firm to advance as well. The engine in racing applications was clearly a step ahead. In a series production car, it was even more startling.

"Of course. That was the reason I did it," Fuhrmann laughed. "So I could have a fast car to drive.

"Since I was the development engineer of this car and this engine...I had the first engine in my own car. This was a normal coupe—you know, every test engineer had a car—so it was nothing special looking. Not built for beauty or comfort. But of course it was a good car because it had this good engine. It was a fast car!"

Ernst Fuhrmann smiled.

"There was a fair in Paris and Mr. von

Hanstein gave me a telephone call and told me I should send my car to Paris. He had to show it to some important customers."

"I refused." He laughed.

"I simply refused. Not possible! I won't give it away. I had some excuse, I don't remember what. Well, then, von Hanstein called on Dr. Porsche and complained about me." He laughed again.

"Dr. Porsche then called on me and said that he would like it if I would rethink my refusal. He was very friendly, but he would like me to send the car.

"So. It was driven to Paris. Several days later on, von Hanstein called on me. He was just that size...."

Fuhrmann leaned over in his chair to place his hands a small distance above the floor.

"The car was completely destroyed by a customer." Ernst Fuhrmann laughed again, harder still.

"So Dr. Porsche came to me at the same time. He was really fair. He said that in Paris, on the Porsche stand, was the first Carrera production car. And of course, this was the nicest one. It had leather seats, I remember, red leather seats, and gold letters on the outside, 'Special Carrera.'

"Everything was special," Fuhrmann said. "And so Dr. Porsche said, 'OK, this car now goes to Dr. Fuhrmann.' And so I had, even before Dr. Porsche himself, the finest Carrera in the company!"

On Maundy Thursday, March 2, 1953, Ernst Fuhrmann's first engine ran in Zuffenhausen. At Chrysler Motors Corporation in the United States, engineers had begun experimenting with hemispherical-head combustion chambers as early as 1935; its first series production application was in the top-of-the line Imperial in 1951. With spark plugs in the center of the Chrysler hemispheres, it promoted greater power because it produced a more efficiently burned fuel mixture. Chrysler's hemis produced their horsepower at higher engine speeds while low-end torque suffered slightly. The engine was a high-rpm, high-performance package.

With the addition of a second spark plug, Ernst Fuhrmann's Typ 547 "hemi"

engine produced similar characteristics. But Chrysler did not stress its 331ci engine to produce 300hp at 5200rpm and its nearly matching bore and stroke of 4.00 x 3.90in made for slower engine speeds. Fuhrmann added dual overhead camshafts, twin ignition, a pair of dual-barrel carburetors, and a roller-bearing crankshaft. Fuhrmann's big bore/short stroke engine, (85 x 66mm—3.35 x 2.60in) produced 112hp at 6400rpm the first time they ran the 1500cc (91.5ci) engine.

Fuhrmann adopted the Hirth-built crankshaft and utilized lighter-section one-piece connecting rods. Fuhrmann's solution to the problem of air-cooling the higher-performance engine was an innovative adaptation. A fan designed by Franz Reimspiess pulled in air from both sides of the fan

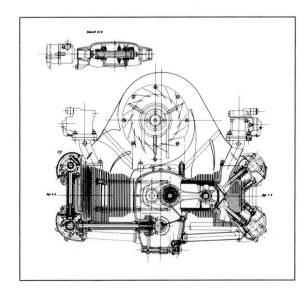

Introduced in fall 1955, the Typ 356A improved the dashboard layout and replaced the V-shaped two-piece windshield with one single piece of curved glass. The crooked shift lever, however, was not a factory improvement. Above, the famous Typ 547 engine was Ernst Fuhrmann's first complete engine design. Measuring 85 x 66mm in four cylinders, the four-camshaft 1498cc engine first ran in April 1953. A highly effective, new cooling fan was one of many improvements. Below, Ernst Fuhrmann's first engine, the Typ 547, utilized a Hirth-built roller bearing crankshaft and double-overhead camshafts for each cylinder bank. His design was derived from Porsche's flat-12 Grand Prix Cisitalia engine. Porsche Werke

shroud. With an inconsequential increase in horsepower consumption, the new fan increased air flow by more than half. Even more revolutionary was Fuhrmann's decision to drive the cams by a concatenation of shafts and bevel gears off the main crankshaft. While this configuration had worked previously on larger engines, notably the final Auto-Union GP and the postwar flat twelve-cylinder Cisitalia, the short camshafts with only two lobes each, suspended from the ends and driven from the middle had caused vibration.

Fuhrmann's engine weighed nearly 140kg (308lb). In its later incarnations, it produced upwards of 180hp. But its terrific complication required 120 shop hours for a complete rebuild. Setting the timing could take eight hours or longer. When the roller-bearing crank was replaced with plain lead-aluminum main bearings, bottom-end reliability increased, as did low-end torque. Rebuilds required a few less hours.

The engines first saw practical use in Typ 550 race prototypes in 1953. It was not a fragile engine. But its repair costs kept it from series introduction in the 356s for two more years. Racing applications, especially the first factory efforts, always came attended by trained mechanics. Customers wanting a higher-performance road car were generally not so mechanically inclined—and some of those who were so inclined often did more damage than good.

Yet the good customers lobbied hard with von Hanstein and Ferry Porsche himself. In the fall of 1955, the model 1500 GS was announced, as part of the new 356A series. It was christened the Carrera in honor of the factory's successful participation in the 1953 and 1954 Mexican road race, the Carrera Panamericana. The new version of the engine was labeled Typ 547/1.

For the autobahn racer competing from Stuttgart to Frankfurt or Munich alongside another equally wealthy enthusiast in a Mercedes-Benz 300SL, the luster faded when all eight of the spark plugs needed changing in the Carrera. Four of them couldn't even be seen. When Germany's winter set in, they found the Carrera 1500 GS had no heater or defroster.

Eventually, as the customer service

mechanics at Zuffenhausen got the hang of plug changes—40 minutes of feverish work—the factory introduced a second, more civilized version, the GS De Luxe. For the Berlin Kurfurstendam cruisers or the Schloss Solitude parkers, the De Luxe offered the necessary frills. For the weekend warriors heading off to Hockenheim or Freiburg, the GS-GT was the weapon of choice.

GT coupes—or Speedsters—had no padding, no insulation. They used light-weight bucket seats, leather-strap lift-up plastic side windows, flimsier bumpers, and—depending on who the buyers knew at Zuffenhausen—even polished intake ports, compression as high as 9.0:1, and fiercer camshafts. The "sports exhaust" let spectators hear Carreras long before they saw them. And long afterwards.

Carreras entered races and won. They won at Charbonnier, at Rheims, at Corsica, in rallies, road races, and hillclimbs. And when they came to the United States, they won in an alphabet soup of venues and events. From Lime Rock to Elkhart Lake to Pebble Beach to Summit Hills to Thompson to Donnybrooke. The US race versions, with a special closer-ratio gearbox and a fantastically high 5.16:1 final-drive ratio, could beat 9sec to 60mph from the start line. The engines were strong enough with 130-135hp, at 7500rpm, that after beating the competition into turn one, the Carreras

In 1955, Porsche manufactured few right-hand-drive 356A-1500GS models, left page; current importer records show only ten right-hand-drive 356A Carrera coupes were offered between mid-1955 and mid-1959. Its price at the time was somewhat more than £3,000—roughly $6,600. Above, by 1959, the Carrera had conquered and divided its markets. For those customers seeking performance and sacrificing comfort, the Carrera GS-Gran Turismo (GS-GT) was strictly business. Aluminum seats were strictly business as well.

beat them to the checkered flag as well.

Yet in 1958, the FIA yielded to pressure and allowed the 1500cc category to grow, to 1600. An engine begun in 1956, the Typ 692, was meant to fill the need.

"That was when I left the company," Ernst Fuhrmann recalled. "They made an engine that was not very successful. It was not my design...."

Ernst Fuhrmann paused, reflecting on the whole matter, then continued. A Porsche development contract with Studebaker had funded the development of his Typ 547 engine. It also introduced Porsche to Klaus von Rücker, Studebaker's assistant manager in testing and development.

"Oh, let's see. I was a young man, very eager. Dr. Ferry Porsche hired Mr. von Rücker and set him in front of me.

"I had nothing against Mr. von Rücker. But I told them, 'You don't need him because I am still here!' This was a very normal situation. Two people would like to have the same position, so one must leave.

"Dr. Porsche thought he would get a man who was experienced in the American way to build cars. To handle a company and so...."

So Fuhrmann left, with a new job almost immediately. But his four-cam engine was already a legend within Porsche.

In 1958, Dr. Ferry Porsche's son, Ferdinand Alexander, joined the firm. He was assigned first to work with Franz Reimspiess. Reimspiess had been one of the designers of the original Beetle engine and gave Butzi his first assignment.

"It was with him," F. A. Porsche explained, "that I was given the assignment—straight out of the parts list—to memorize all the items listed in the parts list....The specifications of screws, the cylinder head, the cylinder itself. All these I had to recite. This took quite a long time, but in this way you knew exactly the specifications and the procedure, the design.

"And then I had to draw the 1500 Carrera engine."

Extra louvers brought air into the Fuhrmann engine, left page. Franz Reimspiess's fan would use all that was left, with only a negligible increase in power requirement. The Stinger exhaust barely muted the raucous racket of a 7200rpm redline in 1959 models. Below, besides the script badges which identify a Carrera as such, a more subtle indicator is the twin oil lines inside the right front wheelwell, which lead from the front oil cooler back to the sump and engine. Headlight grilles were an option on the Reutter-bodied racers.

CHAPTER 5

1955 550/ 1500RS Spyder

Porsche's First True Race Car

Number 90 of 90, this 550/1500RS never turned a wheel in anger. Well, perhaps. Sometime in the total of 634 miles its first owner—a West Coast television executive—drove it, someone must have cut him off. The aluminum bodies were inspired by Glockler, designed by Komenda, first built by Wiedenhausen. Then production went to Wendler, and the car was agressively marketed by von Hanstein and von Neumann. And they were raced by almost everybody who was anybody.

Porsche introduced the 550 Spyder in May 1953. But it had been conceived independently three years earlier.

Walter Glöckler, a Volkswagen dealer in Frankfurt and well-known amateur racer, had examined the open Porsches from Beutler and Reutter and imagined something more "streamlined." With Porsche factory engineer Hermann Ramelow, he built a ladder-type tube frame, fitted Porsche's 1100cc pushrod engine, and used Volkswagen running gear. Weidenhausen Karosserie in Frankfurt built Glöckler's body, something resembling Bugatti's "tank" race car, but with softer edges. His lightweight tank (it weighed 455kg, 1,001lb), won the 1950 German sports car championship for the 1.1 liter class.

Glöckler built again in 1951, now with Porsche backing. The car even wore a Porsche badge over its 1500 engine. Glöckler, obsessive about vehicle weight, shed another 5kg (11lb) in the second car. The new car was nearly as successful and after the season, it sold to Max Hoffman in New York.

Glöckler produced more specials, each one successful, each one more round than the previous car. By March 1953, Glöckler's

Porsche resembled a loaf of bread before baking. Its gentle roundness earned space on the Porsche stand at the Geneva Motor Show.

But located between Frankfurt and Geneva was Stuttgart and as the Porsche factory had assisted Glöckler, it had also observed. The success and the sale to Hoffmann had not escaped notice. Karl Rabe, Huschke von Hanstein, and Ferry Porsche concluded that the aging Gmünd-style aluminum coupes could no longer compete against others with the same ideas and inspiration as Walter Glöckler. Factories were getting involved. OSCA from Italy, Gordini from France, HWM from Great Britain, Borgward from West Germany, and EMW from East Germany were now competitors. At the end of 1952, the three concluded a new car was necessary.

Through that winter, the mechanics worked in Zuffenhausen. Two cars were completed in early spring 1953, bodied by Weidenhausen again. The Porsche bodies were remarkably similar to the latest Glöckler, though Rabe and Porsche ordered removable fastback tops for each car to improve performance on long fast circuits.

Walter Glöckler's cousin, Helm, was offered the first drive in the new Typ 550. In a downpour on the last day of May, Helm won at Nürburgring, finishing 1st in 1.5 liter category in the Eifelrennen. This floated Porsche's hopes and they took both cars to Le Mans two weeks later. Helm Glöckler and Hans Herrmann were entered in Glöckler's Eifel winner, 550-01, car 44 at Le Mans, and factory driver/journalist Richard von Frankenberg teamed with Belgian driver/journalist Paul Frère in 550-02, car 45.

Two months earlier, Frère had raced in the Mille Miglia, winning his class driving a monstrous Chrysler Saratoga sedan. In May at Nürburgring, driving a Formula 2 HMW, he came 2nd, in that same downpour, 1.5sec behind a Maserati. Huschke von Hanstein noticed Frère and offered him the Le Mans drive.

"I went from an extremely big car to a very small car. From extreme understeer to extreme oversteer," Frère recalled. "And

the Porsche was faster, anyway!

"This car was a hybrid; the four-cam Typ 547 engine was already in existence but the Porsche people didn't think it was yet reliable enough for Le Mans in 1953. So they used a quite normal 1500cc pushrod engine, of VW derivation. The lack of an

exhaust system brought more power. It was only very slightly tuned: 82 or 83hp.

"But the engine was turned 180 degrees compared with the production car. The suspension arms of the production car were not long enough to clear the engine. So they reversed them, to have them behind the gearbox. So instead of having trailing arms which toed the rear wheels slightly in, we have forward facing arms which made them toe out. It made the car oversteer more! Very tricky car."

It was Frère's first drive for Porsche and his first Le Mans. In fact, while he had seen the circuit before, he had never driven on it.

"They put Frankenberg in for the first practice, and by the time I had my drive, it was dark. It was absolutely impossible to learn a circuit in the dark—and to learn in a car I had assumed would handle better than a standard 356. I very nearly lost it in the first left-hander after the Dunlop Bridge on the first lap!"

For Frère, the race was frustrating. With fastback tops, the cars reached 200km/h (125mph) at 5400rpm on Mulsanne. Yet through practice, oil temperatures ran high. Additional cooling slots were cut and still 130-140 degrees Centigrade was nearly continual.

The drivers also noticed that at night they could only reach 5200rpm on Mulsanne. Jets were changed, timing adjusted, and the cars went back out. No change. Overnight, a racing engineer discovered that voltage changes affected the electric tachometer. The headlights dropped the voltage to the tachometer by 200rpm. In the end, von Hanstein and Rabe recommended a 5000rpm limit to preserve the warm-running engine.

Frère started and after three hours of steady driving, he was in the middle of the 1.5 liter field. Back out at 10pm, he trailed the leading OSCA by 40sec. Frère slowly reeled in the Italian car and by 11:30, he was within car lengths. An hour later, the OSCA broke, and the 550 soldiered into the class lead.

Porsche had entered the 1953 Le Mans with two primary goals: to win class and to capture the Index of Performance. With high oil temperatures, it threatened the Index. The cars would need more speed, perhaps raising oil temperature even more. Sunday morning, having averaged 148km/h (93mph) for more than 18 hours, they led their class by ten laps. Von Hanstein and Porsche voted to reduce paces to ensure the class win. It disappointed Frère to be unlapped by Austin-Healeys and Frazer Nashs they had passed during the night. When 4pm June 14 passed, Porsche number 45, with codriver Richard von Frankenberg at the wheel, had won the class and established a class record.

Those first two cars were "retired" to Central America. Before shipment to Guatemala, the factory increased their cooling and breathing capabilities. Their new owner, Jaroslav Juhan entered them in the 1953 Carrera Panamericana. Juhan drove 550-01, sponsored by the Cañada Shoe Company of Guadalajara, but broke. Teammate Jose Herrarte, however, driving 550-02, managed to avoid the boulders

The Fuhrmann four-cam. Fed by two twin-choke Solex 40 PII downdraft carburetors, the Carrera engines produced 110hp at 6200rpm, good for 200km/h (125mph) in the 590kg (1,298lb) Spyders. Brushes at the bottom line the torsion bars to keep road grit out of the engine compartment.

Paul Frère:
"This car was a hybrid; the twin-cam Typ 547 engine was already in existence but Porsche didn't think it was yet reliable enough for Le Mans."

and beasts that ended Juhan's race, and won his class. Chassis 550-03 and -04, sponsored by Fletcher Aviation were sent as factory entries to Mexico's 1954 Carrera Panamericana in November. Both cars broke and were returned to Stuttgart.

But back in Stuttgart, some design studies were being considered as a way to entice customer sales. At least one chassis grew a hump. This was a removable panel within the normal deck lid. However, chassis 550-05 and -07 were shown with humps. Known as the *Buckelwagen* or hunchback, this was the first instance of Porsche using a wind tunnel to improve aerodynamics. The Stuttgart Institute tunnel demonstrated the value of the humpback. The finished-product, 550-05, first appeared at the Brussels Show, in January 1954. Subsequently, the two cars alternated in shows in Frankfurt, Geneva, and Paris. One was even painted blue, with red alloy 16in knock-off wheels. The -05 car used the heavy square-tube shock tower mounts and was not developed any further. These two cars did, however, introduce the split body, which

allowed the entire rear end to swing open for access to the engine, rather than through access plates as on the earlier cars.

Kurt Dieterich, a factory chassis development specialist at the time, remembered the second *Buckelwagen*, 550-07. He was a development mechanic during its entire life. It was built as a factory mule and endurance-race practice car. The previous prototype Spyders had bodies by Weinsberg; this was the first built by Wendler to demonstrate its skills.

"I remember that the frame of the racing prototype *Buckelwagen* was changed to pretest racing ideas for other factory 550s," Dieterich explained. "The *Buckelwagen* had the first extra-tube high-step frame changes. Because the frame twisted too much small tubes were added to make it stiffer. These changes were then used in the 1955 race cars and later in all of the last 550s delivered." The car also sported a removable clear plastic bubble top.

Painted silver, with a Porsche basketweave red interior, the racing prototype was used by factory drivers Hans Herrmann and Richard von Frankenberg as a demonstration car, giving Swiss driving school students a thrill while putting on valuable development time. It also was the vehicle the two drivers used to observe potential drivers for a factory team slot. The car then went to the Mille Miglia as the training car.

After the race was won by a Weinsberg prototype, 550-08—not a *Buckelwagen*—the Wendler humpback prototype was shown in Porsche dealerships all over Germany and Austria. While it had actually run in the Tour of Sicily, it displayed the winners' wreath from the Mille Miglia.

The factory stretched the truth a little bit: a plaque identified the *Buckelwagen* as the winning car and urged customers to buy their own Mille Miglia winner just like what they saw.

"Erich Bucklers displayed this car after coming back from the 1954 Mille Miglia," Dieterich recalled, "with the rain mud and dirt as it returned from Italy. This man's nickname was 'The Man Without Nerves' because the car was driven from dealer to dealer during the winter of 1954, without any protection, to take orders for the new

550 Spyder!"

For Le Mans in 1954, four cars were entered, one an 1100cc Spyder codriven by Zora Arkus-Duntov, the Belgian-born, Russian-educated engineer on vacation from General Motors in Detroit. With only 72hp, it was not the speediest of its class but after 24 hours, when speedier cars had broken, Arkus-Duntov had won the class. After Le Mans, he returned with the four cars to Zuffenhausen. The bodies were eventually destroyed and the factory frames and parts were applied to newer race cars. But Arkus-Duntov met Porsche's new chassis engineer, Helmuth Bott.

Bott knew of a paper Arkus-Duntov had helped prepare, called "Manners of the Modern Car." It dealt with roadholding and vehicle handling. Arkus-Duntov accompanied Bott to Malmsheim airport to show him a dozen tests General Motors used to evaluate handling.

"With his tests," Bott recalled, "you could get a very good picture of what the car does on the road. You could measure it and write it down. And if you could measure, you could do better. If you have only your 'feeling,' it may not be the same 'feeling' for everybody else. But with these ten or fifteen steps, you get an improvement that everybody feels!"

Arkus-Duntov and Bott performed the test on a 356, and it resulted in marked improvement. Dr. Porsche then asked Bott to begin the same work with the new race car.

"And so the 550 was my first race car project," Bott explained. "I did all the road holding things. And we picked up 30 seconds on the Nürburgring without changing the power of the engine."

In early 1954, production expanded. After the first nine prototypes were completed, the racing department took delivery of the remaining Weinsberg frames. It kept aside six for its own uses, additional development prototypes and Le Mans race cars. They then began assembling "customer" cars.

Max Hoffman in New York wanted cars to sell and argued that the model must have a name; cars designated only by a number did not sell well yet. Hoffman knew; he was also the Mercedes-Benz distributor for the United States. The "Spyder" bodystyle name had an exotic appeal. The 1955 Typ 550 certainly was a two-seat open car with only an attachable roof and side curtains. Spyder it was.

Aluminum was used for the customer bodies. A spring-loaded trap door, remotely operated from the dashboard, controlled airflow to the oil cooler. The cars weighed about 590kg (1,298.0lb), not quite 60kg (132.0lb) more than the factory cars.

Wendler Karosserie in Reutlingen produced the aluminum bodies. Based on the Weinsberg designs, Wendler's early prototypes had rather more noticeable fenders. The 1955 Le Mans cars and subsequent customer cars were slightly restyled by Erwin Komenda, resulting in lower fenders and using 356 slanted front headlights. By then, the factory had concluded that Weinsberg's assembly techniques were unnecessarily complicated for the lightweight car. While they had built the frames, they would not build the bodies.

While the 550s circled Le Mans in June 1955, improved cars were being constructed at Zuffenhausen. Significant changes were made on this new car, which was initially designated the 550A. At last they had a frame which would keep up with Ernst Fuhrmann's Typ 547 four-cam engine, first seen fitted into chassis 550-03.

The tubular space frame which suspended the rear axle beneath it replaced the ladder frame of the first ninety cars. Rear suspension was replaced with low-pivot Watts-linkage swing arms. The new 550A had gained 40hp to 135hp. A unique four-and-a-half speed gearbox was fitted. First gear was non-synchronized, oddly outside the pattern. This allowed more narrow ratios from second through fifth gears.

Factory cars were campaigned throughout Europe and soon brought Porsche its first great overall victory. Umberto Maglioli won the 1956 Targa Florio, driving a 550A single-handedly. A month earlier, he had declined to race the same car for the Mille Miglia because it was unpainted. A quick coat of whitewash put Maglioli into the car and brought Porsche a 4th overall. It also put the competition on notice.

Cars which had raced through the 1955 season were then brought to Sebring the next spring. This was still the only US race attracting European factory team support. Afterward, von Hanstein would sell off the factory cars, either to Hoffman, Briggs Cunningham, or John von Neumann and Otto Zipper, Porsche's new West Coast distributors.

It was axiomatic by 1955 that if racers sought to win in the 1.5 liter classes, they drove Spyders. At some events, most of the starting field ran 550/1500RSs. At an early 1955 race at Hockenheim, fielded with factory cars and many of the first customers, twenty-one 550s roared away at the start. In the Ost Curve, the East Turn, a huge crash involved fifteen of them, knocking six out completely.

Jean-Pierre Kunstle was a Swiss businessman whose career brought him to California and whose interest in cars brought him to John von Neumann. He bought one of the factory cars from von Neumann after Sebring. By the fall, J-P was a frequent winner. His scrapbook provided witness. The SCCA newsletter reported a race at Palm Springs in March:

"The 1500cc modified race brought the greatest bunch of talent to the grid which has so far appeared on the West coast, to wit: Phil Hill, Carroll Shelby, Ken Miles, J-P Kunstle, Jack McAfee, Cy Yedor, Johnny Porter, Chick Leson, and a host of others of less renown.

"Shelby was in a 1500 Maserati and Leson in an OSCA, and all the others were in 550s. Some show!

"J-P got into Turn One first. And stayed there. He was followed at first by Ken, Phil, and Jack. When traffic settled down, Shelby staged an impressive try with the Mas. Clearly he could circulate quicker than any Porsche. The question was, will the rather fragile Maserati stand the abuse? Answer: not today.

"Shelby passed McAfee, Hill and Miles. He was closing in on J-P when something went pow and that took care of the Italian threat. Ken then set out after our boy. He closed to about 3 seconds but J-P saw him in the mirrors and turned up the wick. As Ken saw the 'Go get 'em' signal from his pit, he signalled back, 'This is all there is, men; we just don't go any faster!'"

The Buckelwagen *was displayed at a Frankfurt dealership. The factory toured the car to promote interest in it and other Porsche products.* Warren Eads archives

Kunstle raced the 550 at Palm Springs. He raced at Willow Springs, Cotati, Santa Barbara, Pebble Beach, Golden Gate Park, Torrey Pines, Santa Rosa, Salinas. Towns up and down the length of California, with oranges, grapefruits, and lemons growing on trees. These were towns John Steinbeck visited, wrote about, or lived in. These were towns with hay bales set in the intersections to mark the turns when race weekends happened.

"You know, I had dices with Ken," Kunstle reminisced thirty-five years later. "He would win Saturday, I would win Sunday. It was murder....

"I bought that Spyder in '55. I was pretty well known by that time. And Richie Ginther and I were going to race one weekend up at Salinas. Rolf Wütherich always took care of our cars. And he was supposed to go up there with us that weekend.

"Rolf called up and said Johnny von Neumann had just sold one of the five new Spyders and that he was going to ride up with the owner Friday afternoon. Fellow had raced a Speedster before but would we, Richie and I, could we show the guy how to drive a Spyder?

"I said I didn't mind so long as he could take care of all our cars.'

"'Fine, sure,' Wütherich said. 'We'll be arriving late at night. You know the guy. He's an actor, James Dean.'"

CHAPTER 6

1957 Sauter Bergspyder

Special Bodies

When is a Porsche not a Porsche, a Spyder not a spyder, a Sauter not always even a Sauter? The confusion continued for decades. This was not the Sauter roadster that inspired the America Roadster.

It must have been confusing. Even before the late 1950s, when entire starting grids were made up of Porsche 550s and the only way to know the entrants was with a program, there was another chance for confusing the entrants.

In 1951 and 1952, there were two Sauters racing cars in Germany. It's possible they even met, knew each other. But sports car competition in Europe at the time was so widely varied, so diverse, that it's just as likely that they only heard of each other years later when people began to confuse one with the other.

Both were businessmen; Heinrich Sauter was in commerce, and lived in Stuttgart. His interest was rallying and his involvement was temporary, although the results did have lasting impact. The other, Kurt Sauter, was a coachbuilder, in Basel, Switzerland. His involvement was career-long. But his impact was fleeting.

Kurt Sauter was a master coachbuilder, having served his apprenticeship learning the crafts and skills of his chosen trade. His career was interrupted by World War II, and while Switzerland was neutral, the army was mobilized to maintain its neutrality. Sauter was called up.

After the war ended, as lives dealt with and recovered from the upheaval, Sauter returned to Basel and got his old job back. But it was a short-lived peace for Sauter. Shortly after returning, his boss announced he would retire and the company was up for sale. Kurt Sauter was able to take it over. Sauter Karosserie was now in business in Basel, doing body repairs and custom fabrications. And the odd racing car.

Sauter had long imagined building his own world-conquering racers. His karosserie adopted some stray Fiat 1100 running gear and suspension, and his first race car was done and running.

Race cars do not only run on gasoline or other fuels. They run on money. And Sauter-the-businessman did not lose sight of his need to keep work coming in. Still, he took time off, campaigning his cars at Nürburgring and Avus from time to time between 1951 and 1954.

Peter Monteverdi, later a builder of his own automobiles, acquired one of Sauter's first Fiat-based racers for his own beginnings. Sauter's cars developed good reputations and it wasn't long before custom-commissioned work followed.

In the winter of 1955, Heini Walter and his friend Werner Brandli approached Sauter. The Swiss racers had in mind a nearly matched pair of hillclimb and short-course road race cars. Walter wanted to go after the European Hillclimb Championship for 1956 and he wanted to use the new Porsche Carrera 1500cc Typ 547 four-cam engine. Brandli, with less experience, chose instead the Typ 369 1100cc pushrod configuration.

Walter had owned one of the early prototype Porsche 550 cars and he had in mind a new custom car. He had seen a new 550/1500RS at a race in Zurich and knew the car's owner. It was the 550 body style that Walter and Brandli wanted Sauter to closely replicate. The three made several trips down to Zurich to see the car and discuss its features: a shorter wheelbase and lighter weight were two requirements for the new Sauter-built Bergspyders.

Walter and Brandli were responsible for

An aggressive, stubby little racer, Sauter's Bergspyder for Walter and Brandli was 120mm (4.72in) lower and 50mm (1.97in) narrower than Porsche's Spyder. But while overall length was within a few millimeters, the biggest contrast was invisible: Sauter's car weighed 70kg (154lb) less than Porsche's.

providing Sauter with all the major components, though Sauter's men produced a tube ladder-frame chassis similar to Porsche's early 550. With one addition. Sauter's men added an additional hoop, which ran behind the dashboard, above the footwells.

Sauter used Volkswagen torsion bar suspension up front, with VW trailing arms and torsion arms since they were lighter than Porsche's. The rear was very much copied from the 550. In addition, the brake drums for Walter's car were drilled with large ventilation holes.

Sauter's numbering system only applied to those cars built entirely from scratch at his karosserie. Something like eighteen cars were built, from the ground up, while another ten to fifteen were rebodies on others' frames. Those retained their original manu-

facturer's numbers. Heini Walter's and Werner Brandli's cars were KS-11 and KS-12.

Kurt Sauter worked mostly from his own imagination in designing the cars. While no reduced-scale formal drawings were ever produced—after all, a life-size model existed barely 125km away, Sauter did finally make a full-scale drawing on his shop wall. It was easier to position the suspension and running gear.

The chassis of each car was jigged. Component layout and the other details could be examined by referring to the real car, which began appearing at local races around Basel.

Sauter had several panel beaters. But one in particular, a man whose name Sauter no longer remembers, was particularly skilled with aluminum. But Sauter was sure of one thing about the man. While his artist

was an Italian from Modena, the similarity with Professor Porsche's experiences in Gmünd ended there. Sauter's aluminum artist did not disappear to the local Bier-stube after each car was completed.

The two cars were completed according to schedule, though they were not cheap. The cost of custom fabrication, to order, was 20,000 Swiss francs. About $6,250. Per car.

Heini Walter had his spyder painted in Swiss national colors, red body with white front deck lid. He and the car were quite successful. He took 1st at the Dubendorf Slalom, 3rd at Ollon-Villars Hillclimb, and 1st at Mitholz-Kandersteg Hillclimb. The car ran consistently and successfully until a hillclimb at St. Ursahne-Les Rangiers when he over-cooked it. Years later, he told a friend he thought Sauter's extra hoop behind the dash saved his life.

The crash nearly totalled the car, and its repair bill—in the days before racing spon-sorships—nearly totalled Walter. It did put him out until the end of the season but only because it took that much time to properly repair the damage. For 1957, Walter went back to Porsche and acquired a Spyder for the next season.

Kurt Sauter's Bergspyder was offered to a variety of talented local drivers for races during 1957. At one point, the car was refit-ted with a DKW water-cooled engine and a radiator and intake were cut into the car's

front end. But sometime later, the original Carrera four-cam engine was rebuilt and restored.

In 1962, at age 48, Sauter relocated his entire karosserie to Gempen, in the Jura mountain range just south of Basel. It's not completely clear whether he still owned the Bergspyder by that time. In any event only three more cars were built after the move. But the move could in no way be construed as a retirement.

Gempen is a small mountain village, reached only by three narrow, twisting roads. Sauter, knowing his customers, simply moved himself to the junction of three potential hillclimb courses, where he could enjoy his own 911 2.2 liter.

When Swiss hillclimb champion Heini Walter set out to take the European championship, he liked Porsche's 550, but wanted it much lighter. He approached Sauter, a coachbuilder in Basel with a known interest in racing. Below left, Walter and his racer friend Werner Brandli each ordered matching Bergspyders—hillclimb spyders—from Sauter. Sauter accompanied Wal-ter and Brandli to Zurich to see a 550, and then Sauter let his imagination do the rest. Sauter took Walter's request for a lightweight hillclimb car to extremes. Everything that could be lightened was drilled. The latticework paid off. The car weighed 550kg (1,210lb). Below, for Wal-ter's car, the four-cam Carrera engine was speci-fied. Its 110hp in such a lightweight, was a formi-dable combination. Bran-dli, with less driving experi-ence, chose the 1100cc pushrod engine instead.

CHAPTER 7

1957 Speedster Carrera GS-GT

Porsche's Hollywood Hot Rod

All John von Neumann asked for was a car he could sell. He had in mind an open car, to see and be seen in along Sunset Strip and Hollywood Boulevard. That they sold throughout the world didn't bother him one bit. Speedsters were stripped to bare bones. The low windshield was removable—another von Neumann specification for racing. The top was a frugal, unpadded, lightweight affair, and the side windows were actually side curtains, fit into small cylinders at the front and rear of the doors.

Johnny von Neumann knew what his customers wanted.

"Imagine, sitting at a stop in the sun! In Los Angeles in the summer! In a coupe? Awful!

"Cut in a vent to blow air? It blows hot!

"So what did the guys want? Well, I knew....

"They want to go, on a Saturday evening in June, down Sunset Boulevard with their elbow over the door and the girls can see them in the car.... And they can see the girls on the walks!"

John von Neumann laughed, then shrugged his shoulders, then laughed again.

"So what's the Speedster?

"It's a boulevard race car. Who needs roll-up windows. I swear, the first time I told them about a car without roll-up windows, they thought I was nuts. Who needs roll-up windows in California?

"'Look,' I said, 'I always put myself in the place of the customer, in the *mood* of these buyers. And I wouldn't sell anything to anybody unless I would buy it myself.' So I said to Maxie Hoffman, 'That I can sell!'"

Von Neumann remembered Hoffman's blank stare. "And Jean-Pierre Kunstle raced one. And James Dean bought one and

raced it. So who was right and who was wrong? In the end they sold what, 3,000 something cars?"

By 1953, John von Neumann was working with Max Hoffman, the US importer for Porsche. Von Neumann was West Coast distributor. The arrangement gave him ties to Porsche, but only through Hoffman.

"I made some arrangements.... Maxie Hoffman never wanted to ship me cars direct from Germany. Because, if he sold, let's say twenty Porsches, then *he* sold them. Even if I resold them. If they shipped me ten and him ten, then it looked very different on the factory records...."

"So I always went to see Maxie, to complain. 'Your cars are too expensive! A Jaguar, 3.4 liter, six-cylinder, dual-overhead cams, 160hp: $3500. Porsche is $4500? To steer like a Volkswagen? To stop like a Volkswagen....

"Modified Volkswagen. And they were not foolproof. Synchromesh transmissions broke. Valves stuck. Lots of problems. We learned how to solve those. But we did just as much research for them as they gave us information.

"I pushed Maxie. He had nothing to lose. I said I wanted a Roadster and I wanted it for less than $3,000. An open car for a price!"

It was difficult for Porsche at first to accept the concept of an inexpensive car. When Huschke von Hanstein first joined the company, one of his tasks was to try to sell the cars as well as organize their competition entries. The Baron called on fellow royalty. An unmentioned class-consciousness pervaded early Porsche history. It was hinted that if you weren't the offspring of at least a Duke, you needn't ask.

But Ferry Porsche and Albert Prinzing knew that Hoffman was selling their cars in America. Reutter Karosserie simplified and minimized the lines of the new convertible and virtually gutted the interior. The frame, suspension, the 1500 Normal engine, all were brought over to this new open car. A lightweight cloth roof was cut, low to the sill (which was itself lowered 37.5mm or 1.5in). It reduced the side curtain area. It also mini-

mized the exposure to the elements, a matter of concern to those buyers outside of von Neumann's region. In its styling, Reutter had created a "chopped-and-channeled" Hollywood hot rod.

Options were available to "customize" the Speedster. The 1500 Super motor could be ordered. A tachometer was not standard equipment. Nor was a heater. Padded seats were available, as were sun visors. But if the car was purchased as barren as Reutter could ship it, the new Speedster sold for $2,995 in Max Hoffman's showroom at 59th and Park Avenue. Europeans couldn't even get one for the first nine months.

Von Neumann wasted no time getting his first one to Los Angeles.

"I introduced it at my house," von Neumann recalled. "I had a house in Sherman Oaks at the time. And I had a swimming pool and I put the first Speedster at the pool. I had a cocktail party for my dealers, invited a few people from the press. It was a beautiful fall afternoon."

If anyone important missed that party, von Neumann quickly found another opportunity. Right after Thanksgiving, he took the car down to Torrey Pines, a road course in a state park near San Diego. When the dust settled and the checkered flag dropped, he had indelibly introduced his $3,000 open car by taking 1st place in the 1500cc class. The next race that day was to be first in line when von Neumann opened his order book.

For his Torrey Pines customers, the Speedster was about to get even better. The standard 1500cc engine was to be replaced by a new 1600 for 1956. In Normal and Super versions, the extra 100cc increased overall power by 10hp. But the real improvement came with Ernst Fuhrmann's Carrera

When Porsche agreed to accommodate Hoffman's request, the assignment went to Reutter who simply cleaned up the lines and features of the standard 356 cabriolet, left page. Without its windshield, it reminded its first viewers of an inverted bathtub. Far left, speedsters were offered with a standard softtop and an optional hardtop. Many more hardtops were delivered than Speedsters with wire wheels. Porsche Werke. Left, actor Paul Newman was one of the first to make a Speedster famous, costarring opposite one in Harper, a murder mystery film with Newman as the title-role detective. While von Neumann was based in Hollywood, he never gave cars to the stars. But he sold many to them. Below, all the interior luxury that John von Neumann could specify was removed from the Speedster. Conceived as a "boulevard" race car, the California distributor asked Max Hoffman to convince Porsche to build "a car at a price"—$3,000—to compete against the Jaguar XK120.

The Typ 547 was Fuhrmann first engine design. He adopted the cam mechanisms from the flat twelve-Cisitalia. Below, in production for nearly five years, and with production accounting for less than a fifth of the total product line, its impact was far, far greater. From a company now known for producing legendary cars, "Speedster" is a household word everywhere.

engine, the Typ 547, soon to be offered as an option to von Neumann's lightweight boulevard race car. However, buyers who specified the 110hp GS package paid a premium price: $5,260.

By 1957, the Carrera GS Typ 547 engine still produced 110hp. But the Carrera GS-GT was introduced in May 1957 for 1958. The body used aluminum panels for the doors and front and rear deck lids. The 15in wheels were aluminum rims with steel centers, with larger vented brake drums fitted at the front. With narrower gears in second, third, and fourth, and with 90kg (198lb) less weight than Porsche's convertible, the GS-GT was

destined for serious competition.

"Well, I liked to race," von Neumann explained. "But my underlying drive.... I'm a person who works best when I am challenged: 'I dare you to....'

"I was tired of these bloody bicycle-fendered MG things running around. In '59 the Porsche had a great engine. The Super 90 engine had an honest 90 horsepower. Which was much better than...."

Von Neumann hesitated for a moment. Sitting in the study of his home in Palm Springs, he was barely two miles up the foothills from some of his earliest victories in Speedsters. Those victories had followed challenges; fellow racers said, "With a rear engine, it can never work."

"Remember, the Porsche had the early synchronized transmissions? They weren't worth a damn.

"On the other hand, the original Porsche had a Volkswagen transmission. A crash box! Drive it like a truck."

He leaned forward, speaking almost conspiratorially.

"I learned one thing. This was my old secret. Call it cheating or just good 'race-manship.' I could, for $60, get new gears cut for the transmission in downtown Los Angeles. Straight cut gears for the old crash box."

Von Neumann's eyes sparked. Part of his marketing strategy had always been to show off the Porsches in competition. Maxie Hoffman had the elegant showroom with shining floors and employees polishing the cars three times a day.

Von Neumann had the boulevards in Palm Springs and Santa Barbara, Torrey Pines and Pebble Beach. The other part of showing off the cars in competition succeeded because he really loved racing.

"...So I could make myself gear ratios for every circuit.

"I could storm out of a corner and pull away from a Jaguar XK120 and they couldn't figure it out." He laughed once again.

"And I could apply it wherever I wanted because I had it lowered. I modified the suspension. With big torsion bars.... Rear wheels splayed way out.

"It was my idea of a boulevard race car."

"Doin' The Continental" was a hit song in the 1940s but not so popular as a Porsche in the 1950s. Introduced in 1955 for the US market, it was another Max Hoffman request. But Ford Motor Company's Lincoln-Mercury Division claimed ownership of the name with plans to reintroduce their own Continental in 1956. Left, the Continentals were sold with 1500 Super or Normal engines. The Super produced 70hp at 5000rpm; the Normal, also known as "die Dame," produced 55hp at 4400rpm. Production of Continentals was limited. A true American market car, most Continental coupes were fitted with a bench seat, split in the seatback to allow access to the rear. Selling for $3,500, sun visors and the Telefunken radio were options. White sidewall tires were optional—but common.

CHAPTER 8

1958 718RSK F2

The Two-Formula Formula 2 Car

When the FIA officially reinstated Formula 2 for 1958, its regulations did not exclude cars with full bodywork. The factory had won some F2 trials in 1957 using 550A Spyders and that success fueled factory interest. Initially one RSK was converted to center steering. "You get through corners rapidly in the RSK," journalist/racer Richard von Frankenberg once described. "Just where you begin to turn into the corner...you begin to feed such an amount of gas...so that the back wheels have just enough slip to put the car into a gentle drift."

The factory really did not understand the races in California. That state and those events were a long way away from Zuffenhausen in distance and in mindset. And to Porsche, the contests at places like Pebble Beach and Palm Springs didn't have an international title; the races in California were not recognized in Paris. So, in the earliest days, when racers in California asked for parts, they got the parts—and they got the bill as well.

For the factory, it was an ideal situation. There was racing going on that was providing some essential development experience and some valuable reputation-building. And it was not costing the factory anything at all. Discoveries made in California made their way back to Zuffenhausen and, confirmed in testing at home, were sometimes incorporated in subsequent models.

It was a factory suspension modification—an improvement over the 550A—that gave the RS its new name, RSK. It's a bit of trivia, now well known: the torsion bar carrier tubes of the front suspension formed a shape that reminded many observers of the letter K. Inside Zuffenhausen and outside, Porsche's design Typ 718 was better known as the RSK.

The front suspension trailing arms were elevated, their pivot points nearly twice as far above the torsion bars as in the 550A. These bars were angled down towards the centerline of the chassis. Wilhelm Hild made these and other changes with a goal of increasing front suspension travel. In those days, with much of Porsche's development testing being done at the Nürburgring, this was understandable.

The chassis—lighter and stronger—was an extruded-steel-tube space frame like the 550A. The brake drums were redesigned, the fins given a 30 degree angle to the axle for better cooling, and the RSK introduced them as the new "turbo-finned" brakes. The rear end of the first RSKs was largely the same as the 550A. However, the rear low-pivot swing axle, a Watts linkage, was mounted on variable-rate coil springs instead of torsion-spring plates.

Other changes were introduced. The steering box was relocated to the center of the front axle and rearward towards the driver. This contributed indirectly to a lower nose, first tried in a short-lived Typ 645, a treacherous prototype known as *Mickey Maus*. A tighter-radius curve permitted the hood to come down much lower and this was carried over from the 645 to the RSK. For endurance races, however, this new design required the use of two extra gas tanks, one in the nose and, for Le Mans, an extra tank in the door!

The center steering box relocation was partially responsible for the overall lowering of the chassis and body height. The other benefit was more critical front-wheel control with symmetrical, equal-length tie rods. While the RSK was designed as a left-driver-seat race car, the new center box allowed for other possibilities, should corporate interest develop.

The RSK first appeared at the Nürburgring on May 26, 1957. While it tested there, it did not race. After that session, small vertical fins were added at the rear to slightly improve stability. Its first competition was at Le Mans, several weeks later. However, on Mulsanne, these winglets provided so little effect that Ferry and Butzi Porsche made

As Porsche advanced its move into Formula 2, Butzi Porsche experimented with shapes. This prototype, 718/2-05, appeared at the Nürburgring. Below right, Edgar Barth gave mechanic/test driver Herbert Linge a ride on Barth's factory center-steering RSK. Jesse Alexander

films of the car in order to analyze its twitchy handling.

It turned out to be elements of the K shape. It induced steering problems: the movement of the unequal-length suspension members altered the camber—slightly negative as the front end squatted, slightly positive as it lifted. In braking this was unpleasant and caused a shimmy. In higher-g turns, this slightly rolled the outside front tire under the chassis, actually reducing traction. So the "diagonal arms representing the K" in the suspension were replaced soon afterwards.

Early in the life of the RSK, engineer Wilhelm Hild did wind tunnel tests to determine airflow over the body. The taped-on wool tufts indicated to Hild that as air passed

over the body it made contact right at the back end. Air pressure gauges confirmed this and Hild placed the engine air intakes there. The back shared with the 550A the removable rear bodywork and access doors to carburetors. In addition, it incorporated a large removable deck lid to facilitate inspections and quick adjustments.

In 1957, the RSK used the 1498cc engines from the 550A Spyder models. For the 1958 season, the Typ 547/3 version was introduced, using larger Weber carburetors. This eliminated fuel starvation in high-g turns. It necessitated making the rear deck lid slightly higher, to accommodate the taller carburetors without cutting holes in the bodywork. The 547/3 produced 142hp at 7500rpm. The car weighed 572kg (1,258lb).

Jean Behra, the French privateer who had taken a new RSK to 2nd overall in the 1957 Targa Florio, brought a car to the Sebring in March 1958. He did not finish. But when he returned in October, he raced with the new 1598cc engine at Riverside in the *Los Angeles Times* Grand Prix and finished 4th overall. Great interest and a strong appetite was created for the RSK in America.

A production run for customers began in 1959. Priced at $8,000, the demand contin-

ued well after the planned twenty-two were completed. An additional twelve were built. Wendler continued the aluminum body fabrication, begun with its contract to produce the 550s. Engine updates took output up to 148hp at 7600rpm for the customer cars, while the factory 1.5 liter entries were tweaked to 160hp at 8000rpm with a special cams. This factory option was made available to certain top privateers like Mexico's Ricardo Rodriguez.

Late in 1959 a few Typ 718RSK factory race cars experimented with an entirely new rear suspension. Porsche's traditional swing axles with Watts linkages were finally abandoned, although the philosophy was not entirely betrayed.

At the time, factory driver Richard von Frankenberg described to a visiting German journalist the evolution in handling from the 550 Spyder to the 718RSK, still called that despite the suspension change: "The old

The center-steering conversion kit was included in the RSK's $8,000 price. It required relocating the steering column from just right of the tach to the center of the body. For center steering, a shorter shaft connected the wheel to the center-mounted steering gearbox.

550 Spyder was a most drastic oversteerer, an automobile that 'came around' relatively early at the back if you were just a bit too fast in a corner. It behaved very honestly in this range of breakaway, however, and it was easy to catch and correct.

"The 550A had the same characteristics, with the exception that its tail end broke away quite a bit later. This motion showed up clearly, and here again you could correct relatively easily with opposite steering lock and application of throttle.

"Today's RSK is still an oversteerer," von Frankenberg said, "whose steering is so close to neutral, however, that in certain situations—for example, going downhill on road surfaces with low friction—it understeers. And since it gives no warning in advance of breakaway, right up to the last instant, in my opinion, the RSK is somewhat more difficult to drive than the 550A. Or to say it in another way, you can no longer drive it so unconcerned, precisely because—and at first this may seem like a contradiction—it has such high roadholding, in the sense of surface grip.

"You get through corners rapidly in the RSK in this way: at the point just where you begin to turn into the corner, you put your foot back on the accelerator and begin to feed such an amount of gas so that the back wheels won't spin—which would put the car sideways in an instant—and so that the back wheels have just enough slip to put the car into a gentle drift.

"If this is done right, you do not have to apply more steering lock. The car will be on a line tangent to the inside of the turn. Be careful. If you apply full throttle too soon, the RSK will reply with breakaway at the back, which costs valuable fractions of seconds."

What replaced the complex old system was something more akin to contemporary Grand Prix car thinking: upper and lower wishbones. But these wishbones were not equal-length A-arms, and the uppers and lowers were not parallel. This created the effect of longer swing axles, while eliminating the camber and track changes of the previous system. However, none of the customer cars were delivered with this new suspension; this would appear in the next year,

1960, in the factory RS60.

"With the RSK," von Frankenberg concluded, "better times can be put up today on courses like the Nürburgring than the 2.5 liter Grand Prix cars could make in 1954. With a smaller engine, the sports car's maximum speed must be lower. So it must be improved roadholding that makes the difference."

Ten of the first customer cars were sold to the United States. Among those privateers in Europe acquiring RSKs were Behra, Count Carel de Beaufort, Wolfgang Seidel, and Heini Walter. Four of these "production" cars were built for European customers with duplicate mount points for the steering wheel shaft, driver's seat, and the foot pedals. The benefit of a center seat position for hillclimb was becoming apparent.

At the same time that the RSK lost the K suspension configuration in 1958, the FIA reinstated Formula 2 racing. It was decidedly lower-key than for FIA's premier series, Formula 1. The maximum engine size was 1500cc, running on pump fuel. For Porsche, this meant its already successful Spyders were eligible. And the regulations did not yet exclude cars with full bodywork.

And at Rheims, France, in an early F2 event, a privateer in his standard, enclosed 550A body demonstrated their obvious aerodynamic advantage. He won.

Next, Edgar Barth and Umberto Maglioli were entered in 550A Spyders in the Formula 2 race within the German Grand Prix at the Nürburgring, August 4, 1957. With spare tires and passenger seats removed, and with smaller, contoured windshields fitted, Barth took both the Formula 2 pole and the class win.

In 1958, Ferry Porsche responded to Hild's and von Hanstein's interest and an existing car was modified. After Le Mans but before Rheims, an RSK was converted to the center-driving position. The headlights and driving lights from Le Mans were replaced with a smooth cover. The rear wheels were also covered and the RSK winglets were fitted.

Racing director von Hanstein, recognizing the image value of nationalism, offered the drive to Jean Behra. And the Frenchman acquitted himself admirably with a 1st

Richard von Frankenberg:
"Since it gives no warning in advance of breakaway, right up to the last instant, in my opinion, the RSK is somewhat more difficult to drive than the 550A."

By 1958, distributors had long been removed from Ernst Fuhrmann's Typ 547/3 cam covers, the ends blocked off with plates. Twin Weber 46 IDM carburetors helped draw 148hp at 7500rpm out of the 1498cc engine. This car, chassis 718-033, was raced by the factory until September 1961, when it was sold. Right page, the aluminum body for the RSK was fabricated by Wendler. Modifications for racing in F2 later included center steering, which necessitated a new engine cover with a center headrest. After production met the factory's requirements, four were eventually offered for sale to privateers with this option.

place finish. At Nürburgring and again at Avus in Berlin, the center-steering RSKs provided encouragement for Hild and von Hanstein. Barth took 6th overall at the Nürburgring and Masten Gregory won his class in Berlin.

The customers, who by this time could purchase 718RSK models, could also order the optional center-steering hardware. By the time summer arrived, four had been sold and Formula 2 races frequently saw all four of the them on the entry list.

The conversion from left seat to center steering could be done in four hours. Owners were provided with the only two parts needed: it was necessary to replace the longer steering shaft with the shorter one and the shorter shift linkage with a longer one. The steering diagonal to the left seat was eliminated by the center placement and the shift linkage diagonal was introduced. During assembly, Porsche had incorporated additional brakeline length to allow for the changes in pedal position.

Two versions of the removable deck lid were shipped as well, with a left headrest and one in the center. With the two factory center-steering cars built first, Zuffenhausen produced a total of six. There was no racing in America for which the center seat was beneficial, so none of the these was originally delivered to US racers.

For 1959, the competition department prepared another car for Rheims. Fins and wheel covers, removed for the Nürburgring and Avus, stayed off in 1959. A higher windshield was required by new regulations. Wolfgang von Trips finished 5th. While the factory might have been discouraged by this result, it was not.

The interest in Formula 2 continued at Zuffenhausen. Still encouraged by its generally good results, Porsche took the December 1958, Formula 1 announcement from the FIA as a good omen.

For 1961, the regulations for Formula 1 would call for a maximum engine displacement of 1500cc. Open wheels were required but the weight minimum was down to 500kg (1100lb). For Hild, Helmuth Bott and engine development engineer Hans Mezger, it was a new challenge. It was met with the Typ 718/2.

By late April 1959, a stubby, cigar-shaped 718/2 Formula 2 prototype had tested at Malmsheim airfield. It was an open-wheel variation on the RSK theme. With a new tubular chassis and its aluminum body, it weighed just 520kg (1,144lb).

It would evolve through 1960 and 1961 as various Typ 787s. Its performance continued to encourage Porsche management. The Fuhrmann 547/3 engine was stressed further. Wilhelm Hild and Helmuth Bott improved the handling. The cigar shapes became more slippery, more fluid from the attention of Butzi Porsche.

The best drivers in the world raced open-wheeled Porsches: Germany's Wolfgang von Trips, Sweden's Jo Bonnier, England's Stirling Moss, and America's Dan Gurney.

Porsche was committed. Porsche was hooked.

Formula 1 was its objective.

CHAPTER 9

1959 356A Cabriolet By Beutler

Special Bodies Again

The business of Carrosserie Beutler in Switzerland was custom bodywork. As builders of Porsche's first cabriolets beginning in 1949, brothers Ernst and Fritz Beutler had long ties with Porsche beginning with the days in Gmünd. Ten years later, they still did custom, open Porsches. The Pur Sang, Pure Blood, was conceived for Duke Carl of Württemburg, based on the lines Ernst Beutler had used for a four-seater of his own. Beutler's car had been based on an Audi, which needed a radiator. But the Duke liked the front-end treatment and specified the same for his air-cooled model.

Ernst Beutler ate thousands of apples during the first decade of Porsche's growth. Yellow Glöcken Apples. Berne Roses, when they were in season, fresh, a day or two from the trees. Jonathans in the colder times. Whatever was available.

This was not a fetish. But it became a habit. A bowl of apples was always full in his design studio. And as he started a new design, he bit into an apple.

A decade had passed since Porsche initially approached Switzerland's Gebreuter Beutler Carrosserie to produce its first cabriolets. After six cars were completed over a span of two months, Beutler, a small coachbuilder, begged off. By 1957, Porsche had produced its 10,000th car and production at Reutter Karosserie was approaching six each day by lunchtime, seventeen every full day.

Yet while Porsche contemplated Formula 1 racing, its commitment solid, the firm had left some production areas out of its objectives. Opportunities still arose for small specialty firms.

Beutler Carrosserie was located in Thun at the northernmost corner of the Thunersee, in the shadow of the Simmentals, dozens of 3,300 meter Swiss mountains.

Twisting 25km south along the north bank of the Thunersee was the more elegant resort community of Interlaken. But Thun was not a resort. Thun was industrial.

The industry of Beutler was bespoke: custom bodywork to order. Ernst Beutler had apprenticed with Graber, one of Switzerland's finest coachbuilders whose lineage dated back literally to coaches. And in 1946, when Ernst and his brother Fritz were able, they rented space and opened their own business.

They did repairs, of course, to help pay the rent. But in those days, car bodies sat on an independent chassis. So, if one had imagination and a certain sense of style, one could have a special automobile—provided one also had a certain-size bank account.

Most of all, Beutler Carrosserie enjoyed making open cars from closed ones. Its first cabriolet was completed in 1947. It was later that year, as business seemed secure, that it moved up to much larger facilities, which it kept for the next quarter century. It was to this new, impressive workshop that Erwin Komenda first came to visit. Later Ferry Porsche came as well to visit the carrosserie that would produce the first production Porsche cabriolets.

In March 1948, Beutler exhibited for the first time at the annual Geneva Motor Show. In 1949, they showed Porsche's open sports car. A few orders followed. But soon after, when Komenda approached the Beutlers about handling series production, Ernst and Fritz declined. The carrosserie had neither the space, the manpower nor, honestly, the interest in regular series production.

Porsche cars, still without a permanent home, continued looking and soon cast its offer to Reutter Karosserie in Stuttgart. But to the Beutlers, they always returned phone calls, answered letters, always kept the door open.

In the years that followed, Ernst Beutler bit into many apples. In 1948, apple number 33 was the Porsche prototype cabriolet. Apple number 34 through 38 were the succeeding five production cars. A decade later, number 81 was another Porsche, this

Beutler's craftsmen made many of the trim pieces for the Duke's custom cabriolet. Difficulty in obtaining factory parts became the mother of invention. The interior is still original, although one driver's seat panel was replaced due to wear.

one entirely a private commission.

As Ernst Beutler later characterized it, "It was in Beutler style. We did more four-seater than two-seater cars. Our clients always asked: a coupe, nice shape, four places."

He had built himself such a coupe in 1956, on a Volkswagen chassis with VW running gear. A client saw it and commissioned an Audi. Beutler returned to the drawing board, took an apple, and, to accommodate the radiator, added a front grille. Another client saw that one, and commissioned another on a VW. Beutler took another apple.

Each car changed slightly. A gentle nudge of line here, a new piece of chrome trim there. More apples, more improvement. Another Geneva show. Another order. But this time for a four seater on a Porsche chassis. Apple number 82.

The Beutlers' bodies, for purposes of weight, were made in Swiss aluminum called "Aluman." This was hand-pounded over tubular forms. Aluman was initially a smooth material that work-hardened with the hammering. This made it quite suitable for Beutlers' assembly technique, butt-welding the panels by hand. But early in 1959, prior to body assembly, Erwin Komenda,

returned to Thun.

This visit was to represent Porsche's interests as the brothers stretched the standard chassis by 250mm to convert it to the four-place coupe. At Beutler, workers made a support to hold the car solidly in place with a hydraulic pump assembly to accurately open up the length. Komenda brought with him some Porsche frame rails, an extension for the gearshift linkage, and some modified wiring.

The car body he saw on Ernst Beutler's drawing boards and being hand-pounded over tubular forms did not appeal to him, and Komenda, the designer of Porsche's 356, said so.

Ernst Beutler recalled the conversation. "We discussed the front, the different bumpers, the different styling. And then they said I had to change 'the mouth,' to have another 'front.' And also...the back, more styled to integrate some original Porsche parts....'

This current coupe was too far along for such massive changes. In addition, it was already sold. Martin Townsend, a customer in New York, was waiting. He was expecting a car "in Beutler Style." But Komenda and his associates were dealing with an upper hand and a stacked deck.

"What they said," Ernst Beutler remembered, laughing now, "was, 'On our chassis, use our engine and keep the guarantee. And, if you would keep the style of the 356, we could help you to always get most quickly the trim parts and others that you need.'"

Beutler understood most quickly that if he didn't follow Porsche's recommendations, trim parts were not the only ones he might have difficulty obtaining. So, while his brother and their staff completed the first four-place coupe, Ernst Beutler returned to his apple bowl.

What resulted was a body style more reminiscent of Komenda's 356. Certain features were exaggerated, elongated to keep proportion with the longer wheelbase and longer roofline, but the Porsche family resemblance was now obvious. The lines were more pleasing to many, but they were less "Beutler."

Assembly time was eight weeks. This took

the forty to fifty body forms from raw flat Aluman to a welded body, ready for painting, next door to their colleague, Lothar Lauenstein.

The Beutler-styled four-place coupe, destined for New York, went first to Geneva for the show in March 1959. On the same stand, Beutler showed drawings of the new bodies on the Porsche chassis. These too generated some interest. But not from everyone.

Duke Carl of Württemberg saw the four-place Beutler coupe and envisioned it as a cabriolet. He had seen the bodywork done for the Audi, with the radiator and grille. The Duke wanted the same treatment. Ernst Beutler returned to his apple bowl and his drawing board.

After the initial contact, Duke Carl arrived in Thun with a complete standard 356A chassis from Porsche. Beutler had prepared for the Duke a scale drawing. Together they changed the lines of the fender and set a date for a "fitting."

"The Duke came once again to sit in the car," Beutler explained, "to check that he fit inside. Because he was very tall." So tall in fact, that Beutler had to redesign the convertible-top roofline to accommodate the Duke's height. "I liked the roofline of my coupe better," Beutler concluded.

Sold for 26,000 Swiss francs (roughly $8,125) finished in steel blue metallic with a beige cloth interior, the car was shipped directly to Württemberg. It was the last of the four-place Porsches in the "Beutler style." Whether Komenda exercised any direct influence is not known. But virtually all of the trim parts on the sole cabriolet were made by Beutler for the Duke.

With the six coupes that followed, the resemblance to Komenda's 356 became stronger and clearer. More and more standard production pieces appeared. Porsche had learned if it made itself clear, it got what it wanted. Thereafter, Beutler never had trouble obtaining parts.

As a four-seater, the wheelbase was stretched 250mm (9.84in), an activity supervised by Erwin Komenda himself. Komenda approved the stretch, but he did not care for Beutler's styling. As Beutler conformed more to Komenda's designs in later four-seaters, more factory parts became available to the Swiss. A bare, running 1600 Normal chassis was delivered to Beutler. Even with his all-aluminum body, the engine choice seems inadequate. A subsequent owner, Janis Joplin, replaced it with a Super 90, to run around San Francisco for nearly ten years. The original engine has been refitted.

CHAPTER 10

1961 Typ RS60LM

Stop The Presses! Get Me Rewrite!

Records indicate sixteen were produced in all and twelve were sold to private racers. For Le Mans, the driving lights were fitted; for the Targa Florio, those spaces accommodated loud horns! The factory continued racing RS60s itself due to its constant development of the two factory cars, even while they built RS61s for privateers.

Paul Ernst Strähle may be as well known among his racing colleagues for his movies as for his driving. Whenever the German was not racing, he pointed his spring-wound 16mm Bolex camera at his friends and their friends.

Strähle often travelled with his good friend Julius Weitmann, generally recognized as one of the greatest motor racing photographers ever. During one of their trips together, they drove to Sicily for the 1961 Targa Florio. When Weitmann drove, Strähle shot a travelogue of Italy through the windshield of his new Carrera cabriolet; when Strähle drove, no pictures exist. He made good time.

For the Targa in 1960, competition director Huschke von Hanstein had the services of Porsche's new update on the FIA regulations, the RS60. Based on the RSK, it clearly resembled it. Yet there were significant differences under the aluminum skin.

The RS60 wheelbase was lengthened by 100mm (3.9in) to 2200mm (86.6in). Space in the rear of the car was allowed—by specific regulation—for baggage, a suitcase of a specific size, 650 x 400 x 200mm (25.6 x 15.75 x 8in). Windshield height was also mandated. Front suspension used torsion bars (indi-

vidual adjustable left and right, on the factory cars only; a solid one on customer cars), trailing arms, an anti-sway bar, and Koni shock absorbers. The rear used unequal upper and lower wishbones, also with Koni coil-over shocks, much like the RSK.

Power came from the Fuhrmann Carrera Typ 547/3. The 1.5 liter engine produced 150hp at 7800rpm. Later versions, 547/4, with 1587cc, rated 160hp at the same engine speed, and then the 547/5—which increased bore by 0.5mm to 88 x 66mm for total overall displacement of 1605cc—produced 180hp for sprint races and 170hp for longer distances.

Records indicate fourteen cars were produced, the first four remaining as factory team cars. The others were sold to privateers—a first, since the customer cars were said to be virtually identical (except for the front torsion bars) to the Werks cars. The factory cars were promptly sent far from home for the season opener, to Buenos Aires where an RS60 took 3rd, then to Sebring where Olivier Gendebien and Hans Herrmann won, and next to the Targa Florio.

For the race in Sicily, the factory sent five cars, two with new 1687cc 90 x 66mm engines. These new engines allowed the cars to use the 100 liter fuel tanks permitted in the 2.0 liter class. Jo Bonnier teamed up with Hans Herrmann and brought the RS60 another victory, Porsches finishing 1st, 3rd, and 5th. However, the cars met with mixed results throughout the remainder of the season, and Porsche came 2nd to Ferrari in the Manufacturers' Championship. The little Carrera-engined cars proved underpowered against the Italians.

Their power and weight were perfect for the European Mountain Championship. Heini Walter and Sepp Greger finished 1st and 2nd—even using the same car in the last event of the season! The big change for 1961 was the introduction of a new engine, the Typ 587, of 2.0 liter displacement. Bore and stroke was 92 x 74mm for the plain-bearing engine, and it produced 165hp in endurance tune.

After the previous season's results, von

Huschke von Hanstein gave final instructions to Hans Herrmann, up on the pit wall, as mechanics finish a tire change at Le Mans in 1958. Codriven by Jean Behra, the factory RSK finished 3rd overall. Jesse Alexander. Below, the nose of the RS60 resembled the RSK, with split fuel tanks. The steering box and brake reservoirs divide the tanks. The twin nuts, visible on the upper torsion tube appear only on factory RS60s. These were fittings to allow suspension stagger, each nut jacking one torsion plate to tune suspension to circuits. Right page, the wheelbase of the RS60 was increased to 2200mm (86.61in). This improved handling as well as accommodating a lower nose and the FIA "baggage" within its overall dimensions.

Hanstein plotted revenge in Sicily.

Three factory cars, a new W-RS and two updated RS60s (known as RS60/61) were entered. The new RS61s had failed at Sebring a month earlier and were not trusted to Targa's challenges. The W-RS and one of the two RS60s, meant for Graham Hill and Stirling Moss, used the new 2.0 liter, its racing debut. The second RS60, for Hans Herrmann and Edgar Barth, used the 1.7 liter roller-bearing 547/4.

The Moss/Hill car was officially entered by Lloyd Casner's Camoradi Team (CAsner MOtor RAcing DIvision), who paid the bills while the Werks mechanics did the work. When Moss practiced, he ran one of the 2.0 liter training cars around the 71.4km (44.6 mile) circuit in 40:28, beating Ferrari's fastest time by 3:15!

Graham Hill, no slouch himself, had never been around the circuit until the previous year, when he pronounced it "unbelievable!" Yet, he won in 1960 in the RSK with Jo Bonnier.

Moss had also won with Peter Collins in a Mercedes in 1955. With Moss and Hill, Porsche was imagining its fourth outright win (Umberto Maglioli was first, in a Spyder in 1956; Edgar Barth and Wolfgang Seidel had won in 1959).

Von Hanstein was jubilant. He organized the team accordingly: Moss was to start and drive the first four laps. Spelled by Hill for two more laps, Moss would return and, it seemed, would drive the last four laps to victory.

Even Moss felt confident. Years later, over a long dinner with some friends, he recalled his feelings early that day.

"I woke up that morning and one of the few times in my life, I felt, 'For today's race, old man, you've got the ideal car,'" He smiled sublimely at the recollection.

"It was a super car," he continued, "perfectly balanced, just really tailor-made for the Targa."

And so it seemed. Cars started every half-minute and his RS60, car number 136, with the large yellow circle on its nose, left a little more than an hour after the first small cars went off. Moss drove furiously during his four laps. He pulled more than 90sec ahead of his nearest competition, Jo Bonnier and new Porsche teammate Dan Gurney, in the W-RS. Thirty seconds behind them was Olivier Gendebien and Wolfgang von Trips in the first Ferrari.

On Paul Strähle's screen, the Targa flickered silently. History filled his dark living room. The young faces spoke volumes.

1960 Bonnier; Hill Le Mans
1961 Barth; Hermann Sebring
1961 Moss; Hill Targa Florio
1961 Barth; Hermann Nürburgring
1961 Holbert Nassau
1982 Jürgen Barth Laguna Seca
136

Stirling Moss pulled out of the pits in the 1961 RS60 after a driver change from Graham Hill. After the pair had led 711km, the rearend seized and the car retired. Moss walked the last 4km. Porsche Werke. Right, chassis 718-044 was raced by Stirling Moss and Graham Hill in the 1961 Targa Florio. Where a fire bottle sits now, Moss stowed his thermos bottle of tea.

Strähle, relieved from his own Abarth Carrera by his codriver Antonio Pucci, went out to film another driver change. After the sixth lap, Graham Hill rounded the pit hairpin and skittered past Strähle's camera, into the Porsche pits. Stirling Moss exchanged places and pulled the yellow-nosed Spyder back out onto the roadway.

However, Moss and Hill were no longer in the lead.

By the time Moss returned to the car, exchanging driving duties again with Hill, Moss found himself 1:16 behind Gendebien who had overtaken Bonnier and Gurney. Yet within another three laps, Moss had eaten up the gap behind the Ferrari and pulled out nearly as much lead. When he rounded the pits beginning his tenth lap, he was 1:05 ahead, the Ferrari lead sacrificed by a long fuel stop and yet another Moss race lap record: 40:41. The noise of Strähle's projector left much to the imagination.

Writers from news services and newspapers around the world knew Moss and knew Porsche. By the halfway point on the final lap, near Bivio Polizzi, when Moss's pace had accelerated to where a sub-40-minute lap time seemed likely, the writers left, hoping to get a jump on their deadlines.

"Moss Wins Targa Florio" was the headline teletyped round the world. Moss's lead seemed indomitable.

One of the features of the new Typ 587/1 engine was its 35 percent increase in torque. The strain of 711km—done at near lap record speed for much of that distance—literally stretched the studs that held together the magnesium transmission side plates.

The imperceptible gap allowed the oil to seep out onto the Sicilian roads. The heat built up. The transmission welded itself tight. The differential seized. The back end locked up. With 3km to go to victory, Moss skidded to the side of the road.

Strähle's silent documentary showed a modest celebration going on in the Porsche paddock. While Gendebien and von Trips had won in a Ferrari, Bonnier and Gurney had come 2nd in the W-RS, and Herrmann and Barth had finished 3rd in their RS60. Strähle and Pucci had won their class.

At the edge of Strähle's frame stood an

ill-at-ease Graham Hill. Center on the scene was Huschke von Hanstein, Porsche's baronial motorsports director. They were calm faces; Porsche had not lost the Targa, but Porsche had not won.

Almost as if by director's cue, Strähle's black-and-white view picked up Stirling Moss entering from camera left. Lean, drawn, hot, with owl-eyes from road dirt sprayed around his goggles, his calm matched the scene. He knew what had happened. Moss and Hill both had reputations for being kind to transmissions.

He went to von Hanstein, and over Moss's shoulder, Strähle's audience saw von Hanstein's expression drop. The competition director put a hand on Moss' shoulder, turned and the two left the party.

Fade to black.

The gas cap, drilled out to reduce weight, perforated the thin aluminum front deck lid which was held in place by twin leather straps. As with the Spyders, the RS60s were built by Wendler in Reutlingen on a space-frame chassis assembled at Porsche. Below, for the 1961 Targa, a new 2.0 liter engine, Typ 587, was introduced. Its 165hp was shoehorned into the aluminum body just ahead of the FIA-required luggage space: 65 x 40 x 20cm (24 x 16 x 8in). The rear crossmember was removable to allow gear changes without removing the engine.

CHAPTER 11

1960 356B 1600 GTL Abarth Carrera

Winner Right Out Of The Box

Its name is larger than the tiny car it represents: 356B 1600 Carrera GTL Abarth/Zagato. Built in a series of twenty-one cars, it was engineered by Porsche, designed by Zagato, and assembled by Abarth. From the first, it was a winner.

Whenever Paul Ernst Strähle talks about the Abarth Carrera, it is simply the Carrera. All the other cars that Porsche named Carrera are just GTs to Strähle.

Strähle was a privateer who raced first with his father in Volkswagens in the late 1940s and early 1950s. And then he took over racing from his father. Closely allied with Porsche's competition department, he has driven as both independent and on many occasions, as a team driver even to the present day, fielding a championship-winning team in the Carrera Cup for Carrera 2 production-based lightweight cars.

Paul Strähle's already deep voice drops another half octave and his pace and diction slows down and spreads out. The word Carrera rolls off his tongue like he is tasting a fine brandy. Cah-Ray-Rah.

Around his eyes, the crow's-feet wrinkles deepen. Good memories. Maybe not always Porsche's fastest car, but with the Carrera in those times, always good memories.

"One time, in Rossfeld, in the European Hillclimb...." He began his speech, his crow's-feet wrinkles grew new toes. "There was a mistake in the regulations and it was not forbidden to go with two cars in the same category."

"Yes, I started with the Carrera and with the GT. And it was possible if I was one of the first contestants in the category, I went up the hill, finished, came back down the return road, then got into the other car and went up the hill again.

"And I finished *slower* in the Carrera. In each run—you got two runs, each car— each time, I was maybe three-tenths, four-tenths slower in the Carrera.

"I don't know. Maybe I made little mistake.

"I didn't win that race. Maybe Sigi Ginders won. I don't remember. I was 2nd. And 3rd."

Strähle's body, stocky even then, was stuffed into the miniature aluminum body. Klaus von Rücker's 1600cc four-cam Typ 692/3 engine was hidden beneath four dozen louvers.

The Carrera, for its striking looks, labored under one of Porsche's most cumbersome names: the Typ 356B 1600 GTL Carrera Abarth/Zagato. Each element of the name was significant, but the "GT" was its raison-d'etre.

The FIA Gran Turismo category was the class that sold cars for manufacturers. Developed in 1957 as a class for production models, the GT cars category had evolved by 1960 into something xenophobically competitive. Brand loyalties extended right up to but did not cross international borders.

Ferrari and Porsche each sought ownership of the GT classes and, to that end, little was spared in expense and effort. Ferrari stretched and stressed Gioachino Colombo's 3.0 liter V-12 in a succession of Testa Rossas.

The Fuhrmann engine, Typ 547, was called the Carrera to honor the company's victory in the Carrera Panamericana. For 1960, the new engine, Typ 692/3A, was used and power output was increased from roughly 100 to 135hp following a slight engine displacement increase of 99cc and other more significant developments. Main bearing journals were enlarged from 55 to 60mm, and the factory switched to plain

The interior strongly resembled the Carrera GT coupes in appearance, using the same aluminum-racing seats. But with its lower roofline, the interior dimensions really fit Italian coachbuilders better than the taller German racers.

bearings instead of rollers. Together with a redesigned intake-cam profile, the new version easily revved to 8000rpm. The 356B GT Reutter-built coupes, lightened through the removal of numerous trim pieces, weighed 848kg (1,866lb). Twelve volts fired dual distributors, one per bank.

The distributors in the early Typ 547 series engines were driven off the ends of the camshafts, which had only two main bearings and so were subject to some whip at high speeds. In these 692 series engines, both distributors were brought together in a V and were driven off the driveshaft. This eliminated the vibration and the unreliability.

Erwin Komenda's continual modification of his 356 body reflected Porsche's awareness of the impact of frontal area on aerodynamic drag as it related to top speed.

FIA rules set a weight minimum of 776.5kg (1,708lb) for the 2.0 liter category and if Porsche was to remain competitive, a new car was needed. But for this 1960 GT contender, the factory went outside for the design and construction. Wendler in Reutlingen were queried about their interest and their ideas. Wendler had done the 550 spyder bodies and was still producing aluminum RS61 coupes at that time.

But Porsche also looked across the border. It took advantage of its longtime association with Carlo Abarth to see if Ugo Zagato's design and fabrication firm might be interested. Porsche knew of the bodies that Zagato had done for Abarth, Alfa Romeo, and Lancia, competitors to Porsche in racing and in sales. Zagato was interested and his bid was lowest. He put young Franco Scaglione to work .

Scaglione's design reduced the frontal area of the 356B by 16 percent, by reducing each exterior dimension by nearly 125mm (4.92in). Production began early in 1960, as bare floorpans were shipped to Zagato's shops in Milan. The bodies, heavy-gauge aluminum hand-hammered over wooden forms, were mostly similar. But of course, these were race cars, so each was slightly different.

In all, twenty-one cars were produced. The interiors, Spartan even by GT standards, were barely large enough for the intended drivers. When the first bodies were returned to Stuttgart for detailing after Abarth's final assembly, seat rails had to be lowered and front wheelwells had to be enlarged. Standard factory instruments were fitted, including, curiously, a Smith's 10,000rpm chronometric tachometer wearing a VDO face.

Scaglione's creation worked. He had pared another 41kg (90lb) off the standard Reutter-bodied B GT, in the process producing one of the most sensuous Porsches ever. Scaglione's lines covered the headlights beneath plexiglass (in most but not all examples), extruded the driver's outside mirror from the fender like a piece of molded clay, and flipped the air up past the windshield wipers with subtle lips. But for reasons explicable only to racing politics, the cars initially bore no Zagato badges, only those of middle-man Carlo Abarth. Abarth had done only final mechanical assembly; his own shops, like Beutler's, were too small to accommodate a "series" production of even twenty-one race cars.

The first Abarth Carrera was delivered to the factory and prepared for the 1960 1,000km of Nürburgring. With only five louvers down low on each side of the round rear deck lid, engine cooling problems quickly developed. By the time the factory finished, they had opened up another thirty-eight breathing holes to feed the fan for engine cooling. An air box, operated from inside the car fed the large Weber carburetors for engine breathing.

As number 1001 was being prepared for its debut at the Nürburgring in late May, the second one, number 1002, was picked up at the factory and taken straight to the Targa Florio by Paul Ernst Strähle.

"We raced as number 16 that year. For the training we used my own GT and also one from the factory. I drove with Herbert Linge. We did one practice session in the Carrera. But we had a very curious problem.

"The people in traffic didn't see the silver cars. We came around a corner in Cerda in practice right at the beginning. The people

Progress to many car makers means their production cars put on weight. Porsche realized this with its new 356B, and chose to contend the Gran Turismo class in a new smaller, lightweight car. With Reutter's capacity strained, the racing department went outside—of the company and the country. Left, power for the Italian-built Porsches was the Typ 692/3A, with bore and stroke of 87.5 x 66mm, the total displacement of 1587cc produced 135hp at 7300rpm. By this time, the twin distributors were driven by a Siamese fitting off the crankshaft. Two Weber 40 DCM 2 carburetors fed the four-cam Fuhrmann-derived engine. In initial specification, Carrera engines used Solex carburetors, the owner of the firm being a friend of Fuhrmann's. Later, however, Porsche returned to Weber carburetors.

The Abarth Carrera's low overall height of 1321mm (52in) and its deceptively short, rakish length of 3983mm (156.8in) show clearly in company of pedestrians who tower over it. Wearing its famous Schondorf registration tag, WN-V1, this is the last of the three Abarth Carreras owned and raced by Paul Ernst Strähle.

heard the car but just didn't see it."

The crow's-feet wrinkles return. The eyes spark like twin plugs.

"If you had a yellow car, a red car, it was OK! So, we made the front orange a little bit and that became the sign of Carrera 16!

"The car, straight from Abarth to Porsche, from Porsche to Strähle, from Strähle to Sicily. We start. It goes. After 8 hours, 10 minutes, 10 seconds, we are finished. Carrera from new car at the factory the same week finishes 6th at Targa, 1st in class."

In 1002 as a privateer, he went to Nürburgring. Codriving with Heini Walter, he finished three places behind the factory prototype that ran the new disc brakes and so had to run GT Sports class. The Strähle/Walter Carrera took 10th, 1st in class.

In 1961, Strähle got the new 2.0 liter Typ 692/3A engine and the disc brakes, and returned to the Targa. This time, Sicilian Antonio Pucci co-drove. Again, 6th overall, again 1st in class. Then six months later, Strähle went to Corsica with Albert Pichet. "Well, I think, if the Targa had been the easiest to win in Carrera, then Corsica was the hardest to lose!"

Strähle settled deeper into a chair. The crow's-feet wrinkles twitched. "The Carrera was not the car for Corsica. The GT was better. From handling, visibility. But *we* think it is better to take the new car.

"So we were in Bastia, in a hotel. The owner was an Englishman. We had two cars, a Volkswagen 1500, red," Strähle laughed, remembering his own story of red, yellow and silver cars. "And we had the

Carrera. The Englishman had a garage in his hotel where we prepared our cars. We used the VW as the training car. Before the start of the rally, this Englishman came down. He said 'Take the Volkswagen. Don't take the other car on the Tour de Corse. Snow is coming! Snow and ice!'

"He went away and we laughed. We thought he was a little crazy. Snow? Ice? Corsica? Volkswagen, on the Tour?

"Well, in the Carrera, there was no heater in the car. No heater for the windshield or for the feet.

"Corsica rallies are mostly mountains. Eighteen mountains more than 1,500 meters. In all, the rally lap is 180 kilometers. Eighteen mountains! You are always in mountains. The island is only 170 kilometers long, 80 wide. So the rally route is 1,400 kilometers in one day and one night. It is all like this...." Strähle's hand flew around the room, randomly, rapidly, like an out-of-control roller coaster. "Nobody who makes a map could make this route!

"And so we took Carrera. And the temperature came to, in Fahrenheit, 10 degrees.

"There were so many holes in the car. In races in the rain, water came in everywhere. In windows, in the body. When it rained, there was always rain coming in the car from the sides and from the bottom. But it would always drain out. We put in big holes.

"But this was 10 degrees. Inside was ice, about 4 centimeters. And the ice didn't go out through the holes.

"We stopped in Corte. It goes up the highest road in the rally, Col de Bayern, it goes from zero to 1,300 meters. The snow comes. In Corte, Pichet bought a bottle of cognac.

"'Pichet,' I said, 'you know, I don't think I should drink this cognac....'"

"Pichet said, 'Ah yes, but..., you see we really don't have the clothes.... After all, this is not the Rally de North Pole!'"

The winner, a man named René Trautman, drove a Citroen ID-19. He jacked up his suspension and got 10km further along the road than Strähle and Pichet before getting stuck in the snow. Because he got farthest, he won.

For Strähle the Abarth Carrera was an almost ideal combination and in 1962, he replaced his first, chassis number 1002, with a new car, 1016. And in 1963, he earned the factory-team drive in 1018, again at the Targa, again with Pucci. Fifth overall, 2nd in class behind teammates Edgar Barth and Herbert Linge.

In the end, Porsche established many things with the Abarth Carrera. Even with tight control over outside assembly, Porsche would chose to stay closer to home in the future. And as a name, the Carrera originally designated Ernst Fuhrmann's engine, but it came to mean more. Its use was not yet exhausted at Porsche.

Strähle's last car, 1018, was powered by the new Typ 587/2 engine, the Weber carbureted 2.0 liter version producing 160hp. The oil reservoir extended through the right rear quarter panel to a quick-fill cap. For some events, auxiliary driving lights were fitted in the front, along side the oil cooler radiator duct. But for the Targa, two horns filled the holes on the silver-and-orange nosed Carrera.

"They couldn't see us," Strähle smiled. "They could hear us."

The sleek Franco Scaglione-designed and Carrozzeria Zagato-built Carrera reduced frontal area by 16 percent over the Reutter-bodied production 356B. The heavy-gauge aluminum bodies were hand-formed over wooden body bucks.

CHAPTER 12

1962 Typ 804 F1

The Pinacle Of Frustration

The pinacle of 1962, a somewhat frustrating year in Formula 1, was met at Solitude, on the east side of Stuttgart, when Dan Gurney raced this car past those pit boxes and the control tower opposite to win before a hometown crowd of 350,000.

At the end of the 1960 racing season, as Porsche prepared the next step into Formula 1, Huschke von Hanstein offered a factory F1 drive to American Dan Gurney. Von Hanstein had great confidence in Porsche's engineers who wanted 200hp out of its new 1.5 liter eight-cylinder Typ 753 engine.

"Huschke approached me, filled me with a lot of baloney," Dan Gurney recalled recently with a warm laugh. "At the time he was speaking to me—I didn't find this out until a long time later— they were making about 127hp out of their new eight-cylinder."

Gurney was in his third Formula 1 season. His first, with Ferrari in 1959, had been in Ferrari's 2.5 liter front-engine car. At the time, Ferrari believed horses pulled carts and engines belonged in front. So in 1960, Gurney went to Sir Alfred Owen's British Racing Motors. The BRM mid-engine car offered Gurney the technological advance but had none of Ferrari's reliability. With teammates Jo Bonnier and Graham Hill, the three drivers finished only one single race each during the season.

Joining Porsche in 1961 offered promise, even if the season was to be run in 1.5 liter-engined Formula 2 cars. Gurney finished 2nd in three events. But, in 1962, after a year of racing "last year's cars," the Porsche team looked like the best decision of Gurney's young lifetime in Formula 1.

"They looked dominant from the standpoint of reliability," Gurney explained. "Over the years, they had refined their 1.5 liter four-cylinder to the point it was making 165hp. With their new eight-cylinder and the new car, it looked to be the opposite of my experience with BRM."

Bonnier and Gurney went with the new cars to Zandvoort, the Grand Prix of Holland.

"For 1962, it was an all new car, but it seemed like it needed aid." Gurney laughed at the problems facing the new car.

"I couldn't fit in it. That wasn't their fault. I looked like a giraffe driving around in the thing. It had reasonable top end power, an OK mid-range, and not-so-good low-end power. But they felt it was brought out prematurely, it wasn't quite ready...."

After the disappointing showing at Zandvoort, Ferry Porsche decided they would not go out again until they could run a Grand Prix distance without breaking down. The team hired Nürburgring for private testing. In charge of the sessions was Helmuth Bott, head of Porsche's experimental section at the time. He took with him Hubert Mimler (who had worked with Butzi Porsche on the car's design), Hans Mezger, designer of the 804 engine, Peter Falk from the competition department, and racing mechanics Karl Dubies and Ludwig Lehner, and factory test driver Herbert Linge.

Bott was known for doing a great deal of his own test driving. He preferred getting his information firsthand. However, he recognized that race drivers could tell him things he couldn't get himself from a car. He learned more, too. For three days, Gurney tested shock absorbers with Herbert Linge on the south circuit. Then they moved to the Grand Prix circuit with Bonnier for the endurance tests.

When the day was done, the cars had completed the Grand Prix distance, fifteen

laps, and in the bargain, set a new lap record, 8:44.4. It was cause for celebration. The car was, at last, dialed in. And at The Old Woodman, a restaurant nearby, they went and celebrated, engineers, mechanics, and drivers.

At Rouen, on July 8, 1962, the results proved the value of the work. But years later, Gurney viewed his—and Porsche's—first GP victory as less than fully satisfying.

"We won that race by virtue of having a troublefree run. You could just wail away on the thing and it wouldn't break. The other guys did. That's not exactly the way you want to win it...."

The British GP followed the French, and after a disappointing showing in England, the next race was Nürburgring where Gur-

ney now held the track record and where Porsche arrived fairly confident after its long testing and the French GP victory a month earlier.

"That whole build-up led to one of the biggest disappointments in my driving career," Dan Gurney remembered, looking at a photograph of the group at The Old Woodman taken years later.

"I ended up being on the pole in the Porsche at the 'Ring in 1962. This was, of course, a big hit with the home crowd."

A contemporary newspaper race report set the scene: "August the fifth dawned like the end of the world. A crowd of some 350,000 cheered by the hope of a Porsche victory, converged on the area of the Nürburgring in lashing rain that must have had a special grudge against motor racing. Black clouds hung low over the Eifel Mountains and the scene looked like something straight out of a Wagner opera."

"It rained the whole race," Gurney explained. "And when you start on the pole, you start on a concrete apron and the other guys start on asphalt. And it just happened that the asphalt had better traction."

That was one problem. In addition, Gurney had elected to not change the setup of his chassis because he felt it was good. Graham Hill, in a BRM and John Surtees, in a Climax-powered Lola, had softened theirs.

"Well, what happened was we started off and I led Hill around for the first two laps. And then a thing happened that scared me.

"The car's battery was supposed to be on the left side, just ahead of my left knee. But it broke loose in the cockpit. It was sliding around my legs and feet. The fuel system was aluminum tanks that kind of fit through the tubes of the chassis. And, you know what happens when a battery shorts out on an aluminum fuel tank?"

Gurney laughed about it thirty years later, sitting still in his dry office in Southern California.

"So I'm thinking, 'Hmmm, it hasn't gone up yet...,' so I decided to try and hold it in position with my left leg. While I was doing that, I lost the lead to Hill, and then a lap later I lost 2nd place to Surtees. I dropped

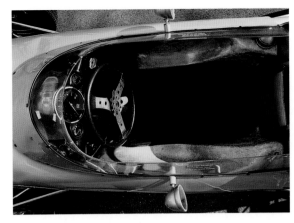

about 18 seconds on them. But once I got it locked into position, I just sort of got back down to driving."

This was "driving" in a car with a six-speed transmission around a 22.6 km (14.1 mi) circuit with 176 corners requiring more than 300 shifts per lap, in the rain.

"And I caught them! I caught up that 18 seconds. But I couldn't get past them!

"What was happening, well, you have to remember, that was a pretty narrow track." Gurney laughed again, at the futility of his efforts. "So while I could actually lap faster than they could, when I got up to them, they'd hold me up in the corners and then accelerate away. I almost ran into Surtees quite a few times. It was a frustrating race. We ran nose to tail for the last five laps. We finished within 4 seconds, the three of us, Hill 1st, then Surtees, then me."

But Solitude, a month earlier, had been different. Helmuth Bott recalled a meeting just before the local event.

"Professor Porsche gave us a very hard task. 'If we don't win this year some more races, then we stop these races.' And our problem was we didn't have the last 10 horsepower," Bott recalled. "By then we had 195, maybe 196. But we never had the 205 to 210 that we had to have to safely win the races that year."

"The Solitude Race was a tremendous event." Dan Gurney slouched back as though he had slid again into the 804.

"There was a hotel and a restaurant up at the hairpin. And then it came back down to the pits, through these sweeps. Very smooth, very fast. Each one looked almost exactly like the others but it wasn't.... It was exceedingly difficult to learn the place because you couldn't practice on it. It was public roads.

"So what happened was that weekend, it was a dual event. They had the Grand Prix of Motorcycles there in addition to all the Formula 1 cars. And after winning that race, part of their ceremony was they took me in a convertible for a victory lap."

Porsche's immediate Formula 1 goals had been met in front of a hometown crowd hungry for a victory. However, at that point, the die was cast: the financial commitment needed to win the championship in 1963 would jeopardize the production cars, a situation Ferry Porsche found unsatisfactory. Butzi Porsche, who had designed the Typ 804, was already at work on what those new cars would be, the cars his father knew the company needed. The moment was over for Porsche in Formula 1. But the moment was unspoiled for Gurney.

"They had this tiny little crowd...of 350,000!" Gurney understated it with a laugh. "These were the locals." In the dry, stillness of southern California, Dan Gurney went quiet. "It was a very special moment," he said softly, "something I'll never forget.

"When they took me around that lap in the convertible, at least 100,000 of them were throwing their hats in the air when we went by."

Above far left, after years of preparation in F2, Porsche entered F1 in 1961 with a car designed by Butzi Porsche. Evolved from his 718/2 and 787, the 804 premiered at Zandvoort, May 20, 1962. Above left, Dan Gurney and Jo Bonnier sat cradled by fuel tanks. The car weighed 455kg (1,001lb) overall, the body only 24.9kg (54.8lb). In places, its aluminum and fiberglass skin was barely thicker than paper. Above, Dan Gurney leaned over Butzi Porsche's new Typ 804 to talk with Ferry Porsche and Helmuth Bott on the grid. After Zandvoort, Porsche sent Gurney and Bott to Nürburgring for more testing.
Jesse Alexander

CHAPTER 13

1965 904/6 Carrera GTS

A Carrera By Any Other Name

In November 1962, after experimenting with making racing driver's seats in "plastic," Hans Tomala, Wilhelm Hild, and Butzi Porsche conceived the idea to do an entire car in fiberglass. Expected to compete in the FIA Group 3 Grand Touring class, the car had to be ready for driving tests before May 1963.

In those days, the entire company was small. The design staff was only seven, including F. A. Porsche. Thirty years later, seated in a small, bare conference room in Porsche Design headquarters in Zell am See, Austria, Butzi Porsche explained how it came about. His hands rarely moved. His deep voice created the images.

"It was my father's wish that I get to know the car body engineering division, to simply gather knowledge 'from scratch.' I knew Erwin Komenda and Franz Reimspiess from my childhood, dating back to Gmünd and even before Gmünd, to the old Stuttgart days before the war.

"I started in the firm working with Mr. Reimspiess, then after nine months, I went to work with Mr. Komenda. He was very strict, he had very formal views about everything, steering wheels for example, doors. So many areas were his...his car body division.

"We disagreed; he would tell me I was doing things not the right way. Many times." Butzi Porsche stared out the window. The memories of 1958 seemed suddenly immediate.

"Despite all that, I was already sure of what I was going to do one day: it was definitely the car body—and specifically, the car body in relation to the engine—I would do the design. In design, there is 'styling,' 'art,' and other terms intermingled. 'Design' means to me that every designing engineer has the opportunity to become at some stage an artist."

F. A. Porsche, speaking in his Austrian-accented German, paused for the meaning to sink in, and then he continued. "Every craftsman who can do more than what he was trained to do is an artist; this is because he develops a degree of 'perfection' that surpasses the level of the acquired skills."

For Porsche, then 28, head of the newly named Styling Department, the opportunity to "surpass" came quickly.

"I was well acquainted with Wilhelm Hild and Hubert Mimler and the whole staff of the racing division. So one day we said, 'Let's make a car!' In those days we were already processing plastic...."

Hild's staff used to pound every racing driver's seat out of sheet metal. But they began to use fiberglass because it took so much less time. The driver came in, sat down and they made the mold. This was done not only for factory team drivers but also customers. It met with wide acceptance.

"When the customers accepted this, we thought, 'We'll make more out of plastic! Why don't we make a whole car?' At first we simply had made parts out of plastic that had been sheet metal in the past. This was faster!" Porsche explained.

Hans Tomala, in charge of the development of a new racing car for the FIA Group 3 GT class, was also aware of the possibilities of "plastic." Willing to break new ground, Tomala coordinated the efforts of the chassis engineers to complete a frame using two large variable-section box struts. They added crossmembers but Tomala understood Butzi Porsche's conviction that the car body could be used to add additional stiffness.

In November 1962, Porsche began to work on the parameters given to the new car, the Typ 904.

"In the homologation," he said, "there was a parameter that a suitcase of a cer-

tain measurement had to fit in to a trunk, there was also an engine specification, we had conceived a wheelbase and wheel track.... But the primary parameter from Tomala was aerodynamics."

"We started off with just the Plasticine model. We would sometimes make subdivisions of the car by drawing lines on those models, sometimes from above, sometimes from the side. And then we would develop it."

Porsche worked not from drawings, but from models.

"That is how this kind of shape evolves automatically. I don't know; it might have been because I wasn't so good at drawing." Butzi Porsche laughed at his own admission. "But in my opinion, this 'touchable' quality is the result more of feel than of, say architecture of line. Feel it, touch it, work on it. It becomes more 'touchable.'"

"With this car, it was an idea from the beginning that the underbody could be *pulled up* above the actual frame part. This is how the edge evolved on the 904. It represents a separating joint between top and bottom." Porsche retrieved a wind-tunnel model of the 904 and continued.

"One can actually see the joint 'run through,' run around the entire car. The concept was to make the underbody, the bottom, out of high-grade steel, constituting a metal unit together with the frame. And the upper body was mounted on top, the top half, made only of plastic."

Porsche's wind-tunnel model used a lighter color below the "joint" to identify the frame. The plastic body above stopped clearly at that joint. Everywhere except at the doors.

"Originally there still existed a door as designed by Komenda, which was 'pulled down' through the structure. But it couldn't be opened at the sidewalk...."

"Come to think of it, it was absolutely crazy." Porsche frowned. This new thought troubled him.

"All this, just for the sake of giving the door a greater resemblance to a 'proper door.' We were accustomed to the idea that the door had to go down relatively low and that it needed to be round at the bottom.... Mr. Komenda had insisted on that."

Porsche stopped again, to examine his model.

"But the doorsill inside the door was so high that to get in we had to climb over the doorsill...."

Butzi Porsche rose and stood over his model, then picked it up, offering a new perspective.

"The 904 is a car that should not only be viewed from the front and the back, but

Regarded by many as the most aesthetically pure race car design, left page, the Typ 904 was the clear result of what can occur when a designer is given a tight deadline and then left alone completely. Below, high-cut doors were introduced with the 904.

Butzi Porsche's interior never betrayed its fiberglass origins. Heavyweight drivers or passengers dared not put a foot foul for fear of penetrating the thin floor. Between driver and passenger shoulders was the ski-binding-type lever that released the rear deck. Below, Butzi Porsche's design intention was to emphasize the joint between the high-grade steel underbody and the upper body, made of plastic. Scale models even showed different colors.

also from above. It is this line, beginning at the headlights, which tops the doors and continues over and through to the back.... It is so important to create such products with all the perspectives in mind.

Porsche stared a long moment at the

"product" he had done thirty years ago. He smiled briefly.

"We could have improved the aerodynamics.... Mr. Tomala even meant to elongate the car, because the aerodynamics would have been slightly better that way, but there was simply...." His voice trailed off.

There was simply no time. And Butzi Porsche had another thought.

"There was something else," Porsche said, reaching for the model again. "These ventilation holes, people call them the 'ears,' in the sides of the hoop. There were only holes, and the idea behind it was not that the cool air was *pushed in* through there, but that hot air was *sucked out*. Ventilation should be located in the back, where the engine was, where the backlight was."

He sighted along the roof line of the model. "The aim was to have the aerody-

namic shape achieve a 'removal by suction.' But there was no time to work that out perfectly.

"That was the beauty of this product. And that is also the reason why the car body remained so unchanged. Because we were told nothing can be changed. This car was four months, working days and nights, from the first Plasticine model to completion of the driving prototype."

Ferdinand Alexander Porsche looked out the window of the second floor conference room once more.

"I think that an advantage was the fact that I was the son, which can entail advantages and disadvantages. People would pay more attention to what I said due to the fact that I had a direct line to the boss.... I would be able to work out a proposition, put it in front of him and say, 'See! That's it!'"

That was an advantage, surely. The disadvantage was surely the burden of expectation. This car, produced from idea to driving prototype in less than half a year, allowed no margin for error, for restarts, for

second chances. It was new technology every step of the way.

"Completing that car, the 904, it was almost like living in an enclosure, like in a monastery. There was only the excitement of creation.... If I had to tell you how many hours that took, I wouldn't be able to...."

"This is true for all my work. There is the process of thinking about it. You can talk about it. But it is ultimately the 'feeling' that motivates you to decide this way or another. This 'feeling,' it's a very important stage."

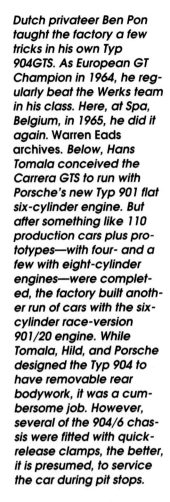

Dutch privateer Ben Pon taught the factory a few tricks in his own Typ 904GTS. As European GT Champion in 1964, he regularly beat the Werks team in his class. Here, at Spa, Belgium, in 1965, he did it again. Warren Eads archives. Below, Hans Tomala conceived the Carrera GTS to run with Porsche's new Typ 901 flat six-cylinder engine. But after something like 110 production cars plus prototypes—with four- and a few with eight-cylinder engines—were completed, the factory built another run of cars with the six-cylinder race-version 901/20 engine. While Tomala, Hild, and Porsche designed the Typ 904 to have removable rear bodywork, it was a cumbersome job. However, several of the 904/6 chassis were fitted with quick-release clamps, the better, it is presumed, to service the car during pit stops.

CHAPTER 14

1966 906 Le Mans

The Long-Tailed Bat: Enter Piëch

After the end of the 1966 season, 906-153 was sold to Swiss privateer Rico Steinemann. Together with his friend and codriver Dieter Spoerry, the two campaigned the car with good results through 1967, though at mid-season, they replaced the LM-wagen tail with a standard short tail. Two of 1996 Le Mans cars raced with new Bosch mechanical-fuel-injected Typ 901/21 engines. These 2.0 liter 87 x 66 mm flat sixes produced 220hp at 8000rpm. The Typ 822 transaxle provided reverse plus five forward gears and the combination propelled the LM-wagens to 295km/h (184.4mph) along Mulsanne.

As the idea first came to him, Rico Steinemann figured he could do it in his own car. His friend and teammate, Dieter Spoerry, was intrigued so arrangements were begun. In early August 1967, after Spoerry had won a prototypes race in Sicily at Enna-Pergusa, they headed back north and stopped at Monza.

Steinemann wanted to challenge several endurance records. His Carrera 6 with two seasons of proven performance behind it seemed a logical choice; Monza with its high-speed banking seemed the likely venue.

"At the time, we didn't work with a computer," Steinemann recalled. "We couldn't calculate whether the car was quick enough, so we went to the track and tested.

"Of course, these records were made in the early 1940s. They were American world records, made in a circle on a salt lake! But the Carrera 6 was so much faster. We found we could easily average nearly 250km/h (156.3mph) where the old records were around 180km/h (112.5mph)."

The competition debut of Porsche's Typ 906 took place on February 5, 1966, at the Daytona 24 Hours. So low (98cm or 38.6in

tall), it made Ford's GT-40 (101.6cm, 40.0in) look massive by comparison. A well-known review said the 906 appeared "shaped from the inside by regulations, from the outside by the wind."

Conceived as the successor to the 904 GTS, the Carrera 6 was the first project to bear the imprimatur of 29-year-old Ferdinand Piëch, named head of Research and Development in 1965. By then, cousin F. A. Porsche's Typ 904GTS was a year old. The 904 had been designed to meet strict homologation requirements, and it was expected that Porsche would have to sell some versions as road cars, for non-races, in order to meet production requirements.

When Piëch arrived at Zuffenhausen, he declared that if Porsche was to make cars for racing, they would be real racing cars. From him quickly came the purposeful-looking no-holds-barred 904 spyder, nicknamed the *Kanguruh*. The Carrera 6 marked the firm's return to a steel-tube space-frame chassis after the interruption of the 904. Only mechanical parts were carried over from the last 904 series: transmission, engine, and suspension.

The Typ 906 Carrera 6 was built to meet the FIA's new Sports Car category in 1966. It required fifty identical examples be built for homologation. But so large a production run out of Porsche's racing shops was taxing and the solution came through outside contractors.

Frames were manufactured by Karosseriewerk Weinsberg who were especially challenged by one innovation of Porsche's engineers: the umbilical that connected the front-mounted oil cooler to its reservoir was two frame tubes. Welding to Porsche's quality vexed Weinsberg. Leaks were discovered in an early chassis that sent oil into more tubes than the designers had specified.

The body also was done outside, by BWR near Karlsruhe, who were slightly less taxed than Heinkel's fiberglass workers had been with the 904. The earlier car was sprayed and counted some fifty individual pieces to make up a body. But BWR had to deal with fewer than half that number, now hand-laid

cloth and resin work, and with a number of pieces being large panels.

Visually, the new car differed drastically from its forbear. The 904, designed by Butzi Porsche in plastic, by feel, had set a benchmark with its intuitive aesthetics. The 2300mm (90.6in) wheelbase, 1534mm (62.76in) wide 904 gave a frontal area of 1.32 square meters and a Cd of 0.33. The 1680mm (66.1in) wide 906 shared the wheelbase but by carefully reading the rules, its narrow cockpit kept frontal area to 1.325 square meters. But the use of 15in wheels and large engine cooling air scoops raised its Cd to 0.35. These numbers were measured before the rear spoiler was fitted and prior to introduction of the front "winglets" that assisted in generating downforce to improve roadholding, but did increase drag.

The 2.0 liter engine, Typ 901/20, in standard form with two three-choke Weber-carburetors, was rated at 210hp at 8000rpm. Actually an extreme development of the

911 series-production engine, it produced closer to 220hp. And just before Le Mans in 1966, the Typ 901/21 fuel-injected engine was installed but it offered negligible power differences.

In its initial, short-tailed version, the car was an out-of-the-box success, winning its class outright at Daytona on February 6, 1966. The low, blue coupe was quickly dubbed the "Batmobile" by writers and

Lacking the grace of Butzi Porsche's Carrera GTS Typ 904, cousin Ferdinand Piëch's Kanguruh Bergspyder has been described as the ugliest Porsche ever, left page. Above left, transporters loaded to depart for the 1965 Targa Florio carried a new Porsche weapon, conceived by Ferdinand Piëch. His new 904/8 spyder, the Kanguruh, contrasted severely with his cousin Butzi Porsche's shapely 904GTS. Above, following its 2nd place Targa finish, the 904/8 Kanguruh ran the Norisring in July. Gerhard Mitter seemed preoccupied with the crash beside him. The stubby bergspyder wore a more efficient windscreen by then. Below, team drivers Jo Bonnier and Graham Hill found the car too twitchy and ill-mannered, bouncing around too much for their liking for the May 1965 Targa Florio. So, Colin Davis and Gerhard Mitter were assigned the Spyder, 906-007—and seven hours later, came home 2nd overall.

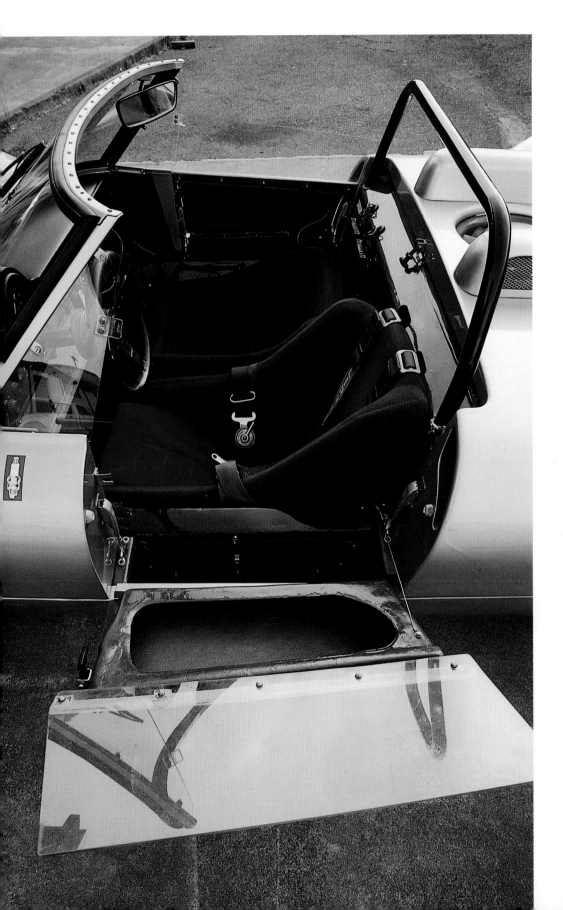

photographers who loved its gullwing doors. By the time Le Mans arrived, the Batmobiles had proven themselves although not always with outright victories. And Ferdinand Piëch had used the Carrera 6 to initiate another innovation: a new car for every major race.

Metal parts—frame members, primarily—developed stress fractures from the race conditions. Especially after such events as the Targa Florio, the pounding of the road surfaces weakened these pieces to such an extent that frame broke in subsequent events. Piëch analyzed the causes of his cars retirements and crashes and concluded that from that point on, all "important" races would be run with brand-new cars.

For Le Mans, Piëch wanted to try something different. The task of designing a longer tail for the 906 for Le Mans was given to Eugen Kolb. Kolb had joined Reutter as a body designer in 1951 and when the karosserie was absorbed by Porsche in 1963, Kolb transferred his talents to the experimental department.

The April 15, Le Mans trials were approaching rapidly. Kolb designed both an extended subframe and other modifications—resulting in an exaggerated body work—a longer, slightly lower nose and a much longer tail. This extra 400mm (15.75in) length allowed a cleaner exit of the air off the body. At this time, Piëch decided to go the entire experimental route and include in the 906 "Le Mans Wagen" project the mechanically injected Typ 901/21 motors. Three of the long-nose, long-tail cars were produced for Le Mans and eventually six other long-nose cars were produced as well.

At a pace typical of the racing shop, Kolb's finished tail designs were drawn on April 7, 1966. The body extensions were hand laid-up by the racing shop from a cannibalized standard short-tail body. The first 906LM prototype was completed seven days later.

Of the three cars built for the 1966 running at the Sarthe, two were injected, one was carbureted. First practice sessions with the long-tail cars revealed the Kolb extensions did increase top speed but also induced a rear lift strong enough that driver's reported hearing rear wheel spin.

Experiments with the standard full-width 906 spoiler caused front-end lightness. Balance ultimately came from two small flap-type spoilers at the end of the long tail and two small front flap spoilers.

Factory records revealed another benefit: improved fuel economy. The standard short tails returned 24.4 liters/100km (9.7mpg) at race speeds while the long tails stretched the gallon to 21.5 liters/100km (11mpg). The slipperier Kolb shape was much easier on engine wear as well, with the long-tail cars consuming half the oil that the short coupes used. And Jo Siffert lapped 6sec faster than the standard coupes.

The success of the cars was beyond even Piëch's expectations. Through much of the 24 hours, the race was run in rain. It took eight of the 7.0 liter 485hp Ford Mk II cars to beat the 2.0 liter Porsches. While Fords swept 1st, 2nd, and 3rd—the other five retiring—Piëch's 906LMs swept 4th, 5th, and 6th. Car 906-153, with factory drivers Siffert and Colin Davis, finished 4th overall and won the Index of Performance. Siffert touched 275km/h (171.9mph) along Mulsanne in his 906 Le Mans Wagen. One lap behind was Hans Herrmann and Herbert Linge, and one more lap back was Udo Schütz and Peter DeKlerk.

To Ford, this victory—its winner covered 4,483km (2,801.9 miles) in 24 hours—was the result of three years of factory effort, and a year later, the US effort withdrew. For Piëch—for Porsche—this was a triumph. The Siffert/Davis 906 Le Mans Wagen covered 4,205km (2,628.1 miles), only 278km (173.8 miles) fewer than Ford.

Le Mans was the harbinger. It introduced a new name to Porsche lexicography and to winner's circles: langheck, the long tail.

As a privateer, Rico Steinemann bought the ex-Siffert factory long tail, 906-153, shortly after the 1966 season ended. The final appearance as a long tail was in April 1967 for the 1,000km at Monza. But during the summer, with Porsche factory help, Steinemann made a short tail for the car, with an eye to the Monza trial.

"The long tail was very quick on the straight, but very much unstable for the Monza banking. You see," Steinemann

explained, "we had to go day and night, with fog and everything. And we wanted a really stable car...so we opted for a Carrera 6 short tail but with the long-tail nose."

Four months later, after his August testing session at Monza had blown up his fuel-injected engine, Steinemann returned to Switzerland and began setting up a world record trial organization. He had a sponsor, British Petroleum, but what started as a small privateer's effort brought a larger realization.

"Everything was getting too big, too expensive. With BP behind us, we knew that

The wheelbase of the Kanguruh, far left, was 2300mm (90.6in), its length overall 3300mm (129.92in), left page. With almost no overhang front or rear, several of the drivers said it hopped and skipped more than it "handled." Hence its name, Kanguruh. Below, the spare instrument panel indicates oil pressure, engine speed, and oil temperature. With an eight-cylinder time-bomb millimeters behind the driver's head, such information was essential. Left, for the 1966 Le Mans, Jo Siffert and Colin Davis raced this car, number 30, chassis 906-153. Piëch's esteem for long noses and long tails was validated. The 2.0 liter 906LMs finished 4th, 5th, and 6th, and it took 7.0 liter Fords to beat Siffert and Davis.

Flat fan revisited, in another super-lightweight Porsche competition car. Based on the 904 chassis, but given 906 numbers, the Bergspyder was powered by the new flat eight-cylinder Typ 771. With 240hp available to propel 570kg (1,254lb), the car was a real handful. Right, two tunnels interrupt the cowl. In front of the driver, the larger housed the tachometer, the smaller for the oil-temperature gauge. Immediately below, an oil-pressure gauge was added during restoration for purposes of engine safety.

from the technical point of view we should not make mistakes.

"Our car had done an entire season. It had been a factory car the year before that. So even overhauling it entirely, there was a risk....

"So I presented the whole project to Ferdinand Piëch, asking for help. I suggested we should take a new factory car, specially built for this purpose. Piëch confirmed our test driving results in Monza."

Piëch authorized manufacture of a new 906 Carrera, 906-162, filled with subtle special features. Based on factory experiences at both Daytona and Monza, a "staggered" suspension was fitted. This increased the car's ride height on the higher side of the banking.

Engine modifications were necessary too. The 2.0 liter six-cylinder fuel-injected Carrera 6 engine required valve adjustment every 5,000km (3,125 miles). This meant removing the engine. The amount of time required would jeopardize the entire goal. Running a world record attempt for four days meant that these valves would run 20,000km (12,500 miles) or more without readjusting.

British Petroleum was interested in the project as a way to promote a new engine oil. They too would be running 20,000km without changing oil. For both companies, the appeal of Steinemann's project was the technical challenge.

So the new 906 was prepared. And in September, Steinemann and Siffert met for testing down in Monza. The testing lasted 12 hours. "Everything was fine and we went back home, very happy," Steinemann recalled. "And that was the big mistake. We underestimated the poor condition of the banking."

Monza banking was parabolic banking, not flat banking like Daytona Speedway. Opened in 1955, Monza followed the style of Avus and Brooklands. In its first days, sports car races were run on the combined circuit of a flat infield together with the banked outer curves. There had been Indianapolis-type races, with American cars in June 1957 and 1958. Those two years, The Race of Two Worlds was run, in the opposite direction, on the banked oval alone. Indy cars could only turn left.

The oval's banking, slightly more than 38 degrees at its steepest, would have accommodated speeds to nearly 325km/h (203mph) in 1955. In 1958, Tony Bettanhausen, qualifying for the "Monzanapolis 500" set a lap record of 283.25km/h (177mph) on the 4km (2.5 mile) oval.

But from the start, there were problems: some pilings supporting the banking sank into the soft soil. Others didn't. Some split. The road surface undulated, rising and falling to the contour of the piling supports. The 1961 Italian GP was the last time the banking was used in competition. The joints between the concrete sections had become too pronounced and the increased suspension loading on the high banking had begun to take its toll. This condition had proven the nemesis of other recent record attempts. Abarth's effort in 1966 failed when the car's suspension broke on the banking.

Steinemann's team for his attempt was now set with four Swiss: Dieter Spoerry, Swiss national champion Charles Vögele, and Porsche factory driver Jo Siffert. The factory's new car was painted in Switzerland's racing colors, red with white. The American company, Firestone Tire and Rubber, agreed to provide tires; they were tire suppliers in 1957 and 1958 for the Indy cars. The entire record attempt quickly assumed an international context.

"At the time, in Switzerland, there was a new daily newspaper," Steinemann recalled. "In order to promote themselves, they sent an editor and a photographer down to Monza for a whole week. And every day, they did stories about our progress!"

By this time, both the factory and Steinemann had carefully and thoroughly read the rules from the FIA that governed such events. In a world record attempt, you could only change spare parts that you had carried with you in the car. And you could only use the tools that you had on board as well. Anything that you anticipated needing to replace—except for wheels, tires, and oil—must have been carried inside the car. They had a box, in place of the passenger seat.

All of which made the car heavy.

At noon, Sunday, October 29, in sunlight only just emerging from thick fog, Siffert headed the specially built, closely watched, internationally supported, short-tail, long-nose, overweight, Carrera 6 out of the pits and north along the Tribune Straight. Up through the gears, he bore off to the right and into the Curva Nord, the north high-speed curve. The car hunkered down, kissing the suspension bump stops under nearly 3 g's of load. It would be the first of 1,250 times that Siffert, Steinemann, Spoerry, and Vögele could *each* expect to enter that banking.

For the first 7 hours, each driver covered the 4km once in every 64.6sec. Within minutes of 9pm, the first record was theirs: 1,000

miles at an average of 225.63km/h (141.0mph). The car, the drivers, the centrifugal force pounded on. At 7000 revs along the straights, lift to 6200 for the banking, back up to 7000, back down to 6200. Back up. Back down. Back up. Back down.

After 9 hours, 57 minutes, 6sec, the second record was broken: 2,000km (1,250 miles) had been done at an average of 216.99km/h (135.6mph). At that pace, a lap was taking just under 66.4sec. Once every 33.2sec, the driver leaned the car to the right and awaited the pounding. Down to 6200. Back up to 7000. Back down. Lean right.

Shortly before 10pm, the car's handling took a decided turn for the worse. The front left shock absorber ripped out of the body of the car. The pounding had fatigued the metal to exhaustion. With only two of the planned five world records accomplished, the attempt was finished. The special car was broken.

Three months preparation and work.

"Should we give up now?" Steinemann remembered a loophole in FIA's famous iron-clad rules.

"I learned that if a world record attempt fails, it can be restarted within 48 hours. Under the same application. And it didn't say it had to be the same car or even the same type of car."

Then Rico Steinemann laughed.

"In the meantime, I knew Porsche had these 911Rs; I just never realized what they were designed for."

Privateer Rico Steinemann piloted his 906LM-wagen through Nürburgring's Karoussel during the 1967 1000km race. Steinemann bought the ex-Werks car at the end of the 1966 season. Rico Steinemann archives. Peter Falk, Porsche's competition director, took up a paint brush to warn the Monza record run team of bad cracks in Monza's aging banking. Rico Steinemann archives. The 906LM designated the long tail but also an extended, dropped nose to increase high-speed stability. Ferdinand Piëch ordered three of these aerodynamic cars built for Le Mans for 1966.

CHAPTER 15

1967 Typ 911R

A Wolf In Sheep's Clothing

The wolf in sheep's clothing, Porsche's 911R was Ferdinand Piëch's experiment with production-based vehicles: how light can we make it, how hard can we push it, how long will it last? Marks of the R: outside dry sump oil fill cap for ease of refill during pit stops, and plastic side and quarter windows, with snorkles to bring the air in and louvers to help it out. Even the outside mirrors were considered for their weight.

It was cool, clear, and quiet in the pits at Monza. The red-and-white Carrera 6 sat, broken.

The front suspension had shattered from nearly 10 hours of pounding on the broken-surfaced high banked turns. A world record attempt at a distance of 20,000km, begun at noon on the last Sunday in October, had gone barely one-tenth that far.

For the sponsors, British Petroleum and Firestone, with a Swiss newspaper on the scene to cover every hour and every kilometer, it was a growing public relations disaster. For Swiss racer Gianrico Steinemann who originated the idea, and his three Swiss friends and codrivers, it was success unrealized, disappointment achieved.

But when Steinemann telephoned Ferdinand Piëch at his home near Stuttgart, it was a new opportunity. The news that might have defeated some, simply inspired the aggressive Piëch.

"'OK,' he said to me, 'I have an idea but I want to calculate it.'"

Steinemann recalled the night as clearly as last night's dinner.

"His idea was that the 911R had to be more rigid than the Carrera 6 so we should be able to do it. With the suspension of the 911 but with the polyester body, the 911R was much lighter; it should be able to withstand the stress.... But was it fast enough?"

An hour went by. A few minutes more. Then a call.

Forget it. The car would be too slow.

Shoulders slumped. Lights went out around the pits and in the drivers' eyes. Another hour passed. With so much to clean up, no one had left.

Then another call. There may be an error in the calculations. The factory will work on it. Go. Sleep. But don't leave Monza.

Later still, the four drivers and the crew met with BP race director Karl Jünker, and listened to Jo Siffert. He had driven a 911R prototype already. It was fast enough, he said, and it could endure the banking.

Monday morning Piëch convened a *Krisenstab*, a crisis staff, and put Helmuth Bott in charge. Bott gathered Paul Hensler from engines, Richard Hetmann from drivetrains, Peter Falk from competitions, and Albert Jünginger from the experimental vehicle section, as well as a calculations man to run the numbers again. Peter Falk recalled clearly the deadline: "The world record rules particularly specified that the attempt can be repeated within 48 hours. By Tuesday, 31 October, 10pm at the latest, a new car had to stand at the start line."

Two of the first production 911R vehicles were in the experimental section in Stuttgart. The start line was in Monza, 400km due south—kilometers measured as the crow flies, not as a transporter drives.

As the five engineers sat together, Bott outlined six questions. To Paul Hensler: Was there an engine?

The 911R production run of twenty cars used fiberglass wherever possible for body panels and plexiglass similarly for windows. It was powered by a variation (Typ 901/22) of the 2.0 liter Carrera 6 engine (Typ 901/20). One of the four Piëch 911R prototype cars in the experimental section had just completed a race at Mugello, taking 3rd overall behind two 910s. Bott's questions were not idle curiosity.

Yes, replied Paul Hensler, but.... After reinstalling the twin-plug Typ 901/22 engine,

Piëch's engineers weighed every piece of equipment going onto the 911R. The individual taillight lenses together weighed nearly 1/2kg less than the standard taillight fixture. Rubber tie-downs replaced heavy metal latches for the front and rear deck lids. Two Weber 46 IDA3C carburetors fed the Typ 901/22 engine. Out of 1991cc (80 x 66mm), the 911R claimed 210hp at 8000rpm. The free-flow exhaust through resonators made the R noticeable even if otherwise it was nondescript.

he discovered that it had been run 100 hours on a test bench. It had been taken apart, measured, and rebuilt. But no one knew how carefully. And there was no time to build a new one.

To Richard Hetmann: Do we have a gearbox?

Yes, but.... Would the fifth-speed gear clusters endure the entire 20,000km. Are we sure which version of the five-speed gearbox is best suited? As with the 906, there were five possible gear combinations. And, do we know yet what maximum speed these fully loaded cars would reach on Monza's steep banks?

Falk again: "The group concluded to install two fifth gears, whereby fourth gear was three percent shorter than fifth. Subsequently, we recommended the drivers always alternately use fourth and fifth gear."

To Albert Jünginger: Can this work be done by this evening?

Yes, but.... Jünginger could do the assembly if he had an unassembled gearbox by noon. He got it.

To Falk: Can we bring sufficient spare parts to Monza?

"It is impossible," Falk replied, "to procure within a few hours the necessary duty paper for a double border crossing. But...a second 911R could be driven as a rolling spare parts warehouse to Monza."

Falk proposed that Heinz Baüerli, the company's chief mechanic, and Albert Jünginger would drive the spare parts car while he and Paul Hensler followed in the actual record-attempt car.

There was one last question, to the man from the calculations section: Was the car quick enough to break the existing records?

With the help of his slide rule and diagrams, the calculator did his sums. Car weighs 823kg (1,810lb); makes 210hp at 8000; to go 20,000km in 96 hours; with gear cluster 28/23. Must be 208.33km/h (130.21mph) with no stops.... Driver's weight? Spare parts weight? Fuel consumption?

No. The car was too slow. It only came to an average of barely 200km/h (125mph) when you consider time for refueling and anticipated maintenance work. A speed of at least 215km/h (134.4mph) was necessary.

Falk's cryptic notes reveal volumes.

"The other gentlemen—with the practice and more trust in the 911R—did not believe this calculation. Mr. Bott approved and signed off on the project.

"So we all put our trust on the Porsche materials and on the Porsche engine mechanics." Later, an error in the calculations was discovered. But, of course, by then....

At 10am in Stuttgart, with 36 hours to go and two cars to move south through two countries, work began. Barely seven hours later, their own work complete, Baüerli and Jünginger left the factory. They were to drive straight through to Monza and, upon arrival, immediately dismantle the "rolling spare parts warehouse" so that its crucial parts—especially suspension pieces, could be stowed on the record-attempt car.

The two chose the most direct route, to Basel, Switzerland, south to Lucerne, to take

Straps raised and lowered the windows in the gutted interiors. In a similar 911R, Rico Steinemann, Dieter Spoerry, Jo Siffert, and Charles Vogele ran 96 hours around Monza to set seventee world records. A spare parts box sat where the Typ 910 seat sits in this car.

the railway/tunnel through St. Gotthard's pass, then through Lugano, Varese, Milan, and on to Monza. But at 6pm, Baüerli phoned from the Swiss border at Basel.

The border police refused to let them drive the car through Switzerland. The car was much too loud. They must instead drive *around* Switzerland, by way of Lyons, France, and Grenoble, then through Turin to Monza. The new route was now nearly 1,000km (625 miles).

Hensler and Falk started in the record car (118-990-01) about an hour later. Forewarned by Baüerli's phone call, they headed the opposite way.

"We chose the way over Austria," Peter Falk explained. "There we knew that Austrians, like French and Italians, had nothing against a good exhaust sound." From Munich to Innsbruck by way of Garmisch, over the Brenner Pass into Italy, past Bolzano, Trento, around the Lago di Garda, and into Monza from the east.

Steinemann remembered this frenzy also. "The first car arrived with a dull motor

noise resonating behind the pit boxes. The wolf in sheep's clothing appeared.

"And then an *unbelievable* work started. Taking apart a car. OK, it was just certain bits and pieces we knew we required. There was a list."

Steinemann laughed at the specifics of the list. "Especially suspension parts. One complete front McPherson strut assembly, and one in pieces (since two complete assemblies would not fit)."

But the new car didn't solve everyone's problems.

"We left a monster problem for Firestone. They could use the Carrera 6 front tires as the rear tires on the 911R. And they had some smaller tires with them so we could start. But before the end of the first day they had to fly in more tires. And they only just made it. Because their plans were based on the Carrera 6."

When Falk and Hensler arrived very early Tuesday morning, the parts car was already dismantled. Its drivetrain gear and many other small parts for engine and electrical

Rico Steinemann: "With great concentration, with caution, we could keep 200km/h.... It needed courage and a quiet hand."

Running 20,000km at 209km/h (130mph), this 911R was home to four Swiss racers for 96 hours. Sponsored by British Petroleum and Firestone Tire and Rubber, the drivers set seventeen endurance records. The record run set a tire-use milestone as well: ninety tires in 96 hours. Monza's surface was brutal.
Porsche Werke

repairs—as well as a large tool package—were ready for the record car.

Some test laps were run on the oval and the two fifth gears seemed to work well. "We learned we could easily run 1 minute 11," Steinemann said. "Of course, the Carrera 6 had been faster, 1 minute 5 or 6. But the average would easily be high enough, between 210 and 215km/h."

Falk wrote: "The restart for the record attempt was on Tuesday, October 31, 1967, at around 20:00 hours; therefore, we conformed to the rules because it was still within the 48 hours."

But Peter Falk's cool, dispassionate notes barely hint at the anxious moments and engineering challenges to come. For Falk, such anticipation took him up onto the banking with a paint can, to make large scale arrows pointing out the worst hazards of the Monza banking.

"We had all sorts of problems." Steinemann shrugged and laughed about the history twenty-five years later. "The weather became worse and worse. From the second day on, we had fog to an unbelievable extent. So bad that one driver refused to continue so long as the fog was there. You could see only 20-30 meters, no more.

"We had rain. Rain and fog. Actually, the rain wasn't so much of a problem with the banking...it just flowed down. But it flowed down onto the back straight. Where we had a lake. With great concentration, with caution, we could keep 200km/h across this lake. It needed courage and a quiet hand...."

"We tried systems to see in the fog. We had burning oil barrels. We had hoped the fog would go up with the fire. It didn't work." Again, Steinemann laughed easily at the memory.

"Then we tried lots of little lights. Like an airstrip. We had small pocket lamps that they put along the circuit every five meters. And because they would only burn for about three or four hours, they had four people circling around all the time changing batteries!"

But it was Monza's banking that challenged and beat them again. At 7,000km (4,375 miles) the first front suspension strut failed. With a complete unit in the record car, replacement took only a few minutes. But it indicated that surely before 20,000km, it would need replacement again.

"It caused a problem because the other one was completely dismantled: time!"

Steinemann looked off into the distance at the retelling of this story. "The chief mechanic, Mr. Baüerli, had a good idea. They dismantled another one from the spare parts car. Since we could decide when to change it, we picked a moment late at night of course, in heavy rain. Because there were always scrutineers from FIA there, and the rule is you can only....

"It was a matter of time. To assemble one from the parts would take 40 minutes. That was time we might need later. So we tried to hide a complete McPherson unit under the mechanic's rain coat.

"And of course, the scrutineer saw it. He made a note and when I was free, later on, he took me aside. 'I saw,' he said.

"He was an old friend, a fellow racer. 'Yes, it's true; that unit came from there; but all the bits and pieces are in the parts box in the car. Which you can see the next time....'

"When it was all over, the scrutineers took the car away to check everything. He came to me later and said, 'All the bits were there; it's OK. You didn't cheat.'"

After 72 hours, the 911R had done 15,115km (9,446.9 miles). Twenty-four hours to go. Five thousand kilometers (3,125miles) more.

With three days done, they still had to do the equivalent of the 24 Hours of Le Mans.

"The only other drama was the one that

When fiberglass is laid up as a single gauge, and reinforced only with wafer-thin bamboo strips laminated to the inside, a front deck lid can be so thin it literally flexes in the wind. What a piece of work had Ferdinand Piëch wrought? Four prototypes and twenty production models were built, weighing 810kg (1,760lb). After Steinemann's record runs, some saw dreams of 500 cars, homologated. Others saw reality: with only twenty-four built, some lingered, unsold even through 1970.

had been foreseen with the two fifth gears. Running 24 hours a day, four days, for 20,000km, flat out, full speed, fifth gear failed on the last day. So we just engaged fourth gear. It saved the attempt!"

The records fell, as planned. Five world and eleven international records: 10,000 miles: 210.28km/h (131.43mph); 20,000km, at 209.23km/h (130.77mph); and 96 hours, (at the same speed to make 20,086.08km—12,505.38 miles).

A seventeenth record was unanticipated. Firestone recorded a world record for tire consumption: ninety tires in 96 hours.

Days later, Switzerland's first race car exhibition was to open in Zurich. The organizers spoke to Steinemann. Arrangements were made to exhibit the car. But this time, Dieter Spoerry drove it all the way. The car, still much too loud to drive on Swiss roads, was now much too famous not to.

The original plans from Porsche engineering called for only twenty production copies of the 911R. After these were completed, Huschke von Hanstein saw them and imagined a larger run, say 500 cars, that would

qualify for the GT category. But the car was only conceived by Piëch as a production experiment, almost a play thing amidst the serious race car efforts of the time, and it all ended after the twenty-four cars.

Vic Elford won the 1967 Marathon de la Route in one, and in 1968, a specially constructed 911 with R components was fitted with a Sportomatic transmission and won the Marathon again. Later in 1969, Gerard Larrousse and Maurice Gelin took 911R 118-990-05 with a specially built, injected engine to the Tour de France and the Tour de Corse and won both. Outright.

A marketing director at Porsche vetoed the large number. He believed it would be impossible to sell 500. He was probably right; some of the twenty were still available in 1970. It was as Rico Steinemann said, "When they were produced, nobody really realized what they were produced for." It would take another five years before the lessons from Piëch's experiments with the lightweight 911R would be applied.

Five years, and a change of company management.

CHAPTER 16

1966 911 Bertone

Special Bodies Continued

Carrozzeria Bertone began work on the roadster in October 1965. It was completed on the eve of the 1966 Geneva Motor Show in early March. Inspired by Bertone's love of sports and racing cars, much of the design work was done by his protege and chief designer Giorgetto Giugiaro.

The truck with German registry pulled into the modern, gated compound at corso Canonico Allamano, 40/46. This was meant to be the first of perhaps a hundred such deliveries.

It was October 1965; a mild autumn in Grugliasco, suburban Turin, Italy. A month earlier, John von Neumann, the western US distributor for Porsche, had visited the same factory. He was there to meet with Nuccio Bertone, to discuss his wish that the carrozzeria built him a series of 100 special 911 roadsters. They were also to discuss in what condition the parts from Porsche were to arrive.

"My advice," Nuccio Bertone recalled, "was taken."

Inside the truck was a 911 in rough finish. It had its engine, running gear, and full electrics. But it had no doors, no hood, no rear deck lid. It had no paint or interior. It had been ordered by von Neumann and had been delivered by Porsche directly.

Porsche had not offered a roadster since its 356C Cabriolet. Out of production now, there was no open Porsche announced to replace it. Von Neumann meant to remedy that.

"He simply requested that I build a Road-

ster," Bertone recollected. "And he gave me full freedom for the project. Since I loved racing and open sports cars—with which I myself took part in races—it was not difficult for me to build an open sports car with a little touch of elegance."

Bertone and von Neumann discussed whether the car should bear any resemblance to the new production car designed by F. A. Porsche and decided it should not. Bertone turned the project over to his designers and modelers, but never drifted far away.

"At different stages of this project," Bertone explained, "all of our specialists took their turn working on this car: stylists, draftsmen, model makers, metal beaters, and workers, fitters, painters, upholsterers, trimmers, and detailers." In his prototypes department, Bertone had nearly fifty employees.

The pace was hurried. The deadline was imminent and implacable. The model and the drawings grew side by side, each one influencing and amending the other every day. A full-scale wood model was developed from full-scale drawings. And then fabrication began.

"We kept only the floor of the Porsche," Nuccio Bertone recalled. "We cut the body that was sent to us. The rest of the car was all Italian." The interior as well, was "all Italian," designed by Bertone's styling staff under his close supervision. Bertone, long known for his clean lines, was equally known for his ability to train promising apprentices: Franco Scaglione, from 1951 to 1959 (who then went on to Zagato and designed Porsche's Abarth Carrera), was replaced by Giorgetto Giugiaro who served as chief stylist until 1968.

The Bertone design lowered the 911 by reconfiguring the dashboard instrumentation, and by evolving Butzi Porsche's rear-deck air intakes into Nuccio Bertone's windowsill air ducts. The engine breathed through new nostrils as the profile was changed.

The headlights were concealed under a slotted cover that echoed the design elements from the rear taillights and exhaust.

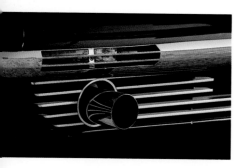

Fitted with a standard 911 2.0 liter engine, a single exhaust was adequate. Bertone's craftsmen did some chassis reinforcement prior to fitting the body. But flex was something von Neumann had feared from the beginning. Porsche was aware of the problem too. Butzi Porsche's solution was to include a rollbar. Below, to lower the car overall required lowering the cowl and reconfiguring the dashboard instrumentation. All the work was done by Bertone's craftsmen.

"It was necessary for aerodynamic purposes," Bertone recalled. "It was also necessary in order to keep within legal height limits of the headlamps. The slots over the outside (low-beam) lamps were built in that way in order to give continuity to the outline of the hood and fenders of the car."

From the start, both participants had goals in mind. For Bertone, it was a chance to further enhance his company's prestige. It was agreed from the start that the car would be introduced on Bertone's stand at the Geneva Auto Show in March 1966.

For von Neumann, it was business.

"You know, with Bertone for the design, he was the expert," John von Neumann explained. "But I knew what I wanted. I was going to try to sell this car."

Yet there were unforeseen problems ahead for von Neumann. Bertone was willing but....

"I had in mind the possibility of producing a certain quantity during the years in which the coupe version of this car was offered (by Porsche)," Bertone said. "But at that time, we were not in the position since we could not build the car in the prototype department at a price that could have been accepted by possible customers."

"Porsche saw the car," von Neumann remembered. "They kept saying, 'You know, you would have to sell this car for about $7,000.' That's what came out of their price calculations. That was provided the factory gave me chassis platforms at the right price.

"My idea was to have them deliver the platforms to Bertone with, let's say, wiring and that stuff in it. That's not such a big deal. And then Bertone would ship it back to Stuttgart and let them put the engines in it.

"The cost of building a prototype varies a great deal," Bertone suggested, "depending upon the characteristics of the car and how complex it was to carry out the project. It took us between 5,500 and 6,000 man hours. The cost of materials did not add up to much.

"As far as I was concerned, it was not a project that I took in order to make money," Bertone concluded. "But it was a personal satisfaction that I wanted."

"I thought I could sell maybe a hundred a year. But I would have had the exclusivity for the distribution. Not the Porsche factory," von Neumann laughed at the idea. "But they laughed at me for the price: $5,000 was high for a car in those days. But I felt sure some people would pay $7,000 for something particular, if it was good looking.

"I talked with Mr. Porsche. He said, 'Well, you know, it has our name on it, so we are concerned to be sure it is going to be right....'"

Von Neumann stopped, letting the words sink in. The highest-quality mechanicals were to be installed in a limited-production body. Porsche had done this many times before. Even in Italian bodies.

"I felt cheated. I knew almost immediately the Porsche factory would not do this. They would have to have it built.

"But the thing that killed it," von Neumann continued with the frustrating story, "was something they already knew. I mean, I was afraid of it, but they knew all about it. When you make a convertible out of a coupe, there is some chassis movement, flexing.

Von Neumann lamented over what could have been bad luck, good business sense, or bad faith, but he drew no conclusions.

"They knew about the project. They gave me the chassis. But they could have said, 'Wait a month, wait two months, we'll give you a reinforced chassis.'"

The Bertone Roadster, in burgundy with tan leather, was finished literally only hours before the Geneva Show debut. Once unveiled, it received encouraging reactions. But it sold not a single issue. Von Neumann had the stillborn prototype delivered to his home in Geneva.

"I've driven it hard in Switzerland. In the rain. I used it as a regular car after the show, before I shipped it back to the States. I would have kept the car had I had a reinforced chassis. I was just afraid it would fall apart under the use I put a car through." Von Neumann laughed again.

"And all the time they were already working on that problem. With their own solution. For their chassis reinforced by a rollbar. They named it the Targa."

A dozen years after John von Neumann ordered up the Speedster, his tastes had matured. This time, he asked for a roadster, based on 911 mechanicals, but designed and built by Nuccio Bertone in Turin, Italy. Von Neumann wanted Porsche to buy the project—from him.

CHAPTER 17

1968 Typ 907K

In Sicily, The Word For Racing Driver Is Pilota

Wearing the livery of the 1967 BOAC 500, the 907 coupe still looks right in wild hills similar to the Petite Madonie in Sicily. But 907s wearing long tails also won the 24 hours of Daytona. It was nicknamed the Mirage as its steeply curved windshield reminded Weissach engineers of the French jet. Yet Piëch's mind had clear visions—of cars with no holes. He proposed a liquid cooling system for the car's brakes and the driver's suits.

Near the end of its life, in January 1969, as Porsche sold off its 907s to privateers, one customer remarked that the slender cabin reminded him of "being in the cockpit of a super streamlined aircraft." Weissach knew the feeling. They had nicknamed the car the *Mirage* after the French fighter jet with its similar bubble windshield.

Driving Porsche's first little fighters was like flight in severe turbulence. Paul Hawkins, the 1967 Targa Florio winner in a 910, went to Nürburgring with Vic Elford to test the new 907L. The 30-year-old Australian already had small car flight experience, having flown a Lotus 33 Formula 1 car into Monaco Bay in 1965. And he had a sense of humor to keep it in perspective.

"We were each asked," Vic Elford recalled, "to do a lap of the long circuit in the 907. That eight-cylinder engine in the back was a lot heavier than the little six in the 910. But the 907 was still basically the same chassis. Not quite, some front suspension changes, but very similar.

"Paul went off and did a lap. When he came back, Herr Bott said, 'So, Mr. Hawkins? How is the car?'

"Paul got out. And in his lovely rough, drawly kind of Australian accent, said, 'Well, Mr. Bott, the back of this car is goin' up and down like whores' drawers at a pile driver's picnic.'"

"Herr Bott just said, 'Is it really?'

The introduction of the 907 advised the world that Ferdinand Piëch was ready to contend for overall honors. It was a redefined race car. While wheelbase and wheel track remained the same as the 910, the body of the 910 was so completely redesigned that the 907L was 50mm (1.97in) shorter—even with Eugen Kolb's longer tail—than the standard 910, and 50mm narrower as well. Ventilated discs eliminated the need for front brake cooling ducts. The result was nearly a 25 percent decrease in aerodynamic drag from the 910 to the 907L.

There were other significant changes for the 910 and 906. The 907 shifted the driver to the right side of the car. Most European circuits predominantly turned right; this aided the drivers in placing the cars more precisely and placed the driver's weight over the inside wheels more often.

But as Elford recalled, "It was pretty well a center steerer," he explained. "Because the cockpit was so narrow relative to the chassis—which was comparatively wide—we were sitting barely to the right of the centerline. The bit of the car that was reserved for the driver was pretty small!"

It was Ferdinand Piëch's attention to drag that relegated 907 drivers to such cramped accommodations. Piëch provided his engineers many such challenges. Helmut Flegl was project engineer on the 907. His memories were particularly sharp.

"Mr. Piëch never was happy when there was a problem that he could only 'tune' so that we must live with it. He wanted to solve the problem," Flegl explained.

"He had strong motivation from aerodynamics. Walking around the pits of Le Mans, he said, 'Gentlemen, so many holes in the body! It hurts aerodynamics! Why not close them?'

"He was that kind of man. A little radical," Flegl recalled, with obvious admiration. "Always looking for a different level of solution. 'Brakes need air,' we said. 'You have to cool them! 'Use a fluid? Have a cir-

culation?' he suggested. 'And this driver's compartment? Can't you close that?'"

There was an edge to Piëch's genius. It was as though he relished slaughtering whole herds of sacred cows to serve as dinner steaks to the very people who revered them.

"The drivers heard this. 'Jesus Christ! You know, we have to breathe in there. It gets hellish hot!'" Flegl smiled.

"'Well, give them oxygen. Use a circulation,' he said, 'to cool them?'"

Flegl smiled again. The irony amused him. Each circulation required a new radiator, a new hole. Driver cooling was done, and discarded.

"There were different ways we could do it," he explained. "Electrical refrigeration? The only thing we could imagine was an ice box. But the ice only went for 10 minutes—it was right next to the oil cooler—and the insulation of the suit was so bad that the drivers complained. They pointed at their bodies: 'Here, I'm swimming; here I'm cold!'

"And for the races, the engineers pulled the boxes out because of the weight!"

Power for the 907 was the Typ 771 flat eight. It appeared first in the W-RS spyders in the 1962 Targa Florio. It proved to be a dependable enough powerplant that it was subsequently used in 904/8 coupes for Le Mans and the 904/8 Bergspyder *Kanguruh* again for the Targa and for hillclimbs. The highly stressed 2.0 liter fuel-injected engine produced 260 bhp for the short runs uphill. With a 5.33:1 final drive and barely 454kg (998.8lb) of weight, the little spyders were geared for 190km/h (118.8mph). A year later, the same engine bored to 2.2 liters, (80 x 54mm) peaked at 278 bhp at 8700rpm. Regeared, the 598kg (1,315lb) coupes ran Mulsanne at 293km/h (183.1mph).

For Daytona, Porsche continued with the long tails. Kolb's bodywork, tapering to a near-knife edge, ran with a slight, flat spoiler. The short-tail coupes were introduced in December 1967, in advance of the 1968 Sebring 12 hours. Both versions shared several improvements.

The front-mounted oil cooler was moved further forward to the extreme front of the nose. The hot radiator exhaust air climbed up over the windshield from a more forward point on the body. A space-saver spare tire

fit up front replacing a full-size spare in the rear as on the 906 and 910.

Daytona was a startling season opener. Early on, a Ford Mustang blew its engine entering the tri-oval from the infield circuit. Gerhard Mitter, running 2nd, losing a tire with a puncture, began to feel it at just that point. Touching the brakes, he found the engine oil and spun into the infield. The flat tire caught and flipped the car onto its roof. Masten Gregory, next through in his Ferrari 275LM, saw Mitter's sparks and braked hard into Dieter Spoerry's private-entry 907L. Gregory went airborne and landed, rolling. Elford then came onto the wall of smoke, dust and debris at nearly 260km/h (162.5mph) and made it through "by sheer luck."

The rest of the night was slightly less dramatic. Jochen Neerpasch, codriving with Elford, became too ill to continue. Rolf Stommelen, codriving with Mitter in the destroyed 907L, stepped in. Then, with barely two hours to the end of the race, Jo Siffert and Hans Herrmann, leaders for much of the race, spent 20 minutes in the pits to repair throttle-linkage problems. At von Hanstein's instigation, each drove the Elford/Neerpasch/Stommelen car for about 10 minutes each. This legally listed them as codrivers.

At the end of the race, Elford's car, racing as number 54, crossed the line in formation with Siffert in racing number 52 and Joe Buzzetta in an aluminum-tube prototype chassis 907, racing number 51. Siffert and Herrmann were listed in 1st *and* 2nd, and Elford, listed only as winner, completed 4,105km (2,656.6 miles) at 170.70km/h (106.69mph) with the aid of his *four* codrivers!

For Elford, the remainder of 1968 driving 907s was a season of drama. The most satisfying was the Targa Florio. While Porsche had introduced its 908 three weeks earlier at Le Mans trials, the firm showed up in Sicily with eight proven cars, four factory 907 short-tail cars with the 2.2 liter flat eights, and four 910s with the 2.0 liter sixes.

Practices were done in production 911s and then drivers had one lap in their real race cars. Elford qualified fastest and when the race started, he was the last one off.

Cars started every 20sec. Prototypes of more than 2.0 liters left last.

"I set off and got to Cerda," Elford recalled. "I used to fly through the village, in fifth gear about 240km/h (150mph). Out the other side, perhaps a kilometer, there was a sharp turn, almost a hairpin, to the left, off the main road and onto another road.

Vic Elford climbs the hills outside of Cerda on his way to victory in the 907 at the Targa Florio in 1968. Codriving with Umberto Maglioli, Elford set successive lap records on each of the last four laps. Porsche Werke. Below, "The Targa Florio was always a blend of rally and race driving," Vic Elford recalled, explaining how he set records lap after lap to win in 1967 in a Typ 907. "In the hills, I drove as though I was on rails, positioning the car exactly."

"And I sort of dived into the corner, touched the gas pedal and the engine went *whoosh*. I thought, 'Something has broken. Halfshaft? Maybe I'd missed a shift?' I put the clutch in again. No, nothing wrong there. So I quickly stopped, got out and found that the right rear wheel nut had undone itself. Still there, just undone sufficiently that the wheel had come off the drive pins...."

Other cars passed Elford. With each minute, he descended further in the overall standings.

"A whole crowd of spectafors jumped off the banks," Elford explained, "and came down and physically lifted up the back end of the car. I tightened up the nut with the huge wrench from the tool kit. And they set it down and off I went!" Elford laughed.

"And I carried on, a bit hesitant, to near the halfway point at Bivio Polizzi. The major teams used to set up unofficial service areas there in the mountains. They didn't have any new wheel nuts but they changed the wheel. We just hoped it was only a little problem.

"I got maybe 10 kilometers down the road and it came undone again. Only this time, it launched me off the road and I punctured the right front tire. Again, people just sort of appeared from the hedges," Elford said, still laughing. "They lifted one end and then the other. I tightened up the rear wheel and put that little space-saver on the front. They set me down and off I went, again!

"You know, that space-saver was really a great tire. I mean, I just ignored it. The car didn't handle too well around left-hand corners, but speedwise.... Along that 5 kilometer long straight along the seaside, I just drove it flat out and it held!"

Elford got back to the pits near Cerda to find Siffert in ahead of him with the same problem. More time passed and more competitors. By the time mechanics could change all his wheels and replace the lock nuts, he was 19 minutes behind the new leaders as he began his second lap. In those days, the Targa was run over ten laps, 71.4km (44.6 miles) each.

"And turns? Thousands?" Elford recalled. "Somebody once told me they'd counted

The Typ 771 engine had first been seen in the W-RS spyders at the Targa Florio, left page. It appeared again in the Kanguruh. The 1967 version, 771/1, produced 270hp at 8600rpm. Bosch mechanical fuel injection was driven by a cogged belt. Left, with Le Mans gearing, the 907 could hit 295km/h (184.4mph) along Mulsanne. Targa gearing was nearer 240km/h (150mph). Elford's last lap speed, a record 119.18km/h (74.49mph) was quick enough. He won with Umberto Maglioli, 3 minutes ahead of 2nd place.

295. Honestly I don't know how many. Apart from the bit along the seaside and the run through Cerda, it was literally left-right-left-right-left-left-right-right-left-right-left all the way!"

Helmuth Bott coordinated the race efforts. Originally, Elford was to drive the first three laps, spelled by Umberto Maglioli for four laps. Elford was to finish the last three. With new tires, Elford drove like a man late for his own shotgun wedding to a Mafia don's daughter. After his third lap, he had climbed up to 7th place, setting a 36:02.3 lap record, a minute faster than the 1967 record.

Maglioli had vast experience on Targa. Driving solo, he won it in 1953 in a Lancia and again in 1956 in a Porsche 550A. When Maglioli took over, Elford relaxed and got a quick meal. He returned to Bott later and saw the times.

"'Hey,' I said to Bott, "if I drive the last four laps instead of the last three, we can win!'

"Bott looked at me as though I'd got a touch of the sun," Elford said with another laugh. "Then he had another look and agreed. 'If you can carry on with 36 minute laps. Can you do that?"

Maglioli was brought in a lap early, having moved the car up to 4th place. And the Englishman returned to the circuit of a thousand turns.

Before reaching the pits after the ninth lap, Elford reclaimed the lead. Lapping in less than 36 minutes—his ninth lap within 2sec of his eighth—he broke one lap record after another.

"The Targa was always a blend of rally and race driving. In the hills, I drove as though I was on rails, precisely, positioning the car exactly. When I got into the towns, there was so much dust and dirt kicked up, I'd just put it sideways."

His last lap, averaging 119.18km/h (74.49mph), was completed in 35:57.48. He and Maglioli won by nearly 3 minutes.

"A little squirt of the gas," Vic Elford said with a laugh, "with that extra 50 horsepower over 910s? That 907 was marvelous!"

But for Ferdinand Piëch, it was not yet enough. More power was coming. And more sophistication in chassis and body work. If the 907 was marvelous, the coming work of Kolb, Mezger, Flegl, and Bott was first going to beg description. And then to defy it.

Vic Elford:
"You know, that space-saver was really a great tire. I just drove it flat out and it held!"

CHAPTER 18

1969 Typ 908 Langheck

Saving Face As A Racing Strategy

Eugen Kolb evolved his long-tail design with the 908 langheck. One magazine reviewer at the time remarked that the cars resembled the speed record cars of the 1930s. But Kolb's long tails had some instability. The back ended tended to lift at 310km/h (193mph)!

"**M**otor racing has never been 'sport' to the Germans. They have always treated it like something designed specifically to show the superiority of German men, machines and method."

Robert Daley wrote that paragraph for his book, *Cars At Speed*. He was referring to the Mercedes-Benz team's first attempt on the Targa Florio in 1922. But the insightful journalist, writing in 1960, also saw the future. Unknowingly, he was describing Porsche five years later.

Ferdinand Piëch had been chief of the experimental department since 1965. From his department almost immediately came the 904 Bergspyders, nicknamed the *Kanguruhs*. And then came the 906 in 1965, then 910, and the 907. Shortly after Le Mans, Piëch learned that the engine displacement for the FIA prototype Group 6 category was to increase to 3.0 liters for 1968. By the time it was official in October, his engineers had already begun replacement engine design. By April 9, 1968, two of these 908 engines were installed in 907 long-tail cars and run at the Le Mans trials.

It took less than four months to produce the flat eight-cylinder, Typ 916. Original engine specifications followed standard 911

dimensions due to the short deadline. They kept the 84 x 66mm bore and stroke. At the 1968 season opener at Monza in mid-April, the four-cam engine was producing 335hp. But it was not a perfect beginning. The firing order set up a fierce vibration at engine speeds above 7000rpm. Hans Mezger was forced to alter the order quickly by redesigning the crankshaft. The cylinder bore was also enlarged to 85mm to more closely approach the 3.0 liter limit. By the season end, output of some engines was nearer 370hp at 8400rpm.

Short- and long-tail coupes were developed, Eugen Kolb clearly profiting from his experience with the 907s. These undulant, sensuously-curved cars struck *Car and Driver* writers at the time as "reminiscent of 1930s record cars." In fact they differed little from the Ford Mark IV. The narrow cockpit of the 907 was retained but tire technology had gone the other direction. In the April tests, one long-tail coupe ran as a virtual 907, while another ran wider tires and 125mm (4.92in) wider bodywork. First runs showed the narrower car was nearly 8km/h (5mph) faster on Mulsanne.

This "adaptation" eliminated the problems of quickly creating a new body. However, the 908 inherited the problems of high-speed stability, which grew worse with the stiffer suspension, wider tires, and body. The tail wandered, particularly when braking hard after the nearly 310km/h (193.75mph) Mulsanne straight. Aerodynamics was something not yet completely mastered.

Helmut Flegl, as a racing department engineer, was responsible for the aerodynamic development on the 907. At that time, with so many of Porsche's most influential engineers directly involved with or very sympathetic toward engine development, Flegl worked under a constant caveat. He was allowed to do as much as needed to the chassis and body so long as it did not affect the drag.

Flegl chose to experiment with fins, wings, and winglets. A small lip added to the extreme tail did not cure high-speed instability, so, remembering an innovation from the earlier RSK, he added small vertical

fins. These improved things slightly. Another test, which Helmuth Bott had done only two years earlier on a 906 mule, offered promise: "whiskers" were added alongside the headlights. These not only held the front end down, they also directed the air more effectively over the car. It still didn't solve the crucial problem: rear end lift. That was another experiment on Bott's 906 *Klappenwagen*, the Flap Car.

Hans Herrmann had driven the *Klappenwagen* at Weissach and then at the Hockenheimring. Bott discovered Herrmann's times varied with the presence or absence of the flaps. Through the most tightly curved portions of the track, the car was quickest with the whiskers and tail wings on the inside of the turn. And slowest when the flaps were used on both sides.

By the end of the day an idea was coalescing in Bott's mind: was it possible to make the flaps act as though they were not on the car's outer side in the outside of the turn? Could these flaps be made to behave as though they were not on the car along the high speed straightaway? Could the flaps react under braking like the air brake on the Mercedes-Benz 300SLR? Could the flaps react to cornering forces?

The driver was busy enough. These various functions could not be controlled by the man trying to steer, brake and shift into and out of each corner. But what if the forces on the car itself could make these aerodynamic devices work?

Porsche was lucky. Rioting in the streets of Paris in May 1968 and a resulting general strike throughout France in June and July postponed Le Mans to late September when all was forgiven and the new President Georges Pompidou replaced Charles DeGaulle. For once, politics in France—although not those of the FIA—benefitted Porsche.

By September, the active-wing 908 long tails were ready. Attached by a lever system

Hans Herrmann and Gerard Larrousse co-drove number 64 to win its class at Le Mans. But they lost overall by scarcely 30m (100ft) to a 5.0 liter Ford GT in June 1969. Afterwards, the langheck was sent through FIA scrutineering where, after it passed its inspection, it received the lead seal on the steering wheel. Right, the Piëch-inspired, Kolb-executed long tail was little more than an aerodynamic appliance, attached behind the rear end to smooth out the airflow as it left the turbulence of 320km/h (200mph). Of the thinest single laminations of fiberglass, its additional weight is more than offset by the top speed gained.

to the rear suspension, the rear wings came up when the rear end lifted on either one side or both, in cornering or braking. At the same time, the front flaps drooped. Tests had concluded that the car's handling had been tamed. The drag was no greater and the top speed of the new cars matched the old wingless versions.

The engine vibration was still a problem. It manifested itself in the bracket that held the alternator. As an attempt not to correct the problem but live with it, a second alternator was fitted, on a separate bracket. But it was not a success. Of four 908 LH cars entered, only one finished, in 3rd, having lost 90 minutes in the pits.

The *klappen* technologies began causing troubles of their own. The whiskers were vulnerable to contact with other race cars, a great likelihood in the early laps. At the Nürburgring, a customer lost a front flap in a turn and slid off the circuit; he was killed in the crash. Factory drivers might be quicker in responding, but could Porsche only outfit its factory cars with front whiskers? The customers who paid so much money wanted their car as much like the factory version as possible.

Then at Le Mans in June 1969, the rear wings came under scrutiny. At the same time as the 908 LHs were racing at Le Mans in September 1968, Porsche's new "sport car" was in final design form. Bott and Flegl had equipped the Group 5 Typ 917 with the same active-wing system from the 908 LH cars. But by 1969, the growth of "aerodynamic devices" had caught the FIA's attention.

In Formula 1, large wings mounted high above the cockpits had appeared on struts, which were strong yet spindly looking. One month before Le Mans, on May 4, 1969, in Barcelona for the Spanish Grand Prix, Graham Hill and Jochen Rindt each suffered bad crashes after their wings came off the cars. A third car similarly disabled went into the spectators. The FIA reacted immediately, but laboring under a large public outcry, its reaction was indiscriminate.

For Monaco two weeks later, a provisional ban outlawed all wings that were "not a fixed or integral part of the bodywork." One

week later, the provision became permanent: "any *separate* aerodynamic surface which may exert a vertical thrust" was illegal. "Separate" meant wings whose only attachment to the body was through a flexible joint. The ban never specified size, merely movability, and position.

With *Klappenwagen* winglets, Porsche believed the matter was different. Racing director Rico Steinemann argued the case against the ban: Porsche's winglets were small; if they were to come loose, the car would still be drivable; the 908 had run with them previously with no problem; and finally, the 917 was homologated with them by its own inspectors.

The FIA remained firm. Steinemann, cast in the role of Porsche's ambassador of good will as well as motor sports director, approached Ferrari, Alfa Romeo, Matra, and Ford's John Wyer. He proposed a jointly signed letter recognizing the wing problems, pointing out a problem with the new regulation banning all movable wings without regard to size. Matra agreed. Alfa Romeo and John Wyer agreed. Enzo Ferrari, after ranting on the telephone for several days, concluded that Ferrari was Ferrari and he would sign no papers with other teams.

The letter had no effect anyway. Piëch then threatened to withdraw Porsche from

Helmuth Bott kept the flight-prone long tail on the ground with rear wings reacting to suspension in braking and cornering. Below, looking more like a land speed record car, the earliest 908 langheck was fast enough but aerodynamic flaws lifted the rear end. Porsche Werke

No mirage this, the 908 langheck *continued the tradition begun with the narrow-cockpit long-tail 907s. In fact, the newly designed engines—3.0 liter displacement flat eights—premiered in the 907 during the April trials for the 1968 Le Mans. Final versions of Eugen Kolb's long tails retained the 907's narrow cockpit but ran wider tires. The bodywork was widened 125mm (4.92in) to fit. Still the car challenged Piëch's with its holes. The box cut to the right of the oil cooler access cover was Piëch's ice box, complete with a pump for the driver's suits.*

Le Mans. The organizers, who anticipated a great battle between Ferrari and John Wyer's Ford team, wanted Porsche to race. Steinemann knew this and proposed a strategy to Piëch: go to Le Mans. Fix the flaps solidly on the 908. And on the 917, keep them movable, as approved and homologated by the FIA.

Porsche arrived. The Le Mans organizers greeted them happily. The FIA inspected them politely. An offer was made to demonstrate the handling of the 917 without its wings but the inspectors declined. It was not necessary they said. They believed, they said. Faces looked the other way.

Steinemann years later characterized it all as a matter of face. The FIA did not react quickly enough to the proliferation of high wings on Formula 1 cars. After the Barcelona tragedy, the FIA's reputation was hurt, face was lost. To recover, it reacted. It overreacted. When it became aware of its error, it could not back down without further loss of face. Steinemann's diplomacy avoided the issue. By giving up the winglets on the 908 without fuss, he kept the winglets on the 917 by reminding the rules-makers of their own approval prior to Barcelona. In diplomacy, one does not lose face if one simply turns the other way.

Robert Daley's assessment, seen years later from a face turned wise with hindsight, may seem harsh, unsympathetic, unkind. More likely, it may be simply unfair. Because in truth, as any racer knows, one can replace the "Germans" in Daley's statement with participants of any nationality.

One does not race to finish second. But Rico Steinemann knew that one cannot win if one does not race. There have been occasional, individual "sports" in motor racing. But even to those gentlemen, the object of motor racing was always to show off their superiority. If not one year, then the next. At the end of the 24 hours, Ford was superior at Le Mans in 1969. But Porsche's fixed-wing 908 long tail was 2nd—by scarcely 30 meters after one of the longest, closest, most exciting 23rd hours in memory.

However, even before the 1969 race started, Steinemann and Piëch each knew definitely that 1970 was going to be their "next year."

CHAPTER 19

1970 911ST/GT Monte Carlo

First, You Get It Backward

The Monte Carlo Rally starts from eight locations all over Europe and converges first on Grenoble. From there the cars run the first 36 hours of special stages, through the mountains. From that result, the top sixty cars go out on another all-night loop, about 640km (400 miles). Von Hanstein trusted Elford. Teamed with codriver David Stone, they finished 2nd in their first attempt in 1967. Von Hanstein, elated, reported to Piëch and for 1968, the effort included a second entry. Elford and Stone won outright and that cinched Porsche's commitment.

"What you do if you're on ice and snow—and you often are in the Monte Carlo Rally—first of all you turn it sideways. To slow it down, because you get that much more tire patch on the road instead of only a little bit. This very last approach, say, the last 20 or 30 meters...you actually approach with the car pointing the opposite way to the turn."

The man prescribing this action was Vic Elford, winner of the 1968 Monte Carlo Rally. This was the same Vic Elford who used to terrify some codrivers by taking most blind fly-overs flat out.

"I only did when I knew from our pace notes which way the road was going...and I haven't been wrong yet." Some of his colleagues called him reckless; Elford preferred "determined."

"You keep the car balanced with controlling the slide, but then you overcorrect and that has the effect of making the car spin right around. You get the car right out there, not quite backwards but definitely with the back overtaking the front.

"But when you actually get near to the apex in the corner, you're still going too fast to get around. So then you start pouring the power on. With the limited-slip rear axle, this

is pushing the car back into the corner. So, at this point, you are absolutely hard on the power.

"But it takes a bit of practice...."

Elford smiled at the understatement.

The car Elford best demonstrated this with was a 911T. He had never driven a Porsche before 1966, when he approached Huschke von Hanstein about running a rally program for Porsche. Von Hanstein recognized Elford as a current team driver with Ford and agreed to take a chance, to provide Elford a car for the Tour de Corse.

Elford returned to London, borrowed a production Porsche from John Aldington, the distributor, and learned how to drive a Porsche. There was no practice car in Corsica, so Elford ran in a rental car for two weeks to learn the route. The rally car arrived, on a trailer behind a van.

"When we opened up the van, it was full of wheels and tires. And that was it. Wheels and tires." Elford smiled broadly, the wrinkles in his face deepening to contours like Corsica itself.

"I said to Huschke, 'That's great. Car looks great. But where are the spare parts?'

"And he said, 'We don't have spare parts. Porsches don't break.'"

The laugh lines deepened further in Elford's face.

"And I said, 'C'mon Huschke. You're joking! Every rally car breaks. Even a Porsche has got to have something that's going to break sometime....'

"'No,' he said. 'Porsches don't break.'

"And he was absolutely right!"

The car delivered to Elford was a 911 with the Rally Kit II option. This option changed carburetor jets and venturis, provided a much smaller air-cleaner cover for the carburetors and fitted an oil-breather catch tank to capture the overflow forced up by high-g turns. The car, gutted of production interior amenities, boasted an additional 15hp. Elford and codriver David Stone took the Porsche to 3rd overall in Corsica, and von Hanstein offered the pair a full factory car for the next event, the 1967 Monte Carlo Rally. A second car was prepared for Gunther Klass.

Interiors were gutted. Drivers were given Recaro bucket seats while codrivers lashed themselves into standard sports seats. Bjorn Waldegaard's codriver, Lars Helmers, has his own custom-made competition seat.

Elford led through every stage but the last, where unexpected heavy snow dropped him to 3rd at the finish. Still, that was good enough for von Hanstein and he convinced Piëch to continue the remainder of the 1967 season on a rally-by-rally basis.

Elford and Stone again placed 3rd in the 1967 running of the Tour de Corse, only this time they were competing in one of Piëch's

lightweight prototypes, the 911R. This car, chassis 306-681S, was one of the four special prototypes constructed by the experimental department and entrusted to Elford.

For 1968, the FIA reclassified the 911T as a Group 3 car, same as the 911S. The factory looked at both cars and dropped the Rally Kit from the S model. The T, being 52kg lighter, was the natural choice and when it was delivered without sound deadening, that saved another 25kg. The new 911T Rally Kit included the 160hp 911S engine; interiors were comparably Spartan, suspension was lowered, and the brakes were drilled. For Elford and Stone, the car was tuned to 180hp.

The Monte Carlo Rally actually starts from eight locations all over Europe and normally converges first on Grenoble, the gateway to the French Alps. From there, the cars run the first 36 hours of special stages through the mountains, about 1,600km (1,000 miles). From that result, the top sixty cars go out the next night on another all-night loop, about 650km (400 miles).

"When we got back from the first loop, I was lying 2nd." Elford lit a cigarette as he recalled the long night. "Gerard Larrousse was leading in an Alpine and one of the reasons (that I was 2nd) was that I had had a massive spin in the Chartreuse and wiped all the lights off the front.

"Then, I couldn't turn around again. So we had to back...going the right direction but in reverse, I had to go down the road for about 3 kilometers. Until I could find somewhere big enough to spin the car around and carry on."

Ready to set off on the last mountain stage, Larrousse had a 20sec lead over Elford and codriver David Stone. Elford was edgy, worried about the weather and he complained to Stone that he couldn't seem to get his "rhythm." Driving up to the start of the third special stage, Stone did his best to calm Elford. Stone reminded him of the accuracy of their pace notes so far, and that the weather forecast was good.

"Forget the ice and snow," he said, "and forget about Larrousse. You know you're the fastest in the mountains, so forget about everything except the last mountain circuit. And we'll just do it."

With the five-speed transmissions, the 938kg (2,064lb) car was geared for a top speed of slightly less than 210km/h (131mph). But that was unloaded and on the flat. Carrying spare wheels and tires, Elford, Stone, and other equipment, the weight was more like 1,110kg (2,442lb), and top speed was more like 190km/h (120mph).

"We set off over the Col de la Couillole. It's a 26 kilometer test." Elford dragged deeply on a cigarette and closed his eyes, retracing the route in his memory. "Up one side and down the other. Up is pretty tight and twisty. Down is very fast. *Very* fast. We were doing 190km/h downhill. And there was ice and snow on that one.

"We got to the end. We clocked in and then went off....

"It took me about five minutes more to light a cigarette. Then David and I analyzed it all on the way back down to the main road. 'How many corners do you think we could have gone around quicker?' I asked him.

"'Well, I think three,' David said.

"'Nope,' I said. 'Two.'

"'Christ,' Stone said."

Elford and Stone had done the 26 kilometer (16.25 mile) section in 17 minutes flat. Exactly 1 minute faster than Larrousse. Porsche had won the 1968 Monte Carlo Rally.

For 1969, the factory entered four cars, 911S cars, with Elford and Stone attempting a repeat. Pauli Toivonen, Björn Waldegaard, and Elford's rival from 1968, Gerard Larrousse, ran the other cars. With Lars Helmers codriving, Björn Waldegaard won; Larrousse took 2nd. Toivonen and Elford did not finish, due to accidents.

For 1970 the entries were run in new

Until Vic Elford proposed it to Huschke von Hanstein in 1966, Porsche had not thought much of rallying. Yes, Erich Böhringer had finished 2nd in a 904GTS in the 1965 Monte. But that was as a privateer. Elford meant a factory effort. When this 1970 911ST won with Björn Waldegaard driving, it was Porsche's third victory.

cornering technique worked that he sat down and, trained engineer that he is, he worked it out.

"Do you know about the triangle of forces?" he asked "Well, it's just that. The resultant force is the third side of a triangle. At any point in this corner, two forces act on the car. One is momentum—that is the way you were aiming it when you arrived—and the other is the force you're applying through the rear wheels onto the road, which is going at a different angle.

"The result," Elford explained, cracking a broad smile, "at any instant in time, is the third angle. So as you go further around the corner, it follows, changing infinitesimally—and instantaneously—and at any speed."

Elford smiled again.

"It *does* take quite a bit of practice."

Evi Butz Gurney got a firsthand education with the triangle of forces at the same time Elford was mastering it. Evi Butz was head of the press department for Porsche from 1965 through 1968. She is now married to Dan Gurney. She recalled other cornering techniques and another running of the Monte Carlo Rally in 1968:

"Elford and Stone had taken off on the last special stages from the Col Terrini. For the rally, they closed those special-stage roads, and all the support vehicles had to go around the route, on public roads." She shook her head as she remembered a long-forgotten ride.

"Sometimes the routes were more direct, but sometimes they were much longer. Huschke von Hanstein wanted very much to meet Elford at the end, to see for himself how his drivers and his car finished. For Huschke, this was important. It would be a big feather in his cap if Porsche won. He'd hired Elford, he'd arranged for the cars....

"So we leave, and Huschke is trying to beat these guys. Now, we are on ice, in a Porsche, in the Alps, in the middle of nowhere. Through the whole night to get to Monte Carlo.

"We also had with us an older gentleman. He was folded up into the back. He knew speed. He was fifteen times German motorcycle champion. But Huschke is driving like *we* are in the rally. Downhill, on ice. We are really going around corners, the

911ST models, with the standard 2.2 liter engines producing 180hp at 7800rpm. A modification to the GT version, for racing applications, used special Mahle pistons and the 1mm larger bore and 10.3:1 compression ratio; output jumped to 230hp at 7800rpm. For the rallies, the choice was to stick with the less highly stressed version.

These ST cars were lightened before assembly, using aluminum for the rear deck lid and door skins with the front and rear bumpers and hood available in fiberglass. The three works 911STs each weighed less than 910kg (2,002lb) by eliminating such ballast as the glove compartment cover, the ashtray, and the heater ducts. The driver was fitted to a Recaro bucket seat while the navigator used a standard "sports" seat. Rally fuel tanks of 100 liters (26.4 gal) made up any weight saved by the deletions.

The factory, in an expression of confidence, added 10 percent to the 1970 Monte Carlo Rally budget to cover the cost of a victory banquet. Björn Waldegaard and Lars Helmers did not let them down. For the third year in a row, Porsche had won the Monte.

But by this time, enough people—competitors, journalists, and spectators alike—had asked Elford just how his spectacular

Huschke von Hanstein: "Porsches don't break."

back end is out so far. Below us is just air! For a long way down.

Evi Gurney laughed again. "This older gentleman—he was about 65—he kept yelling to me, 'Miss Butz, why don't you ask Mr. von Hanstein to slow down?'

"I was just a young girl, I was 26," she said. " I yelled back, 'Ask him yourself. He might listen to you!'

"You know, to this day, Vic Elford thinks he won Monte Carlo.

"Well, a Porsche won it. But we did it. We are the ones who won the 1968 Monte Carlo Rally. With Huschke driving."

For 1969, Porsche sent four 911S to Monte Carlo. The rally cars competed with 180hp at 6800rpm in an automobile homologated at 840kg (1,848lb)!

CHAPTER 20

1969-1971 Typ 917

The Ulcer, The Widowmaker, The Champion

"The car," Vic Elford counselled, "was unbelievably dangerous to drive! Nobody had ever built a car that would go even remotely close to those speeds. In 1969, we ran 350km/h (219mph) down Mulsanne. The 908 long tails did 320km/h (200mph) and the short coupes barely 305km/h (190mph)!"

It was familiar behavior. It was a rules maker's game. Again.

The FIA, first upset and then aghast by the success in 1966 and 1967 of American immigrants, sought to return European racing to the Europeans. Rules for Prototypes class from 1968 would be limited to engines of 3.0 liter displacement. While it would eliminate Ford, it would encourage Matra.

But the FIA also changed its Group 5 and Group 6 regulations. It modified production requirements for homologation to fifty cars. It had been cheated on, run around, and lied to. Yet here was a gift to the manufacturers. The FIA expected merely to encourage them to continue racing existing sports cars—Ferrari's 250LM, Ford's GT40, Lola's T-70—without incurring the hardship of producing more cars. Yet the requirement was high enough to discourage anything new.

In the spring, Porsche went to Paris to appeal. "Yes, OK," the FIA agreed, "it's a sizable number. Make it twenty-five cars...."

It was not entirely selfless. Racing spectators flocked to see the great Ferrari-Ford battles. The FIA knew the value of big crowds to the circuits and to the sponsors.

The FIA never expected the 917.

Rico Steinemann, Porsche Racing manager at the time, knew FIA dramas first hand.

"We showed our car at the Geneva Show in March 1969. We had all the bits and pieces for the twenty-five cars required. We knew the homologation dramas.

"They had been happy either with declarations that cars would be built, or seeing customers' orders, some existing, some already in production, and some only in bits and pieces.

"We had, by the end of March, produced half a dozen cars. All the bits and pieces were in the factory. There were stories we all knew, laughed about. Stories where homologation inspections took place in long rooms with mirrors at one end. Stories where ten cars were viewed in the morning, inspectors were taken for coffee, then to another place to see ten cars. A long lunch with wine and then another place to see ten cars. Afternoon coffee, another place, ten cars. Dinner, wine, desert, coffee, the last ten cars. The same ten cars all day....

"When the technical committee arrived, they saw six complete and all the parts. On the spot, they approved. They went home, wrote their report. The full committee read it and decided, no!"

Steinemann went to Ferdinand Piëch and Helmuth Bott. The FIA wanted to see twenty-five completed cars? OK, they would see twenty-five completed cars. But if others could have fun, so could Porsche.

"Because the racing mechanics were busy with the 908s for the actual racing season...we put together apprentices, messenger boys, office people, secretaries. Just enough people, taught just enough to put together twenty-five cars." Steinemann clearly enjoyed telling this story, nearly every other word punctuated with a laugh.

"We worked from the idea that we wanted twenty-five cars there. Since there would be changes after homologation, after further development work, no matter. We wouldn't race these 'secretary cars' anyway.

"In fact, except for the one or two test cars, all these cars were undrivable. And

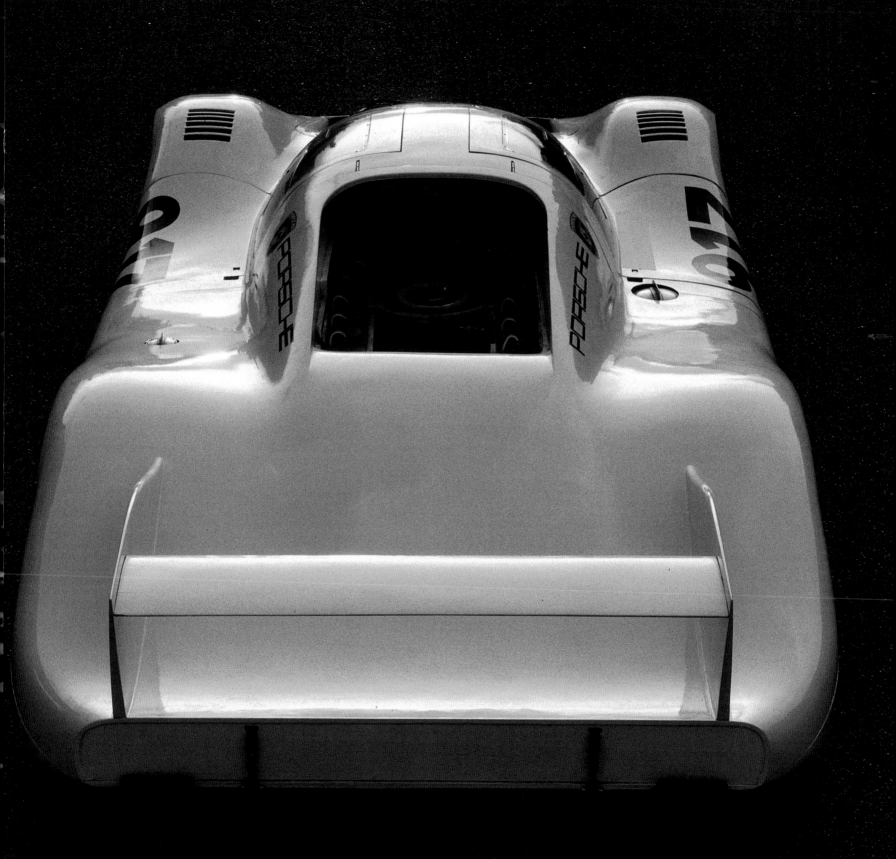

not safe. Yes, you could start the engine. Yes, you could engage first gear. Yes, you could go 5 meters. No more. These cars had been put together by bookkeepers.

"The real race mechanics made sure that engines would run and that we could engage first gear," Steinemann explained. "So the inspectors came again. But they had become so suspicious about seeing twenty-five actual cars, they wanted to see if all the engines would run.

"You know the famous picture, the twenty-five 917s all lined up? Parked close for the inspection? The car's turning was not so tight. There was just enough room to go forward and reverse. So we could look at the inspectors and say, 'Go ahead! What do you wait for? You can start and drive any one!

"We didn't tell them they wouldn't go around a city street let alone a racetrack!

"The cars passed. And all the cars

except for the actual test cars were dismantled again. Eventually, after development work, each was reassembled by racing mechanics."

And Steinemann learned a lesson about the FIA he would not forget.

"The idea of twenty-five identical racing prototypes? Ridiculous? It's fine for production-based cars. A Porsche 917, a Ferrari 512, these are not production cars. One million Chevrolets is production."

The 917 project started mid-1968 and Helmut Flegl was involved from the start. Having worked on aerodynamic development of the 907 long tails, he was also involved in the evolution of the 908 from long coupe to stubby roadster. He was natural for a new big sports car.

"And here, I did especially the 917 body. And this was a bad result...." Flegl's admission stopped conversation. History confirmed the engineer's assessment. Such candor was unexpected.

"The downforces weren't correct. The drag was good. But you should remember the 917 was designed from the beginning as a long tail—which had a tail you could remove."

Flegl spoke softly, for emphasis, not secrecy. The words repeated history, explained it, revealed it. "But the short tail was never really tested in the wind tunnel," he went on. "It was just put on the racetrack. And the aerodynamics were just wrong. It had tremendous rear lift. And this was found at the racetrack.

"The motivation behind the 917," Flegl summarized, "was to go for the first time for the World Championship. Mr. Piëch said, 'This is my goal. We go for the championship.' Before those times, we had excellent cars. The 908 could win Le Mans. But really to win the championship, you needed major luck. The 917 should be the car. It would be the luck.

"So he gave directives, the strategic approach, as a leader. But in 1969 we couldn't do it. It was just too brief. For 1970, we went with the 917 to racetracks where the short tail was the right car." Helmut Flegl let his words trail off. The 1970 season became another matter altogether.

Ferdinand Piëch had other directives,

other strategic approaches in his mind. After losing at Daytona with the 908, Piëch and Steinemann discussed what was possible. Piëch understood racing-car development, believed that more could be accomplished and that a 917 program for two years longer could prove valuable and interesting.

However, Piëch also had other ambitions. As Steinemann summed it up, Piëch wanted "To be the best. Everywhere."

Steinemann: "Piëch's strategy was to win the sports car world championship, win Le Mans, go into Formula 1, win the Formula 1 world championship, and then go to Indianapolis."

Steinemann didn't blink.

"This can be said," he decided aloud. "It's over twenty years ago so...."

"We discussed this. After the 1969 season, we would concentrate the development side on these new things. We needed someone to race our cars in a way that we don't waste time, so that our people can fully concentrate on developing new things.

We needed somebody excellent.

"We'd been beaten at Daytona by the John Wyer team. They had excellent organization, they had a powerful sponsor behind them, Gulf.

"Piëch said, 'Do you think...?'

"I said, 'Yes, I think....'

"'Well, you know all these people,' he said to me, 'speak the languages, I authorize you to have secret talks....'"

At Sebring, in March 1969, Rico Steinemann went to call on John Wyer in his trailer. Wyer was shocked at first. Yet Steinemann sensed Wyer's second reaction: interest. The Gulf Mirage, a 3.0 liter Cosworth project, was in difficulty. Ford was no longer interested. Wyer was at loose ends.

Saturday, Wyer won again. The previous night, however, Wyer and Steinemann solidified the arrangement to present to Piëch. Immediately after the Spa 1,000km, Wyer and Gulf executive VP Grady Davis flew to Stuttgart. They met Piëch and Ferry Porsche, and signed the agreement. And by that time, the 908s had begun winning again.

Rico Steinemann: "You know the famous picture, the twenty-five 917s all lined up? We put together apprentices, messenger boys, office people, secretaries. Just enough people, taught just enough to put together twenty-five cars."

The FIA invented the 917 in its worst nightmare. Changing their Group 5 and 6 regulations to require fifty cars for homologation, then to twenty-five, was meant to encourage existing manufacturers to continue old models, not to undertake new models.

But the 917s had yet to prove Piëch's vision.

"Between Spa and Nürburgring, the whole thing was completed," Steinemann explained. "They got the material at no charge. From the moment everything left Stuttgart, it was on their expense. We split drivers; we paid Siffert and Redman, Wyer paid Pedro Rodriguez and Leo Kinnunen. We wanted to keep our drivers for our future plans...."

Brian Redman, Jo Siffert: Formula 1.
Jo Siffert, Brian Redman: Indy 500.

The aerodynamics came under scrutiny in October with Peter Falk, Helmut Flegl, and John Horseman.

At Zeltweg, Austria, they pursued the problems. Flegl and Falk had brought along the 917 PA Porsche+Audi spyder prototype whose flat rear deck surface had emerged from Tony Lapine's design studio. It evolved during a ten-week period over the summer resulting from the shape of the 908/2, the "Flounder." The spyder was 4sec quicker around the track. With identical chassis and

drivers, it stood to reason that the body configuration made the difference. Horseman's crew raised the short-tail coupe rear bodywork to match the spyder using aluminum pieces. It stabilized the coupe and lap times dropped quickly to near those of the spyder.

Flegl explained. "This new short body end—where the car had been critical before—was redesigned. Back home, in wind tunnels, this perfected the short body. It was a big change."

In the summer while Lapine took up his design pencil, other things were changing as well. One morning, Steinemann was called to join Piëch, Bott, and a bookkeeper in Ferry Porsche's office. The men heard that 30 million DM had been spent for racing the 908 and the 917. The 1969 entry at Le Mans alone had been something like 5 million DM. And Porsche could not afford it. While the 908 project had spanned three years and the 917 would span three more, the costs of presenting new cars at each major race had caught up with the competition department. To ensure victory at these events, Porsche had entered six, seven cars. With travel and housing on the road for vast racing teams, the costs had become insupportable.

For Ferry Porsche and his sister, Louise Piëch, this was an element of the schism that would eventually split the family and the company. For Ferdinand Piëch, it was a setback that suggested additional obstacles that could confront him. Frustrated in his Indianapolis and Formula 1 dreams, he would begin racing 917s through his mother's Austrian import distributorship, Porsche Konstruktionen Salzburg.

When the 917 was first introduced in 1969, it had the suspension-activated flaps. However, even with these, Rolf Stommelen had his hands full testing the car March 29 and 30 at the Le Mans trials.

When Porsche returned in late June, the FIA challenged the flaps and Steinemann diplomatically encouraged a solution: the 908s running in Group 3 would fix their flaps while the 917s, which had been homologated with them, could run the active ones. To Vic Elford, it made little difference.

Elford first saw the car at the Geneva Show. It was love at first sight. He had always loved big cars, powerful cars. Then at Le Mans in June, he drove it.

"The car was unbelievably dangerous to drive!" Elford was matter-of-fact about the car, one that Gerhard Mitter had nicknamed "the Ulcer" and that Brian Redman, after his first drive at Spa, decried as "the Widowmaker."

"Nobody," Elford continued, "had ever built a car that would go even remotely close to these speeds. In 1969, we ran 350km/h (220mph) down Mulsanne where the 908 long tails did 320 (200mph) and the short coupes barely 305km/h (190mph).

"Because of the newness, they simply hadn't had the time to get it right. It used to load up heavily on the back end while we were on the power. But when you got to the end of the straight.... You couldn't take the kink flat out. Couldn't even think about it. You couldn't just take your foot off. If you did, the car would come up in the air at the back. It would start steering the car. At 350km/h (220mph)!

"What we had to do, even at the kink, was come very slowly off the gas pedal and get it balanced once again. At any of the fast corners, we couldn't go deep on braking because we had to come very gently off the gas pedal and onto the brake pedal to keep it balanced."

Elford smiled slightly now; as if remembering the self-conscious feeling of a first dancing lesson, he remembered dancing with the 917. "Coming into Mulsanne, with the back end of the car waltzing, that was all perfectly under control. That was just the limit of braking." The smile broadened quickly.

"But such was the ability of Mr. Piëch's engineers in the following year, 1970—indeed, in that white car, number 25, the one in the Steve McQueen film—I went flat out, through the kink, at night, in the rain, at 392km/h (245mph).

"And that, let me tell you, was exciting. The first time. In a dangerous way. Exciting to be able to do it. It took a few laps before I got to that point. But once I got up the courage to do it...."

Elford paused, inhaling deeply on an ever-present cigarette. Exhaling, the smoke

At Daytona in 1970, John Wyer's Gulf 917Ks set the pace. Pedro Rodriguez and Leo Kinnunen (2) battled their own teammates Jo Siffert and Brian Redman (1) in a memorable race. Dale von Trebra archives. Above the inside rearview mirror, a "skylight" was cut into the roof for Daytona. The driving position inside the 917 was so deep that without it, racers could not see their way around the banking.

In 1969, the 917 ran Mezger's Typ 912/00, the 4.5 liter, 580hp engine. Gulf Oil sponsored the 917 in the World Manufacturer's Championship, with Pedro Rodriguez, Brian Redman, Jo Siffert, and Leo Kinnunen driving. The Siffert/Rodriguez rivalry provided spectators with great racing.

Vic Elford:
"The car was a monster."

surrounded him like early morning fog on Mulsanne. "It's difficult to say what it feels like. It's just unique. I think I was the only one who ever drove the long tail flat out through there. You've just done something that nobody else in the world has ever done. That nobody else in the world can ever do...."

With similar possibilities, Tony Lapine's design studios found their own opportunities. Lapine joined Porsche in 1969, after 17 1/2 years with General Motors. He worked first in Detroit for Harley Earl, the great stylist of the sheet-metal-and-fins era. Then Lapine became head of design at GM's German subsidiary, Opel, in Russelsheim, suburban Frankfurt.

At Porsche, Lapine's designers were limited from massive changes that could affect drag or aerodynamics. Yet they could make small changes in appearance and had complete influence over the paint treatments. Lapine's sense of humor led to the memorable 917s.

"The 917 Salzburg car in 1970, that was easily inspired," Lapine explained. "We did wind-tunnel flow visualization. Put india ink dots on the scale model. They fire up the fan and you see where the ink gets rolled by the wind. The cars would be all streaked."

But that car, Piëch's Le Mans winner, was tame in appearance.

"You can do these things," Lapine laughed at himself and at the memories, "but the main ingredient is that you cannot take yourself too seriously. When you do, you risk appearing comical.

"But when you intentionally do something comical, you take the words from those who would criticize...." Lapine stopped. His gaze stopped on a vase of irises, then at a painting of them opposite.

"The Hippie Car at the same time, of course, well, it was psychedelic. But those are the colors I love. Irises. And white.

"Race cars are on tight schedules to be finished. The later they finish, the more up-to-date development they have. A good racing team has the car finished, ready, just at the start of the first training session. The last thing done is the paint.

"With the Hippie we only got two colors

done, purple and white, at Bauer factory in Stuttgart. When it arrived, everybody said, 'Ugh! Ohh, Jesus Christ! White with purple? This time you guys overcooked it...!'

"And we agreed! They didn't know we had green paint with us. And after night training, we had from 1am to 7am to paint the rest.

"The mechanics arrived the next morning. Everybody said, 'Ahhh! Now that's more like it!' That was for number 3, Larrousse and Kauhsen. Next year, when I saw Willi Kauhsen at the Targa, I said, 'Just wait. Next time you drive a pig!'

"He laughed. I was serious.

"You see, that car was particular. It was 1971. We had it in our wind tunnel, a kind of competition. There were three teams. The engineering/aerodynamics team from Weissach, our design team from the studio, and a third team, the wind-tunnel crew, which was under contract from Mr. Piëch. This was Charles Deutsch and the lads from SERA, in Paris.

"Mr. Deutsch was on the committee, the

"You should remember," Helmut Flegl explained, "the 917 was designed from the beginning as a long tail—which had a tail you could remove. But the short tail was never really tested in the wind tunnel...the aerodynamics were just wrong. It had tremendous rear lift!" The 917 went through many configurations as coupes. They were first shown with a plexiglass covering over the engine like the 908LH. When this starved the engine and fan for air, the cover was removed, recalling Butzi Porsche's "sugar scoop" treatment on his 904 GTS. Fender louvers equalized low pressure.

Ferdinand Piëch sent Rico Steinemann to offer John Wyer the Porsche 917 team. Wyer, finishing the Ford GT program, accepted at Sebring 1969. Later, John Horseman, Wyer's lieutenant, went with Flegl to Zeltweg, Austria, to test. The handling of a new Can-Am spyder showed the way to change the coupe's rear deck.

rulemaking committee for Le Mans. and other things....

"The tests went on. And in the end, we definitely had the best results. Which was announced, honored. But, for sound political reasons, Mr. Piëch suggested we give the edge to the tunnel crew, the Deutsch crew should win....

Lapine began to smile. "For us it was satisfying enough just that we had won. We couldn't change anything. Then Mr. Piëch said, 'But, you can paint it.'

Lapine's smile erupted again into laughter. "Well, the French were aghast. The sponsor, Count Rossi, dropped 10,000 Marks! Dr. Porsche was miffed.

"Dr. Porsche said, 'You know in the old days, it was so simple. The Italian cars were red, British cars were green, French cars were blue. German cars are not pink.'

"I could only say, 'Well, we have a sponsor. And in any event, it will be the most-photographed car!

"And Mr. Piëch was delighted." Lapine

laughed again, delighted himself with the story of the short, fat-tailed pink pig.

Vic Elford remembered the bodywork and Lapine's paint schemes. His own rides were in less-controversial-appearing cars. He theorized aloud: "I think I was the only factory driver," he suspected, "who actually enjoyed driving the 917 long tails in 1970 and 1971. Those cars required a lot of precision. You had to drive like it was on rails. Most drivers in big sports cars would get a bit sideways, if it was possible. I never did and that was probably why I was the only one who liked it.

"Because with that long tail, even in 1970, the white one in the McQueen film, you couldn't change your mind if you'd committed it to a corner. If you'd made a mistake, you were pretty likely to have an accident.

"The car was a monster. It was not...." Elford halted, mid-sentence. A thought occurred to him, one which needed careful handling, a cautious commitment to the line he was to follow.

"I think Porsche may have made a kind of moral mistake in selling the first 917 to John Woolfe in 1969. Everybody on the team was finding it a monster handful. And put in the hands of somebody like that....

"But, he was a victim of circumstances as well. The first day of practice he had problems with it. Second day of practice more problems. Digby Martland was to be John's codriver. He got in two laps, which rather seriously frightened him, and he begged off. Linge was drafted. The crew solved the problems and Rolf Stommelen— the man with more hours than anyone in a 917—qualified the car.

"Which gave poor John a good position. Well up the grid. That was the last year of the running start. Linge wanted to do the start, should have done. We all tried to persuade John. But he wanted to.

"And then to add to the misfortune, he made a good start. He was up in the top dozen. Just getting swept along. You can't get out of the way. You just go, dragged along with them."

Elford paused. With Dick Attwood, he started in number 12, the car that would last 21 hours and retire in 1st place, with a bro-

ken transmission, after dragging the rest of the field through a long summer night. He continued, speaking more softly.

"We got round to White House on the first lap. White House, even in an easy car, was not an easy corner. And in a 917, it was hell."

Stommelen in a 917 led Elford in a 917 who led Siffert, Schütz, and Herrmann in factory 908s. Jo Bonnier in a Lola came next. Seven cars later came John Woolfe.

"We used to come down, doing about 290km/h (181mph). We take off over the bridge and change down to fourth gear in the air. Go through the righthander with the car drifting. And let it swing out through the lefthander and then slide out to the wall. When it got to the wall, we simply stopped it with a flick of the wrists.

Elford hesitated again. He was describing the first 3 minutes of the first 24 hours of 917s at Le Mans in 1969.

"John couldn't do that. He got it sliding through the corner. It just slid and carried on sliding. It was under control, it just carried on sliding until he hit the wall.

"Then it overturned, spun around, and just broke in half."

Thwarted by budget constraints, Ferdinand Piëch still hungered for competition. While John Wyer operated the Gulf 917s, Piëch began racing 917s through his mother's Austrian distributorship, Porsche Salzburg. Wyer's blue-and-orange cars lost to Piech's red-and-white car at Le Mans.

CHAPTER 21

1972 917/30 Can-Am

Porsche's Adjustable Flyer

The differences between the 917/10 and 917/30 extended from nose to tail and amounted to nearly a completely new car. Charles Deutsch's SERA research and design group in Paris were hired to codesign and wind-tunnel test the nose, body, and rear wing.

George Follmer smiled. "I was absolutely scared witless!" Then he laughed. "I had a stacked deck. I'd never been to Atlanta. I'd never *seen* Atlanta. And now, Mark Donohue's lying in the crash house up there with a bad knee.... I didn't know the crew. Didn't know the engineers. Didn't know the car!

"Hey, I'd never driven a car with that kind of horsepower! I mean, at that point we had probably 850 to 900 horsepower....

"I drove out early in the morning with one of the crew. We'd gotten permission to go out on the track with my rental car so I could find out which way the track turned!" Follmer laughed again, recalling what could have seemed like sheer folly.

It was a Thursday morning. Mark Donohue had shown to the Can-Am world the potential of Porsche's 917/10 at Mosport, the season opener. Even though he didn't win, his charge back up through the field after his long drawn-out pit stop, alerted the McLaren camp that the game was afoot.

"And so this pressure," Follmer continued. "When you drive for the Captain (Roger Penske), you are there to perform a service. To do it his way. Which was fine! I'd done it before. I'd driven for him in previous Can-Ams. I drove for him in '67, drove Trans-Am. That was not the problem.

"The problem was that car. That awesome car."

Porsche's 917 coupes had aerodynamic problems that were virtually solved in a testing session that introduced factory drivers Jo Siffert and Brian Redman to the new 917 spyder, the PA, Porsche+Audi's entry in the Canadian-American Challenge series.

During the summer of 1969, Jo Hoppen, Porsche motorsports director in North America, learned of the creation of Porsche+Audi division as a part of Volkswagen of America. He suggested the factory build a Can-Am spyder to promote the cars. Hoppen planned for a three-year program. Siffert's interest helped propel the program to fruition.

The spyder and coupe chassis were identical, as were the engines. And testing the two at Zeltweg, it was only the lap times and ease of handling that differed and pointed the way for future coupe development. It also clearly showed Weissach engineers they were on the way to North American victory. Joining the season in late July, entering only half the races, Siffert and the new 917PA (917-028) finished 4th in the standings. The spyder ran the coupes' 4.5 liter 580hp flat twelve-cylinder engine.

But with only 580hp, Porsche knew it would be weak in 1971. Options were explored. A flat sixteen-cylinder engine with versions ranging up to 7.0 liters—the Can-Am/Group 7 regulations wrote no limit on engine displacement— was developed and tests produced 755hp. But Hans Mezger and Valentin Schäffer also tried turbocharging the existing flat twelve with Piëch's encouragement as the more technically interesting of the two projects.

After great frustration and much work, the turbochargers—twin Eberspacher units adapted from truck applications—were tamed. Engine output soared to 850hp from the 4.5 liter and 1,000hp from the new 4.9 liter engine.

The chassis, up to the challenge of 580hp, needed modification to handle nearly twice that. The body was redesigned

to keep the extremely light front end on the ground. To balance that effect, a vast wing was suspended across the rear deck, cantilevered slightly out, effectively lengthening the body through the air.

In 1971, Siffert again joined the Can-Am season late. Sponsored by STP, he took a 5th, a 3rd, and two 2nds. A second team was proposed for Roger Penske using Sunoco sponsorship, but this never materialized. The factory then committed to a full season for 1972. But tragically, Siffert died during a non-championship race and the motivating and guiding light behind this effort was dimmed.

The factory was familiar by this point with outside teams running their entries based on John Wyer's success with the Gulf coupes in 1970. It also knew of Penske's operations. Porsche struck a deal with Penske to do the same with the Can-Am spyders for 1971 that Wyer had done with the coupes. L&M tobacco was to sponsor, Mark Donohue was to drive, and Penske, ever the realist, bought a spare car. He needed it by the second race.

"So this pressure, the car, the track...." George Follmer smiled again. "The first time I came in, I was ringing wet. And it wasn't because it was hot!" Follmer laughed at his case of nerves. But the nerves steadied and with each lap the car became more familiar. More laps, more seat time. Follmer qualified the car 2nd and on Sunday, race morning, another practice session/tire warm-up gave Follmer another few minutes.

"When we started, Denny Hulme had the outside, which was considered to be the line for the first corner.... But he didn't get there first!" Follmer also got to the finish line first, learning, literally on every race lap, better and better how to drive the car.

"It was the kind of car you just drove into the corner on the brakes. There was no compression and downshifting didn't do a thing. So you set the car with the brakes, and then hit the throttle.

"You'd hit the throttle right at the beginning of the turn. And that would probably get you through the corner, probably to the apex, and then from that point on you start having the power! But you *had* to be sure the thing was going in the right direction

because when it came in...I mean it didn't just come in trickles. It went from 400 to 850hp pretty quick!"

While Follmer learned to overcome the engine's turbo lag, the one thing he could only master was its twitchiness. "In a corner like the old Turn 9 at Riverside—well, in a lot of corners everywhere—it was just a walk. You just walked the car through. You'd start in and the nose would set and then the back end would begin to move. You'd correct that and the nose would begin to move. You were constantly sawing the wheel....

"And then the wind! You were just constantly walking the car. People didn't see it but you were doing it all the time. It wasn't any chassis stiffness kind of thing." Follmer shook his head. "It was just too short...."

Helmut Flegl, the development engineer on the entire 917 project—coupes and spyders—was well aware of the problem. At the beginning of that 1971 season, Penske and Donohue tested at Mosport. Throughout the day, with one adjustment after another, they got lap times down below their expectations. In fact, they got things so well sorted out that making changes began to detract from performance. The results were telexed back to Flegl at Weissach where they were duplicated and then further developed.

"The range of where the car worked was pretty narrow," Helmut Flegl recalled. "Which is dangerous because you can lose all performance very quickly."

The season began and, aside from Donohue's accident due to a mechanic's error, the car performed extremely well. To

The 917/30, left page, was more easily recognized in America in Sunoco blue and yellow. Mark Donohue flashed around Can-Am circuits with nearly 1200hp Throughout Europe, Müller commanded the same respect in Martini cars. The InterSerie ran regulations similar to Can-Am. Müller was champion. Left, the 1972 Can-Am season championship had been decided. Racing at Laguna Seca on October 15, 1972, George Follmer needed only to finish 2nd but teammate Donohue, in the number 6 L&M 917/10, slowed his own pace for the last two laps. Follmer won the race and the championship. Here at Riverside, Follmer and the 917/10 ate up the back straightaway for the season's finale. Bob Tronolone. Below, by 1973, the engines had increased in displacement and been turbocharged successfully. The variable-wheelbase test car ran the InterSerie with a Typ 912/51.

At the end of 1972, the 917/10 wheelbase was still just too short—2300mm (90.5in). Flegl imagined interchangeable inserts behind the driver, ahead of the engine, to lengthen the wheelbase in 100mm (3.94in) increments. It proved far too time consuming. A compromise 200mm (7.87in) plug was inserted. In 1972, George Follmer won the Can-Am series in a 917/10, driving "that awesome car." For Herbert Müller and Mark Donohue, the car became even more awesome. With a 2500mm (98.4in) wheelbase, the handling improved markedly. The 250 additional horsepower did not hurt, either.

some extent, Follmer's performances gave Flegl the luxury of thinking about what might be the car's weaknesses. He recognized in theory that the wheelbase was the most influential parameter in handling. He planned that before anything else, he would examine that factor.

"The car had a wheelbase of 2300mm (90.6in), which is very short," Flegl explained. "This was normal for Porsche but for the racing world, it was just very short. There were reasons. Because weight is important... when you make a wheelbase longer, weight might be hurt and the size of the car....

"And the aerodynamics! We never liked the big wing! That came as a result of a strategic approach: Don't hurt drag! Really!" Flegl, a chassis man, shrugged. As an engineer interested in the total vehicle, Flegl understood trade-offs. "So the big wing, that cost a few pains. But the car worked—we were winning—so it was accepted.

"And then there was the long tail. That was Mark's idea. He said, 'Porsche's knowledge has always been in long-tail cars. Why don't we make this a long-tail car?' So

when it came time to plan for the winter, we proposed work on the wheelbase."

Discussions followed. Could they vary the wheelbase of an existing car? How much should it be: 2400mm, 2500, 2600? No one knew. Flegl recommended trying all three, slipping extensions into the driver's compartment, so that the steering equipment and the drivetrain went unchanged.

But that opened a can of worms. Flegl and his team knew you could not change wheelbase by itself. Other things were affected. "But our approach became 'Don't touch this car *except* the wheelbase.' So we made the three pieces that bolted between the front and rear, with a throttle cable, a shift linkage. But nothing else changed. A true scientific experiment.

"I had the idea that we could change things back and forth within a few hours. It didn't work. But we had to be sure that the pieces would fit so we made a jig. The jig was put to the front end and the rear end of the car. It supported the engine. But it took so much time, we began to realize we could do the changes and there would be no time for the driver to actually drive....

"So we judged to have the 200mm

(7.87in) piece to make 2500mm (98.4in) overall. Well, the mechanics worked a day—or something like that—to have it fitted. We realized our plan to quickly exchange pieces...well...." Flegl shrugged again. He knew theory, yes, but he knew testing required the engineers to leave the ivory towers and come to the track. The car must run!

"Then, it turned out that with the 200mm insert, it was just so much better than the standard 2300mm length, that we said there is no need to do the rest. We could live with that.

"And then later on, we worked on the aerodynamics, with the nose and long tail for the new car, the 917/30."

The 917/30 was a nearly unique situation in motorsports history. Because it was designed for and raced by only one driver—Mark Donohue—it was designed particularly to his liking. He convinced Flegl to graft a 917 Le Mans-style long tail onto the spyder, seeking higher top speed while willingly sacrificing some downforce. The top speed went from 340 to 385km/h (212.5 to 240.6mph).

Flegl elaborated: "The 917/30 nose was very much influenced by what we had learned from the 917/10. And there, we were unhappy with the sensitivity of nose height. You could lose all the downforce by the nose being a little too high." Flegl spelled it out with little drama. The car was extremely sensitive to suspension adjustment. The SERA nose, long tail, and large wing produced so much downforce as to compress the suspension to the bumpstops. "And where there were bumps, the car became critical."

George Follmer remembered the situation with a little more immediacy.

"I remember one time at Riverside in Turn 6, I came up and let the car slide across, you know, the way we always used to kind of cross that apex: go way out and drive her off? It was kind of an outside apex, maybe a little further out than you'd normally expect.

"Well, I did it in the Porsche. I was following Mario Andretti, and I really wanted to get by him. And that was a pretty steep drop off at the exit to 6, heading back up

toward 7? And I came out and took the front right off the ground."

Follmer laughed, imagining what he must have looked like in Andretti's mirror.

"I went down between 6 and 7 like a boat...it got a little light. I really wanted to blow off Andretti. He'd been blowing my doors off at Indy for a long time....

"Well, I didn't exactly pass him on two wheels...." Follmer paused to let the image sink in.

"It goes back to what I said about the car not having any front weight. I tell you, it got my attention! I just kind of gently got out of it and it came back down. Just landed like an airplane.

"And then that 1,000hp came on and I blew him off."

Flegl's and Penske's development work with Donohue succeeded in controlling the handling. In 1973, the 917/30 won the Can-Am Championship. After a fitful beginning, Penske's Sunoco team won the last six events. Donohue retired at the end of the season and soon after, so did Porsche.

The SCCA limited fuel consumption to 73 gallons per 200 mile race, due to concerns with OPEC's oil embargo. Only one final accomplishment—with no fuel restriction—awaited. A world closed-course speed record had been set in 1974. Donohue believed the 917/30 could beat it. After blowing several engines—Mezger and Schaeffer had designed the Typ 912 for on-off full power, not steady on—a new engine appeared with a second intercooler.

At Talladega, Alabama, on a 4.26km (2.66 miles) banked oval, Donohue set a new record on August 9, 1975: 353.79km/h (221.12mph). That was the sign-off for the 917 Can-Am cars.

In Europe, the Inter-Serie, roughly a Can-Am equivalent, had run in 1974, Herbert Müller winning the season in Flegl's adjustable prototype. And then it was done. Environmentally and economically, the turbocharged racers had served their purpose and proven too extravagant, a liability.

Ironically, only a few years later, environmentally and economically, the turbochargers would become an asset.

The 917/30-001 prototype spent weeks as the development mule for the massive changes to the 1973 Can-Am entry. Its wheelbase was modified—a test Helmut Flegl conceived to try to further improve handling. After it retired as a development car, Herbert Müller ran it in the European InterSerie in 1974 for Martini & Rossi. And won.

CHAPTER 22

1982 Typ 916

A Most Special Wish

They started life as Volkswagens, derided as Vopo's in the European press. Porsche sold its own version, the 914/6. In the United States, they were called Volkswagens for the rich. Then Ferdinand Piëch put his hand into it, "inventing" the Typ 916, fitted not with a 911T engine but a 190 hp 911S. Eleven were built, and then a twelfth.

There was no doubt this project was to be a Volkswagen. But in order to attract attention, VW head Heinz Nordhoff meant it to adopt some of the best, most trendsetting ideas of the day. It was to be mid-engined, like Ferruccio Lamborghini's startling Miura or Ferrari's Dino 246.

By long-standing agreement, VW's research and development department *was* Porsche. Nordhoff wanted his new car to be developed by Porsche, and to utilize the suspension and rack-and-pinion steering from the 911. This new car would profit from the false starts in chassis reinforcement made on Porsche's Targa. This new VW would be a Targa, but a stiff one. And it would look like something completely new, like a sports car, seating only two.

To contain costs, it was to be powered by Volkswagen's 1679cc Typ 411 fuel-injected engine. The four-cylinder Boxer motor produced 80hp at 4900rpm. Unfortunately, it sounded like a VW.

In exchange for its development work, however, Porsche would be allowed to market the car with its own badges and its own six, the 1991cc Weber-carburetted 110hp 911T engine. It would not sound like a Volkswagen.

Then Heinz Nordhoff died in April 1968. Kurt Lotz, his successor, didn't know much about Nordhoff's project, but he didn't care much for it. Through fits and starts and countless meetings, the details and agreements once presumed settled had to be resettled. One result of this turmoil had been the creation of the Porsche+Audi Division to handle sales and distribution in the United States.

Nordhoff's legacy was to be confusion in the extreme.

This new joint-venture car, called Typ 914, was no more a simple project. The bodies were made by Karmann in Osnabruck. Those cars destined for VW engines remained there for assembly; those becoming Porsches were shipped back to Zuffenhausen and put onto the 911 assembly line.

Those becoming Porsches carried an extra burden, however, which was never anticipated by Porsche management in all its cordial dealings with Heinz Nordhoff. VW under Kurt Lotz raised the price to Porsche for the 914 Karmann bodies. When all the math was done, the unit cost was higher than for a 911 body. Zuffenhausen's bright enthusiasm for this project—for what was considered internally to be a viable replacement for the entry-level 912—dimmed measurably.

By the time the cars were introduced in September 1969 at the Frankfurt Auto Show, VW's 914 was offered for 11,995DM ($3,870). Porsche's visually identical version with the six-cylinder was priced at 18,995DM ($6,125). But worse than showing these two side by side, was the fact that only a few feet further away was the least-adorned 911, at 20,000DM. For only 1,000DM more—$325—buyers got a "real Porsche."

The 914 was panned. It died in the press. Writers called it a suitable replacement for the Karmann-Ghia but it was not by any reach a 912. Abuse clung to it. Officially known in Europe as the Volkswagen-Porsche, it was nicknamed the *Volksporsche*, the People's Porsche. Press director Huschke von Hanstein begged journalists not to refer to it as the "Vopo." Suggestion offered, suggestion taken. Vopo it was.

The twelfth 916 was begun in 1979 in Rolf Sprenger's Sonderwuncsh "Special Wishes" department. A young master mechanic had his own special wish to upgrade his 914/6. To confuse viewers, he used the cloth inserts in his new leather seats. A special rollcage stiffened the chassis to retain his open roof.

And that stigma came off the ships with each car entering the Port of New Jersey. It attached to the Porsche version, the 914/6, because of its identical looks. In the United States, it was labelled "The VW for the rich."

Total production for the 914 was 115,596 cars over its five-year life, astonishing considering the enthusiast press' dislike; but for the 914/6, it was a disappointing 3,353. That the Porsche suffered from VW—both in internal business matters and external image matters—was obvious.

But even as the Frankfurt Show opened, Porsche remained curious about the car. On September 10, 1969, engineers at Weissach squeezed the 3.0 liter flat-eight engine of the 908 into one of the evaluation mules, number 914 111. Detailed in Kraftfahrzeugbrief Nr. 37 341 086, the hybrid was intended to "evaluate the boundaries of the mid-engine concept."

The evaluator was none other than Ferdinand Piëch, Porsche's chief of development at the time. Running the engine to 8500rpm increased output to 350hp and it was judged that this was the boundary in an 1,350kg (2,970lb) car. Seven days later, chassis 914 006 was fitted with a slightly detuned version of the 908 eight-cylinder, rating 260hp, and this was presented by the factory to Ferry Porsche on his 60th birthday.

His hand-written driver's manual advised "running the car between 3500 and 7500rpm. To prevent fouling the spark plugs, it is recommended to leave the motor to turn freely occasionally." Idling in rush-hour traffic was not what the writer intended.

Ferry Porsche knew what was meant because he put nearly 10,000km on the car before it was retired to join his nephew's car in the Porsche Museum collection.

Piëch experimented liberally with the chassis. The factory's first attempts with turbocharging 911 engines coincided with testing and development of the 914 chassis. Piëch had one of the two 2.0 liter experimental turbo engines fitted for a short while.

FIA regulations offered an outlet for sporting use for the 914/6. Marketing was anxious for racing successes to help promote the model's lagging sales. And so was born the 914/6GT, fitted with the Typ 901/35 engine. A dozen were turned out by the factory but many dozen more were assembled by privateers from parts offered by the competition department. One factory outing with three 914/6GTs resulted in a 1-2-3 finish for Gerard Larrousse, Björn Waldegaard, and Günther Steckkönig in the 84 hour Marathon de la Route staged at the Nürburgring in August. Another saw two-time Monte Carlo Rally winner Waldegaard in one for the 1971 Monte running. After a heroic effort in some of the worst weather in years, he finished 3rd overall.

In early 1972 the 914 Evolution appeared, a brief star in an otherwise dreary chapter for Porsche: it was called the Typ 916. The new number signified a complete break from the VW project.

The 2.0 liter 911T engine was replaced with the 2.4 liter 911S version. Horsepower jumped from 110 to 190hp at 6500rpm. The Targa top was fixed solidly, welded into place, to eliminate all flex. Brakes and shocks were lifted from the 911S. Front and rear sway bars and 175mm (6.88in) wheels front and rear held the car to the ground, while front and rear track were widened 21 and 27mm (0.82 and 1.06in) using spacers. Carried over from the 914/6GT were the trademark flared fenders, widening the body nearly 90mm (3.54in). Leather filled the passenger cabin and the car was available only with the best radios Becker or Blaupunkt had to offer.

The car became what Weissach and serious Porsche enthusiasts expected. A high speed (top of 230km/h, 143.4mph) Gran Turismo, with quick acceleration (0-100km/h—62.5mph—in 6.7sec), it was a blisteringly fast go-kart. It even had a hand-built price, 40,000DM ($12900), or 9,000DM more than the 911S. The car was "available," but "only friends of the house" could order one.

There was talk of a larger production run, of showing the car at the Paris Auto Show. There was talk of competing for sales against Ferrari's Dino 246. But two weeks before Paris, the project was hidden in a desk drawer. Further production was canceled. It was believed no one would pay for the car what it cost to build plus a reasonable profit. Eleven had been assembled in 1972; five were snapped up quickly by Porsche and Piëch family members, and the other six slipped out to friends. There were to be no more.

But the exception to the rule came to work for Porsche in 1974, as a mechanic in the engine-assembly department. Bernd Oergel owned a 914/6. He knew of the eleven 916s.

Five years later, he was transferred to Customer Service, to work for Rolf Sprenger, the creator of the *Sonderwunsch*—the Special Wishes program for customers. Oergel had a special wish of his own.

A year after joining Sprenger's department, he began a metamorphosis. Working on his own time and with only the help of his brother Walter, he transformed number, his car, number 2,451 of 3,353 into number twelve of eleven.

Everything was replaced based on factory manuals, changed to factory-original, factory-correct specifications for the 916: the engine, suspension, body panels, instrumentation, oil cooler, even the space-saver spare tire in the front trunk were replaced. "Working," as he recalled, "every spare minute, day and night, for eighteen months," he added leather in the interior but retained the 914/6 checkerboard cloth, to confuse observers who might think it was merely a look-alike 916. But this was no

With 911S running gear, the 916 could reach 235km/h (146.8mph). Acceleration was equally fast—0-100km/h (62.5mph) in 6.9 seconds. The 190hp 1,080kg (2,376lb) package with its extremely low center of gravity, could literally spin circles around normal 911S production models.

mere poseur.

Improvements in tire technology and chassis and suspension developments had occurred during the nearly ten years in which Oergel wished for his 916. These allowed him to use adjustable anti-sway bars and 50 Series VR-rated tires. His car became an "evolution."

It was a 1982 Typ 916.

Everything matched—or exceeded—factory specifications except one item: with help from an engineer friend, a roll cage was built that exceeded even the factory's torsional stiffness specifications for the 916 from 1972.

Bernd Oergel's *Sonderwunsch* go-kart kept its open top.

CHAPTER 23

1973 Carrera RS
1973 Carrera RSR

Singer Develops A Legend

On Monday, January 29, 1973, the FIA inspected the 528th Carrera RS and certified the car legal for Group 4 Grand Touring. Yet, because of paperwork delays, the next weekend, the two racing versions, RSRs, started the Daytona 24 Hours as prototypes. Sunday, February 4, when the endurance race ended, Peter Gregg won in a 911, Porsche's prototype RSR.

When Dr. Ernst Fuhrmann returned to Porsche as Technical Director in 1971, he found a company in transition and in search of financial equilibrium. The previous year's sales had been slightly more than 300 million DM (and motorsports had spent a tenth of that). He also found Helmuth Bott in charge of Research and Development.

Plans that had existed to replace the 911 had to be scrapped. Funding for Porsche's new car was coming from research and development work that Weissach was doing under contract to Volkswagen. The changes of management at VW affected Zuffenhausen. It was apparent to Fuhrmann that the 911 still had development potential. And it occurred to him that a way to demonstrate its continued vigor—a new racing program based on the 911—would be beneficial. In fact, it was also the only racing program that the financially ailing company could afford.

While Fuhrmann had not been at Porsche to witness the creation and development of Piëch's 911R, he knew of its existence and he knew of its specifics. Within the next year, a Group 4 car was conceived, a name from Fuhrmann's own history was resurrected and rumors were leaked.

British journalist Denis Jenkinson called it "an incredibly honest motor car"; German writer Jerry Sloniger suggested that perhaps this car ought to have its name—Carrera—written backwards on it nose, readable in other's rearview mirrors, because it appeared so quickly on the scene.

Series production for the Carrera RS 2.7 liter coupe had begun in October 1972, at the same time as the public introduction at the Paris Auto Show.

On November 27, 1972, the FIA gave Homologation Number 637 for Appendix J, Group 4 to Porsche KG for model year 1972-1973. Four versions of the car were created. The H was the homologation version of which only twenty were built; the M471, the RS *mit Sportausstattung*, was the sport equipment model, the Lightweight; M472, RS Touring; and M491, RS *mit Rennausstattung*, the RSR.

The foundation of it all, as with all Porsches, was the engine, in this case so extensively modified as to be virtually new. While the production 911S for 1972 was still a 2.4 liter, the RS 2.7 was bored out 6mm to 90mm. The standard 911S offered 180hp; the RS, Typ 911/83, produced 210hp at 6300rpm. The body was lightened through the exclusion of sound deadening and insulation materials and in some cases undercoating. In some further cases, lightweight interior panels were used. Still, the front and rear bumpers, the front spoiler, and the rear engine lid spoiler, the new *Burzel* (the ducktail), were fiberglass. The H weighed in at 960kg (2,112lb) with fuel; the RS Lightweight was 15kg heavier, 975kg (2,145lb).

The RS Touring car was equipped mostly like 911S models but with the ducktail rear spoiler and wider rear fenders. Not immediately visible and also common to the Lightweight, were such features as supplementary forged-alloy front axle support, reinforced rear axle trailing arms, gas shock absorbers, 7mm spacers for the rear axle wheel mounts, torsion bar housing reinforcement, the thinner Glaverbel window glass, and forged-alloy wheels. The S interior and trims added 100kg (220lb) to the total, bringing the RS Touring to 1,075kg (2,365lb).

While most of the Carrera RS Sport and Touring models appeared in white, nine other standard colors were offered and fifteen special colors at extra cost (as well as a "match-to-sample" specification at significantly higher cost) came out of the catalog. The trendsetting Carrera graphic on the car came from Tony Lapine's design studio.

Porsche needed to produce and sell 500 in order to meet the Group 4 homologation rules. In order to do that, the first 500 cars were all assembled as Lightweights. When

each car reached Point 8 on the assembly line, with all necessary pieces in the car so it would function fully but not yet ready for customer delivery, it was taken to the Zuffenhausen town scale. There, at an independent facility, each car was weighed and certified. The cars were then returned to the factory and split off either for final inspection or returned to assembly to fit the customer options.

Offered at 33,000DM, barely 10 percent more than the 911S, all 500 copies sold at the Paris Auto Show. Another batch of 500 was approved, the price increased 1,000DM, and those sold too. And another batch, and then another until eventually 1,580 sold in all variations. This quantity permitted homologation into the FIA's Group 3.

The Group 4 legal RS allowed Weissach an additional measure of creativity, and created the first of the 911-based RSR legends. Norbert Singer was the man who Fuhrmann and Bott assigned to create this legend.

Singer had joined Porsche in early 1970 at age 30. He had earned a master's degree in Mechanical Engineering, Aviation and Space Technology, from Munich Technical University. His first work at Weissach involved development of the 917 coupes, especially the aerodynamics of the long tail cars competing in the World Championship of Makes. This new project was to be his first assignment as project manager. Fuhrmann's (and Bott's) first goal was to contain costs. Singer's first goal was to have two cars ready for the Daytona 24 Hours, February 4, 1973.

An entirely new powerplant, Typ 911/72, displaced 2806cc. New pistons increased compression to 10.5:1 with the result that the 911-based engine produced close to 308hp at 8000rpm. But the 975kg homologation weight was still a disadvantage.

One of the first RSRs was delivered to Roger Penske for Mark Donohue and George Follmer to drive. Another went to the Brumos team, to be driven by Peter Gregg and Hurley Haywood. No one expected much beyond additional development results out of a production-based car racing against the prototypes from Alfa Romeo, Matra, the Gulf-Mirages from John

Wyer, and Reinhold Jöst in a 908.

Singer went along to Daytona to keep an eye on his new cars.

"I remember it was...well, we were running 12th. And then the prototypes got problems. The Gulf dropped out. The Alfas. The Matras, I don't remember exactly. The Jöst 908 had a leak in one of the fuel cells."

Singer, a serious and brilliant engineer, is also a man quick to laugh. And retelling the story of this race car brought back many laughs.

"Jöst's 908 had two tanks, one on each side. Each tank held 60 liters. But with the leak, they could only use one tank. They had to plug the crossover line. It took them time to plug the lines and now it meant they had to stop every 20 minutes for fuel.

"We had the two Carreras. Donohue's car had an engine problem in the night. But Hurley's car, well, they could run an hour between pit stops for fuel. And Hurley, he loved Daytona at night. He was faster in the night than he was in qualifying! So we won. The RSR number 59 won Daytona!

"You know that little Burzel? It came from the production people. It actually did some good for the road cars. But for the races, we needed more downforce. That wing got much bigger." Singer began laughing. "What we did was make an extension on it...at Monza...."

Norbert Singer's old friend, Klaus Reichert, joined in the laughter at this point. Reichert, for years Porsche's staff photographer and number-two man in the press department, had been at Monza and remembered.

"Vallelunga was the first European race," Reichert explained. "Our two Martini

The Carrera RS, left page, was introduced at the Paris Auto Show, October 5, 1972. Production was planned for only enough to meet homologation needs: 500 models. All were sold by the end of October. Within six months another run of 500 was sold out. Throughout 1973, nearly 1,580 were sold. The evolution from costly prototypes to production-based race cars had begun successfully. Left, development of the RSR was Norbert Singer's first assignment as project manager. After the lavish racing programs with the 917's, Singer's instructions included keeping an eye on costs. The first two cars produced went to privateers at Daytona: Roger Penske for Mark Donohue and George Follmer, and Brumos, for Hurley Haywood and Peter Gregg. The 1974 Turbo RSR was the next step. Porsche Werke

The Typ 911/72 was an entirely new engine. Displacing 2806cc, the flat six produced 308hp at 8000rpm versus the 210hp of the RS. With the same lightened body as the RS, but with heavier brakes, a larger oil tank, 31.5gal fuel tank, rollcage, and other modifications, the racing version weighed 17kg more, 917kg (2,017lb) Bodywork was lightened wherever possible through the use of fiberglass panels for the rear decklid, front spoiler and decklid, and front and rear bumpers. The first 500 cars were assembled and then taken to Zuffenhausen city scales for certification of their weight. After weighing, the cars were returned to production. Some remained as lightweights, option M471, which specified gutted interior as well as other modifications. The rest went on to become either M472 touring cars or M491 full race cars. Below, after introducing the new RSR at Daytona in February, 1975, Peter Gregg and Hurley Haywood campaigned the Brumos Racing effort throughout the entire Camel GT series. They won Daytona by fifteen laps. At the fifth race of the season at Riverside, May 10, Gregg finished 3rd behind BMWs. Yet the new RSR was so consistent, Gregg still won the series championship. Bob Tronolone

& Rossi Carreras were the only two cars that qualified. When they finished the race, they had won GT class, 1-2. None of the customers could qualify. They all went home Saturday night.

"At Monza, the second race, Singer was told by the course stewards that he had been protested. By a Porsche dealer! An Italian, named Bonomelli."

Singer laughed: "We had replaced the

148

rear suspensions where it was fitted to the body, where the torsion bar was...we replaced that with a solid part. It was a kind of plastic, teflon, actually. He thought it was not legal...."

Reichert jumped back into the story. "But, you don't file a protest just before the start of the race! Because while you argue with the scrutineers, they start the race. And you are still in scrutineering!"

Singer started to chuckle. "So, we thought, 'What do we do? We can't replace it with a production part because we didn't have anything else with us.' So we decided to change class!"

Singer's chuckle elevated into a hearty laugh.

"Herbert Müller was racing with us in those days. I think he had been with Ferrari before, because he spoke fluent Italian. So I went up to the tower with him and we said, 'Well, we want to change the class.' From GT to prototype. Against the Matras!" Singer and Reichert both laughed at the irony.

"The course steward just looked at us. This is just before the race! Then she signed the request and we rushed out before she could realize.... We went to the grid immediately!

"This was the first time we really knew we needed a little more downforce from the rear. We needed better weight distribution. When you make a Carrera light, you can only lighten the front. You still have all the weight in the rear. So we put up a few extra pieces for a rear wing, very large, like this." Singer made a high wall with his hands. "And we went out. As a prototype you can do what you want."

Singer laughed again and turned to Reichert. "You remember Le Mans trials?" he asked Reichert. "The big discussion about wider tires afterward in June?"

Both men laughed. Another story, sweet in the telling.

"There was a practice session at Le Mans in April. There is normally a two-day session there and we raced with the narrow homologation tires there. I think it was 11 or 12 inches. And for the race in June, now we're a prototype. We widened the rear tires to 15 inches. Just a little bit."

Reichert picked up the story. "Yes, but the top speed dropped by 15km/h. And you must remember, Mr. Fuhrmann was an engine man, basically. He got a little upset!"

Singer's laughter continued. "He wanted to know how he could make us more power—by this time we had 3.0 liters and had gained 20-25hp, and still the car was slower on the straight. How can you do that?

"But the laps times were equal. What we lost on the straight we compensated in the corners. And you got the average lap times constant. With the narrow tires, you start off quite fast but the tires go away. Very fast, then after two laps you lost a lot. Therefore, overall, it *was* faster. But of course, if you are looking for a faster lap time *and* a faster top speed, then you have got nothing....

"I remember Mr. Fuhrmann was really disappointed about the top speed. And on Saturday morning before the race, he was just resigned. He came up and said, 'OK, just tell the driver we race *flat out* from the first lap. Twenty-four hours.'

"And I went to Herbert Müller and said, 'Well, OK, you can make dinner reservations. Mr. Fuhrmann wants flat out. It'll be a short race." Singer and Reichert laughed once again.

"Peter Gregg's car had brake problems and a problem with the butterfly. The BP Carrera driven by Gregg and Guy Chasseuil had all the problems you can have in any race. And all with that car. And Jöst and Claude Haldi...Jöst stopped! He didn't see the fuel light. He just ran out of fuel!

"And Müller! Müller and Gijs van Lennep in number 46 had no problem at all with the car. Absolutely no problem. Flat out. Twenty-four hours. They finished, I think, 4th overall. Müller's car had no problems...."

Both men laughed again. "That spoiler, Herr Reichert?" Singer looked at his old friend. Reichert stopped, mid-laugh.

"You know, we called it the Mary Stuart collar. In the old days, the clothes had those high, wide collars? Like the Queen?" Reichert knew part of the story. "Yes," he asked, not knowing the rest of the story.

"Well," Singer started, seriously now. "You were there. Some of us referred to it as Klaus Reichert's idea. We thought it was really just your idea for good pictures!"

The Mary Stuart-collared RSRs rumble through Teloche. Norbert Singer, following in his 911, pulled out to shoot the 1973 Le Mans team on the way to the start. Car number 46 won. Kerry Morse archives

Ernst Fuhrmann: "Just tell the driver we race *flat out* from the first lap. Twenty-four hours."

CHAPTER 24

1976 Typ 934

Sharpened Like An Old Wood Pencil

Group 4 regulations allowed widened body-work and the adaptation of stronger suspension and brake assemblies. Because the category was production-based, a high minimum weight of 1,120kg (2,464lb) was specified. The car sold for 108,000DM.

"You know," Tony Dron said, looking up from his luncheon plate, "that 934 was just like an old wood pencil." He paused, this man who possesses equally the skill to turn a phrase or a lap record. And he waited the obligatory two beats. "It had been simply sharpened and sharpened and sharpened until there was no wood left!"

The car was Porsche's Group 4 Turbo RSR, the Typ 934, announced in March 1975, but homologated to the Appendix J regulations in time for the 1976 racing season. This was the penultimate development of the production 930 turbo.

Dron, editor for *Thoroughbred and Classic Cars* magazine, was coincidentally 1984 Le Mans class winner codriving a Typ 934. His assessment was based on three seasons of campaigning the same chassis, with owner Richard Cleare, in which virtually everything except the outside skin and the floor pan was replaced.

The 934 engines, Typ 930/71 (Bosch K-Jetronic injection) and Typ 930/73 (Kugelfischer mechanical injection for the United States), were subject to the new FIA Group 4 regulations. These rules allowed larger engines from production based automobiles but at a penalty of greater minimum

weight. The engine displaced 2993cc, with bore and stroke of 95 x 70.4mm.

Intercooling would condense the air and improve power output. However, managing the airflow through an already cramped engine compartment was another matter. The air-cooling fan had already been layed flat. The idea of an air-to-water intercooler was proposed, tested, developed, and eventually adopted. Behr provided dual intercooler radiators, which were mounted in the front spoiler, a long way from the engine. This complex system dropped the intake air temperature from about 150 degrees Centigrade (302 Fahrenheit) to just about 50C (122F), and with revised fuel-injection and intake ports, the engine produced 485hp at 7000rpm, when it was introduced (540hp at 7000rpm in the IMSA versions for 1977).

Group 4 regulations permitted very few modifications other than adaptation of stronger racing parts for suspension and brakes, and some widened bodywork. Minimum dry weight was 1,120kg (2,464lb). Once the interior was gutted and fiberglass front and rear deck lids, doors and fender extensions were fitted, some of the 934s actually ran with functioning electric window lifts from the 930 street turbos to bring the weight back up. But mostly, judicious placement of ballast served the purpose. The cars were introduced for 97,000DM, but sold finally for 108,000DM.

By mid-1977, the thirty-or-so 934s were competing with more than 500hp. This was accomplished by replacing the electronic fuel injection with the mechanical injection. And, with steady and continuing development over the years, Richard Cleare was eventually coaxing 620hp out of his. But for Dron, the biggest improvement was in its overall manners—not only engine performance but also handling.

"When I first drove the car, we got a class win at Silverstone. But the turbo lag was unbelievable. At Silverstone, you'd come up to Copes and turn in. And then you'd put your foot on the accelerator straight away and you'd go the whole way through the corner, past the clipping point

Some kind of unusual race car, this 934. With full road-going bumpers yet very wide fender flares, 14in tires, and BBS wheels, the car was based on the production 930 Turbo. This homologated it for Grand Touring, Group 4.

and right up the exit, and *then* the hammer would come down. It had 525 brake horse-power, or so. And it would just go *bang*, squat and go."

Dron smiled broadly. "You had to time it so that this came in where you were going straight. Because if it came in early, it would turn you right around. And if it came in after that, you were going to be very, very slow."

But Dron learned how to make it work, and with Richard Cleare they relayed their experiences and comments on to Lars Schmidt at Porsche. The turbo lag steadily decreased in their car. By 1984, at Vallelunga, Dron and Cleare felt the car was closer to what was imagined from it.

Dron, with three seasons in the car by this time, knew it well. "I thought I was God in that car by that stage. I thought I could do anything in a 934." But Dron was about to *see* God instead, in one of those moments racers remember and spectators never forget.

"There is a very twisty infield section and very fast corners out the back. And the left hander that goes out of the back stretch

goes down. It's flat out.

"And I'm going for a time in practice and there's a back marker, just in the way. And I thought, I can just go flat out through there. Just go past him. Past him on the left!

"And I got it wrong!

"I started to spin at 130mph (210km/h) in this big heavy car. Now this corner is sort of a dog-leg left. And coming out of it, the car turned around just enough that I was sort of looking over my shoulder. The road is off there and I'm travelling sort of backwards toward the Armco. And still rotating.

"I remember thinking, 'This is a high-risk moment!'

Dron smiled puckishly.

"Well, I took my feet off everything and swung the wheel around hard, and then hit the brakes, locking everything up. I lifted off the brakes again, the front came around and I continued straight ahead....

"I was very pleased to get away with that one. The marshals were quite...." He laughed. "You know, I wouldn't care to try it again...."

When Cleare and Dron took the car to

152

Le Mans, they took two engines, a 3.0 liter and a 3.3 liter. The scrutineers challenged them on this matter, not because of the two engines but because two different rear wings were homologated. For the 3.0 liter configuration, only the flat spoiler with the rear flip was legal; for the 3.3, the "tea-tray" type with edges all around, was allowed. Cleare complained but the FIA scrutineers were adamant.

"The funny thing," Dron recalled, "was that using the flip spoiler made us faster—by about 3 or 4 seconds.

"But at that speed, you could really tell the difference. On a normal road-going Porsche 911, you're glad of having any of those spoilers above, say, 110mph (175km/h). But at Le Mans you could tell in an instant which spoiler you had on.

"On the straight, with the 'tea-tray' the car is completely stable and absolutely straight down Mulsanne. With the flip...well, in those days, there was a crown in the road and no chicanes. So, when you settled onto the left side of the road, the car adopted a little 'attitude,' the nose pointing up toward the crown and you'd have to steer a little bit of opposite lock to go down the straight. If you had to change lanes or pass somebody, it wasn't a problem, you sort of climbed up and over, you could feel the air coming over the back and it would alternately go from this side to that side, to this, to that, just very slight. And all at about 200mph (325km/h).

"But honestly, it was OK. The car felt lovely. It never really felt as though it was going to go off the road. Well, once...."

In the early 1980s, racers tended toward ever-stiffer springs to make the cars into go-karts with full bodywork. It was thought that this was the best way to understand and manage the effects of downforce brought about from vacuum-cleaner-nozzle-shaped front spoilers and rear wings the size of the great outdoors.

"Of course, we had no wing at all," Dron laughed at the futility of it. "But Richard Cleare decided that for Le Mans he was going to use these super-stiff springs. So he went out and warmed up the car, cautiously, because it was his investment, his car, his springs. And he believed in them. Fervently.

"When he came back in, he was pleased. He sent me out, telling me, 'You'll probably be a bit quicker than me, but I think you'll like it!'

"I thought, 'Great! This'll be good, this'll be nice!' And I got out on the straight....

"Now, the other difference, in those days, Mulsanne not only had the crown in the road, but just before the kink, there was a bit of a rise. And it went up a little plateau and ran along, I dunno, maybe a few hundred meters. Then it dipped through that right kink.

"And I went barreling down the straight and the bloody thing took off.

"And I was off the ground long enough that I could count one, two, three. And then, sometime later, I came down. Now I don't know how far you go while you count in the air at that speed...but it was a bloody long way. I mean, I actually had to lift off the throttle at that speed to stop from damaging the engine!" Dron laughed again, remembering his low-altitude flight.

"So I brought it back to the pits and I just laughed. And I said, 'Take them off, you bloody fool.'"

Tony Dron's experiences in Richard Cleare's 934 were certainly not those of many critics. To them, the car was too heavy and they simply referred to it as Porsche's smaller, lighter tank. But Dron dismissed much of that criticism to lack of experience—either not enough hours in a 934, or not enough hours in one as well sorted as Richard Cleare's car became.

"The basic quality of that 934 was magnificent," Dron spoke of the car with sincere admiration: "It did all those miles and kept running like a train. By the time we stopped racing it, it had done six years of endurance racing. The floorpan was gone. The next time in the shop, we should have stripped out the floor and welded in a new one! It had gotten to the point where there was no 'wood' left."

"You know," he said calmly, "I actually did work out once in an idle moment of insomnia, that I'd probably spent about four hours out of my life on opposite lock at over 150 (240km/h)...."

A smile cracked across Dron's face.

"Most all of it with that 934."

Not only were full road-going bumpers retained to meet the minimum weight, top, but once the cars had been gutted, many kept the stock door panels, and some even retained operating electric windows in order to meet minimum weight. In the United States, Group 4 cars competed in Trans-Am and in 1977, they were legal for IMSA. Above, Porsche's 934 raced in SCCA Category II in the 1976 Trans-Am series. First National City Travelers Checks sponsored Vasek Polak's number 16, driven all season by George Follmer. After eight races, Follmer owned the championship.
Bob Tronolone

CHAPTER 25

1978 Typ 935/78 Moby Dick

Rules Are Meant To Be Interpreted

The FIA Regulations of Race Cars Appendix J announced that cars for Group 5 had to look like the production car on which it was based. "But it was funny," Norbert Singer recalled, "because the regulations said 'The fenders are free!' That left us a lot to play with!" Recalling his first FIA inspection of the 935/78 Moby Dick, Paul Frère said ruefully, "Norbert Singer saw a magnificent loophole.... When I saw that, I was very upset. But again, Singer showed us our own regulations."

For more than twenty years, an unusual and unorthodox program has been going on at Weissach. The department had no clandestine name, no complicated multisyllabic German word obscurely relating to its function. Funded through the engineering department, it has been populated by some of Germany's most learned minds.

Analysis of the written word, the search for hidden meaning, deeper significance in pursuit of higher truths, usually falls to literature departments at universities. Works of "literature," subject to the most vivid interpretation, generally have been written by humanity's most creative writers.

Norbert Singer would categorically disagree. History's most creative writing, subject to the most diverse interpretation—if one accepts Singer's view—would be found elsewhere. With a passion other scholars devote to Dostoyevsky, Elliot, Goethe, or Hemingway, Singer recommends several volumes of literature variously known as Federation International de l'Automobile, Division Commission Sportive Internationale, Reglements des Voitures de Course, Appendice J.

This work has been carefully examined in institutions of higher learning throughout the world—in Weissach, Germany; Modena, Italy; Venice, California; and Midland, Texas, to name but a few.

Norbert Singer, Porsche's Manager of Racing Car Testing and Operations, found the whole thing funny.

"We were a very small group. It was not really a racing department like you would expect. And the only chance we had was to read very carefully the words and the letters in the rulebook. And this we did."

The regulations that had brought about Porsche's Turbo Carrera in 1974 were to change in 1975. The FIA had announced that cars for Group 5 had to look like a production car but manufacturers "could add aerodynamic things." The regulation was postponed until 1976 and so Singer and his engineers began to work more carefully on the new car.

"The regulations changed quite a bit from the Turbo Carrera. We could go 'on the basis of the 911' but it ended up completely new," he said.

"From the outside, you could 'discover' the 911, but we flared fenders out front.... We changed the engine, the gearbox was new, wheels of course, 19 inch rear tires. The weight, there was a sliding scale from the engine displacement. We needed a minimum of 970kg (2,134lb). We were pretty free.... We could do a lot that we wanted but we had to have the basic design of the production car. But it was funny because the regulations said 'The Fenders Are Free.'"

Singer was Porsche's "Man of Letters," a student of the writings of others.

"What they meant of course was 'free' to flare, to 'add aerodynamic things.' But that left us a lot to play with. Which left the FIA officials a lot upset.

"And when we came to Mugello with this new car, the 935, we had the scrutineers for three hours! We expected long discussions, so we hurried to the scrutineering bay and we were first in line.

"So everybody, all the rest of the field, had to wait. Three hours. The practice sessions started. And nobody could go out!"

The lessons learned from Singer's 1974 program with the turbocharged 2.1 liter RSR,

Under the front deck of the 935/78, the massive fuel cell with overflow tank and the oil and brake reservoirs look familiar. But Singer's fenders, flattened through careful interpretation of FIA regulations, were only an obvious clue to the many other differences.

Jürgen Barth: "With the boost turned up full on this car, we had closer to 900 than 800. When that power came on, you needed to hold on!"

were put to good use with the development of the 935. Using an entirely new purpose-designed engine, with bore and stroke of 92.4 x 70.4mm, the displacement was 2.86 liters, rating 4.0 liters with the turbocharger. Titanium connecting rods, twin-plug ignition, and a Bosch fuel-injection system aided by a KKK turbocharger generated something like 590hp at 7900rpm. Two works 935s were constructed for the 1976 season, sponsored by Martini & Rossi, chassis 935-001 and -002.

The tail of the 935, however, was not part of the "free" fenders and it was in this technicality that the creative writers got back at Singer. Both 1976 cars had been equipped with air-to-air intercoolers. These didn't fit within the profile of the series-production 930 rear compartment and wing: "Mechanical parts should not protrude over the original bodywork." The creative writers stuck to their letters, and Singer and his engineers had to adopt air-to-water coolers that had to be plumbed into the rear fenders. The

result was less satisfactory but now legal.

For 1977, the regulations changed again. This time, Porsche's man of letters was invited to join in the curriculum discussions. Singer, a perceptive student, merely sat and took notes.

"There was a meeting in Paris where BMW came up and said that Porsche had an advantage with our rear engine and the exhaust. The others had the front engine, and the regulation said the exhaust must come out *after* the middle of the wheelbase." Singer listened intently to their concerns. "That means you had long tubes running to the middle of the car. And with a race engine, you want a short exhaust."

Singer explained the essence of BMW's complaint. "When you have a normal car, with exhaust tubes underneath, you can't lower the car as much as the Porsche where there is no exhaust. So they asked to change the regulations to allow a hole cut through the rocker panels to get the exhaust through. So they could run the same ride height as the Porsche. The FIA people said, 'OK, made sense; equal chances for everybody.'

"They made the regulation to cut these rocker panels. Their meaning was to get the exhaust through. But it was quite freely written. So we cut the entire rocker panel, everything! And that put the car down another 7 or 8 centimeters! The car started where the door started!" Singer leaned over to the ground. "The race car was this high!"

For the 1977 season, Singer's group was able to redo virtually the entire car. FIA regulations prompted continued interpretation. Relocating the front and rear bulkheads prompted the most striking bodywork yet featured on a production-based Porsche. Two cars were constructed for the season, 935/77-003 and -004. After a serious crash at Mugello damaged -004, a new chassis, -005, was rushed to completion. The /77 engine got a second turbocharger, which reduced the lag therefore improving throttle response, even as weight limits remained the same.

Then, for 1978, another FIA ruling was interpreted. "Body structure" constituted only the area between front and rear bulkheads, that is, the engine firewall and the cowl. Singer replaced the structure outside those two walls with a light alloy tube frame. He took advantage of that loosely worded rocker-panel regulation and lowered the entire car 75mm (2.95in).

A new engine was introduced, internally known as the Typ 935/71, with a displacement of 3.2 liters. This was the most radical engine yet produced by Porsche since Ernst Fuhrmann's Typ 547 Carrera 4-cam. The 935/71, with four valves per cylinder, water-cooled twin-camshaft cylinder heads, and the twin turbochargers, produced 750hp at 8200rpm at racing boost. This larger motor required a higher minimum weight, now up to 1,025kg (2,255lb), 55kg (121lb) over the 1977 model. But all of this was absolutely incidental to its appearance.

Sitting on the test track at Weissach without its familiar Martini colors on it, the vast white car looked like a beached whale. In a department led by a man of letters, the car was quickly nicknamed "Moby Dick."

Norbert Singer continued. "When we

had, at the end, let's say, designed the car. I went to Herr Bott and he got very nervous. 'Are you sure you can do this?' he asked."

"Well, by the letter, I am quite sure." Singer answered.

"'Yes, well, but maybe these people have a different meaning,' Bott wondered."

"Well, I know their *meaning*, and I know the *letter*."

Jürgen Barth, as factory test and development driver, was first to drive the white whale around Weissach. The engine's power quickly earned his respect.

"It was the first car I ever drove where I had to hold on to the steering wheel with both hands," Barth recalled. "You see, in their best tune, the standard 935, with full boost, could make 650hp. With the boost turned up full on this car, we had closer to 900 than 800. When that power came on, you needed to hold on!

"But it was the handling that was even better. The normal 935 was a handful. But this car, it was lower, the weight was lower with all the metal cut off. Even with this extra length, it was just perfect. The weight was only in the center. All that extra length was just aerodynamic appliances."

Only two of these were built, 935/78-006 and -007. They incorporated every loophole Singer could find. With their elongated

"It was the first car I ever drove," Jurgen Barth, factory test and development driver, explained, "where I had to hold onto the steering wheel with both hands. You see, in their best tune, the standard 935, with full boost, could make 650.... With this thing, we had closer to 900!"

The 935 for Group 5 had been introduced in 1976, only two built. For 1977, Norbert Singer, Porsche's Manager of Racing Car Testing and Operations, began making every "legal" modification possible to improve speed. Reading the rules with great care, he stretched the FIA's envelope...and patience.

Paul Frère:
"Norbert Singer saw a magnificent loophole—and we couldn't stop it!"

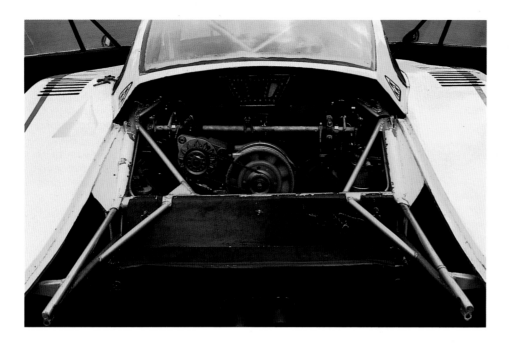

The most radical engine since the Typ 547, the 935/71 displaced 3.2 liters. Its dual-overhead-camshaft, four-valve cylinder heads were water cooled. With twin turbos, it produced 750hp at 8200rpm. An FIA rule described "body structure" as what was between the firewall and the cowl. All else was "aerodynamic aids." Right, it was Norbert Singer's Great White Long Tail, Moby Dick the result of the most careful reading and tightest interpretation of the loosest-worded regulations. Porsche Werke Far right, the doors were giant NACA ducts, venting air in to cool the rear brakes and the engine and for turbo and intercooler breathing. At full boost, Moby Dick wielded nearly 900hp and ran 365km/h (221mph) along Mulsanne. Porsche Werke

noses and tails, they stunned the FIA scrutineers.

"We learned we could have a pre-scrutineering," Singer explained. "We invited two or three of the CSI (Committee Sportive Internationale) people to Weissach, to show the car. And at the end of the meeting, they could give us a kind of piece of paper, it's called the 'passport,' which shows that it's a legal car.

"One of those people was Paul Frère, and he is also a friend. And when he saw the car, he couldn't believe what he saw!"

For Frère, vice-president of the technical committee at the time, it was more difficult than that. He had not been the creative writer whose letters Singer so carefully examined; Frère was more like the visiting professor, invited to monitor the final exams.

"There was a definition somewhere," Frère began, "saying that the body of the car was the part comprised between the front and rear bulkhead, something of this sort. We had already modified another regulation saying that the floor of the body could be raised up to the sill of the door. So Singer saw a magnificent loophole where he could raise the bottom of the car and drop the whole thing between the front and rear—which is what he did—and we couldn't stop it!

"But the doors! To get better streamlining, to get a better flow to the rear wing, he covered the original doors with a fairing. He kept the original shape of the doors, the original doors, even, beneath the fairing."

Frère shook his head, remembering his disbelief. "When I saw that, I was very upset. But again, Singer showed us our own regulations."

The words allowed "aerodynamic devices" that did not extend beyond the bodyline of the car. Viewed from the front, past fenders that were "free," and that allowed fairings out over wider tires, the doors did not protrude beyond the perimeter of the car. The year before, Singer had added an additional rear window to enhance airflow. The original roofline remained intact beneath the modification. While this modification did not merit enthusi-

astic response from the CSI, it was, according to its own book, "legal." The precedent was set, the man of letters argued.

Splitting the technicality, the FIA prevailed and Porsche had to remove half the cover, revealing half the door beneath. For Singer, it was not ideal but it was acceptable.

The long-tail, wide-fender, flat-nose, twin-turbocharged partially water-cooled car went out for practice at Le Mans. Most of Singer's creativity had been retained and the work proved its worth. The car, Porsche's most powerful to date, was also its fastest. Along Mulsanne, Rolf Stommelen touched 366km/h (227.5mph) through the speed traps. But little problems kept the car from achieving its anticipated success. While it won Silverstone handily, it only finished 8th at Le Mans, delayed in the pits too

long by an insignificant oil leak. For the remainder of the season, 935/78-006 was entered at the Norisring and at Vallelunga. Consistently running fastest overall, it retired from each event while leading the field.

The customer-variation 935, available since 1977, continued to campaign for the Group 5 and IMSA championships exclusively after 1978 with great success. For Norbert Singer, regulations were changing again and Porsche had other needs for his reading skills.

Was he frustrated by the FIA's uncanny ability to change the rules on him, to legislate away his loopholes?

"No, not so much," Singer explained. "If it puts you out of a series, that is frustrating. But at the beginning, if it happens, it gives you confirmation. You did it right! Not by their meaning, but by the letter."

An FIA hearing, presumably to benefit competitors, enabled Norbert Singer to lower the 935/78 floorpan 75mm closer (2.95in) to the ground. Every feature raised eyebrows with FIA scrutineers. Singer read the FIA regulations carefully. And he understood. Not always their meaning but he always understood their letter.

CHAPTER 26

1981 Typ 936

The Hunting Dogs Are Black

"We have a lot of spare parts from the 917 in stock," Ernst Fuhrmann said. "It should be easy to make a sports prototype car out of the parts." From mid-October 1975 to early April 1976, it was not easy. Norbert Singer's crew was already racing Group 5. Number 12, the five-year-old 936-001, driven by Jochen Mass, Vern Schuppan, and Hurley Haywood finished 12th, behind Ickx and Bell, winners in number 11, 936-003. The new engine, a Typ 935/75, was an offshoot of the Indy project, displacing 2.65 liters and producing 620hp at 8000rpm. Twin turbo boost was 1.6bar.

"It was during one of our many meetings," Norbert Singer recalled. "Ernst Fuhrmann quietly asked, 'What do you think about these new Group 6 regulations?'

"This brought all conversation to an immediate halt."

It didn't surprise Fuhrmann. It wasn't as though Singer's people didn't have enough to do already. It was mid-September 1975. They were well involved with two other nine-thirty-something projects. So when the boss asked, everyone just looked around. Finally the looks came to Singer.

"'Well, we really don't know. We're preparing the 935 for next year's world championship.... We know of course there is a sports prototype class but....'"

Ernst Fuhrmann let the words trail off. He knew also. The FIA's competition arm, the CSI, had made rules encouraging "silhouette" racing, classes based on the series-production automobiles. A Manufacturer's World Championship would be contested in Group 5. This dovetailed perfectly with Fuhrmann's budgetary constraints. He was virtually prohibited from another lavish 917 project. He spoke slowly and asked everyone around the table what it would take to build a car to do the program.

"We have a lot of spare parts from the 917 in stock," he suggested. "It should be easy to make a sports prototype car out of the parts."

Then everybody spoke more rapidly. "Well, we can't do it." "We're already doing Group 5." "We're supporting the privateers in Group 4...." "Adding another series!" "There is no time."

Everybody had excuses.

Again, Fuhrmann listened appreciatively. The words trailed off. He had come to know the CSI, which was in Paris. And he knew Renault, which was continuing work on its own sports prototype. And he knew there was still activity from Milan, from Alfa Romeo. And then there was Le Mans! The organizers were still open to sport prototypes. They had chosen to decline World Championship status for 1976. Le Mans was still the place for manufacturers to prove the worth of its products.

Fuhrmann recalled an old Austrian proverb: "We don't carry the hunting dogs." It meant "We don't miss the first scent that starts the hunt." He expected the French and Italians had similar sayings.

"OK, I'll tell you," he said to no one in particular as he left the room. "We'll do it."

Two weeks later they met again. They discussed it another time. Fuhrmann listened again. And concluded the same. "We do it!" But this time, he waited a few more minutes.

"Look," he suggested, "you take the parts from stock, make a new space frame, just make a body...."

Singer jumped in. A loophole had opened, an opportunity had landed in his lap.

"Well, with a new body we need a wind tunnel...."

Best shot delivered. But Fuhrmann emerged unscathed.

"You have a lot of experience. You don't need a wind tunnel. Just make it!"

And so, as Norbert Singer recalled, they did.

"That's it. That's the whole story. Took us half a year. Started in November. And the car was running in March. The first time in

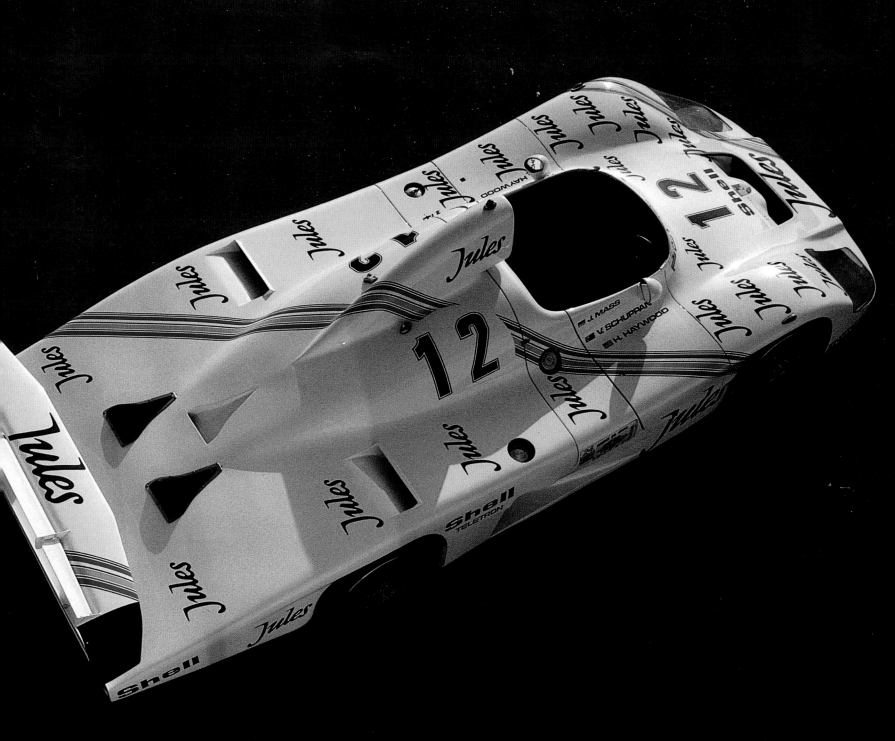

were allowed at all where visitors were usually not allowed anyway.

A testing date was set for the circuit at Weissach. Even on the home circuit, Fuhrmann was concerned.

"This was a real secret, this car." Norbert Singer recalled. "Nobody should know. Nobody was to know we were doing a new sports car. So Mr. Fuhrmann had the funny idea to paint it black. Nobody should see it when it is running!"

This worked well enough at Weissach. Flegl, Singer, Helmuth Bott, Paul Hensler, and Peter Falk all watched on a cold March morning as Hubert Mimler drove the car the first time. The car performed well enough that another test, an endurance test, was planned immediately, at Paul Ricard for mid-February 1976.

"With it all painted black, no signs on it, we went down to Paul Ricard to test." Singer laughed heartily. He was telling the story; he knew where it was going. "It was an official test day for the 935, announced. But we also had along with us the 936. In the trailer.

"The day before our test was a Formula 1 test. It was finished and all the people left. Well, nearly all. We had the 935 out and just as we were rolling the 936 out of the trailer, Yorn Pugmeister came around the corner." Pugmeister was on staff for *SportAuto* magazine; fifteen years later, when Singer recalled this story, Pugmeister had become Porsche's press director.

"It was unbelievable! We just couldn't cover the car. It was standing on the lift of the truck. Just there! Just there!" Singer shook his head and laughed at all the ironies.

"So he came up and said, 'What's this? Here is the 935 but are you doing sports cars as well? Is this a new one?'

"And a few minutes later, the guy from *L'Equipe* came around the corner too!"

L'Equipe was France's daily sporting newspaper, *SportAuto* was a German monthly. Singer knew Fuhrmann's plans to publicly introduce the car in three weeks at the Nürburgring 300km race. He proposed that if Pugmeister could get rid of the Frenchman, Singer would give him the "exclusive" on the new prototype. *SportAu-*

Paul Ricard, testing. The first time in the Nürburgring, racing." Singer shrugged.

Helmut Flegl was named project director for the 3.0 liter sports prototype, and the 936 came together as a parts-bin collage. From the 917 racks came brakes, springs, shocks, sway bars and an unused five-speed transaxle gearbox. Looking further, Flegl's team found wheels, steering pieces and suspension uprights from other 917 bins. The design, engineering and appearance of the aluminum tube frame chassis closely resembled both cars. The engine was a direct evolution of the 911 engine, coming from the 2.1 liter single-turbo RSR. It produced 520hp at 8000rpm, entirely adequate for the 700kg (1,540lb) car.

The fiberglass body, made by hand, blended mostly features of the long-tail 917s with some aerodynamic tricks of the 917/30s. The most notable was the Can-Am car's large horizontal rear wing.

But the car was kept a secret. Fuhrmann held a tight lid on the project. No visitors

With race boost set (by the knob at right) at 1.4bar, the 936 driver had 520hp at 8000rpm at his call. Total weight without driver was 720kg (1,584lb). Chassis 936-001 won Monza, Imola, and Enna-Pergusa in 1976. But it was the new 936-002 that would win Le Mans. As Martini & Rossi number 4, this car, 936-001, won in 1977.

to's deadline could have pictures in print just before the 'Ring.

Pugmeister succeeded. He convinced the man from *L'Equipe* that the car was nothing more than a vintage racer being hauled back into France for some rich collector. Pugmeister was the only one with pictures of Ernst Fuhrmann's secret hunting dog.

When Count Gregorio Rossi di Montelera, Porsche's racing sponsor, saw the car all in black, he loved it. He had his company stripes and logo painted over the black, and at the Nürburgring, Rolf Stommelen premiered the unusual, if malevolent, Martini & Rossi "Black Widow."

The first race gave Stommelen *and* Rossi problems. The accelerator cable broke on the 936, ending Stommelen's race early. But the event was run in a deluge, and under the darkened skies, Rossi's Black Widow was difficult to see and harder to photograph! The Count, disappointed by its poor performance and poorer press coverage, ordered the car painted white before the next race.

Between the new color and Flegl's modifications to the throttle linkages, the hunting dogs were set free. The 936 won Monza, Imola, and Enna-Pergusa; the three victories in the seven-race series gave Porsche the championship. For Le Mans in June, a second 936 was entered, 936-002, which featured a new large, vertical air intake, while 936-001 retained its traditional spyder bodywork.

For Ernst and Elfreide Fuhrmann, who lit candles when their sons had major exams and their cars had important races, it was a long night under the warm orange glow. The candles lasted through Sunday's dinner. Le Mans was a Porsche apogee. Jacky Ickx and Gijs van Lennep won overall in the 936-002 Group 6 spyder, Rolf Stommelen and Manfred Schurti driving the Werks Martini 935 won Group 5 honors. Rounding out Porsche's success, three privateers drove a 934 to win Group 4.

For 1977, Fuhrmann decided to concentrate the 936 effort solely on Le Mans. Over the winter of 1976, 936-001 and -002 underwent numerous changes reflecting the

Ernst Fuhrmann: "We have a lot of spare parts from the 917 in stock. It should be easy to make a sports prototype car out of the parts."

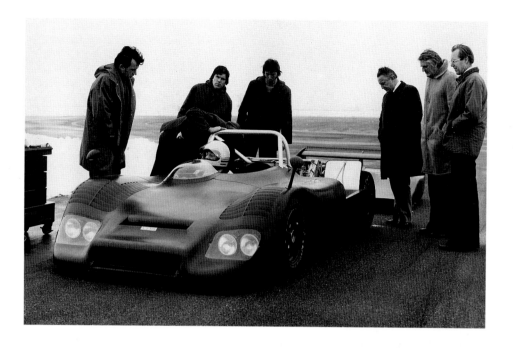

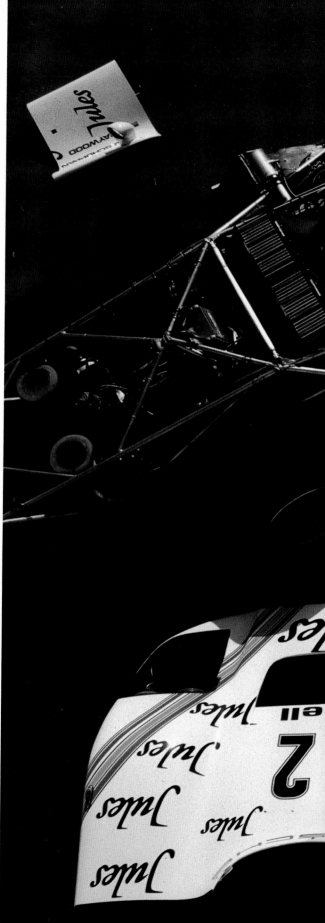

Above, Helmut Flegl, left, and opposite, Helmuth Bott, Paul Hensler, and Peter Falk look on while Weissach technicians check fluids after Hubert Mimler's first run in Ernst Fuhrmann's prototype, the 936. As a top secret project, Fuhrmann ordered the prototype painted black. Testing at Weissach proved the car ready and capable. But the aerodynamics soon required an higher air intake. Porsche Werke. Right, chassis 936-001 tested at Paul Ricard in late February. In five months, the 936 had gone from Ernst Fuhrmann's suggestion to competitive prototype. Further development in March led to its debut at the Nürburgring, April 4, 1976. A top secret project within Weissach, Fuhrmann ordered the car painted black.

management strategy. Twin turbochargers were fitted, however, using a single waste-gate.

This time it was the turn of 936-001 to triumph. But it was not without a struggle.

With -002 out early, Jacky Ickx joined Jürgen Barth and Hurley Haywood. The crew of -001 soldiered on after a nearly 30 minute pit stop to repair an injection-pump problem. It returned to the race in 41st position. Through the night, it regained one position after another, keeping the pressure on the lead Renaults until they all retired. However, with barely 45 minutes left of the 24 hours, codriver Hurley Haywood pitted with a seized piston. With only a single Renault Mirage far back in 2nd place, Fuhrmann reasoned a gamble was worth it.

Fuel and spark were cut off from the seized cylinder and Jürgen Barth was to go out, somehow manage to do two more laps and claim the race. Mechanics got Count Rossi's colorfully striped white car started and Barth motored slowly. He kept to the road edges and crept on to Porsche's fourth Le Mans win. It would be 1981 before a 936 Porsche would win again at Le Mans.

That winner, 936-003, was an entirely new chassis that had been constructed for the

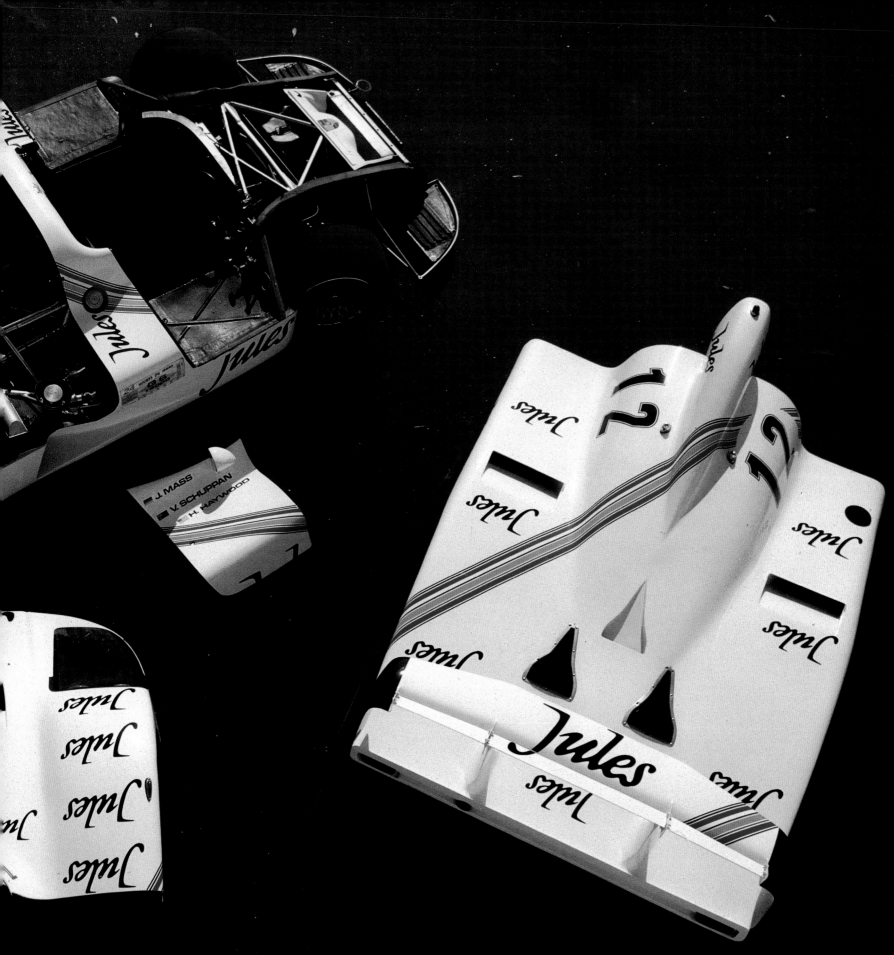

The engine, right, a Typ 911/78, was basically a development of the 2142 cc engine. Faced with the tight deadline, Norbert Singer's team raided parts bins, finding wheels, steering, and suspension pieces from the 917. Below, As a top secret project, Fuhrmann ordered the prototype painted black. Far right, at Le Mans in 1978, 936-001 continued its development role, introducing new bodywork and the 2.1 liter four-valve engine. Basically a completely new car, it finished 2nd, still with Martini sponsorship. It was not until 1981 that 936s again ruled at Le Mans.

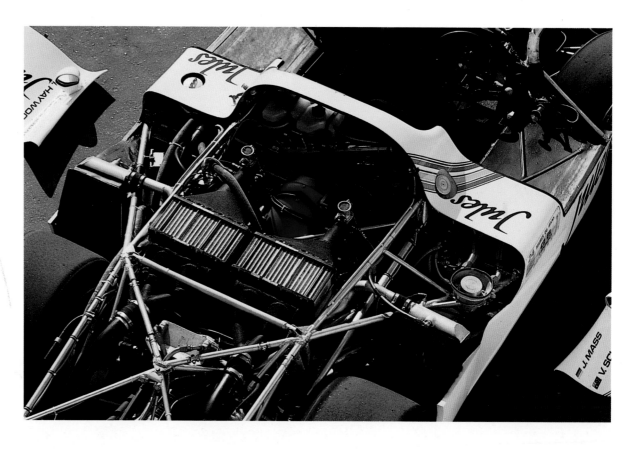

1978 race. The intervening years taught the Weissach engineers some painful lessons about gearbox strength. Fifth-gear pinions proved to be the weak point, leading to near misses in 1978. For 1981, the entire gearbox was replaced, using a development from the 917/30, capable of handling nearly twice the 936 engine's output.

The engine too was changed for 1981, using a development from the 1980 Indianapolis effort. The new engine, with four valves per cylinder, displaced 2.65 liters and produced 620hp at 8000rpm with its twin turbos boosted to 1.6 bar. New sponsorship from perfume manufacturer Jules put Jacky Ickx across the finish 1st for his fifth and Porsche's sixth Le Mans win.

That was the end for the 936. Group 6 and 5 were due for replacement for the 1982 season by a new category, Group C. Weissach's intentions were to chase that championship with the same energy as its predecessors. The ill-fated Indy car engine had won at Le Mans. It accomplished

4,796.9km (2,998 miles)—nearly the equivalent of six nonstop runnings of the Indy 500—in 24 hours.

The engine would meet its new fate. But it would be in a closed car with two seats in a brand-new category. Fresh for the scent, Ernst Fuhrmann's new dogs already knew all the old tricks.

CHAPTER 27

1980 924GTP
1981 924GTS

Porsche's Best-Kept Secrets

Al Holbert and Peter Gregg were to drive the 1980 924 GTP at Le Mans. But Gregg was injured in a road accident and Derek Bell, already with many testing miles in the car, was drafted from the English GTP team. Despite a top end of "only" 288km/h (180mph), the cars ran well until valves burned on two of the three entries.

"Volkswagen's history, because it was a different type of company—inaugurated by dictatorial orders—never really required an advertising department."

Tony Lapine, his deep voice filled with mirth, delivered a history lesson. As all history is complex, its many elements interwoven to create a tapestry with many textures as well as colors, this history teller attempted to follow one color, one pattern, one theme through to the end.

"Think about it," he continued. "The German labor union let its members buy stamps, keep a little book. And when they filled so many books, a Beetle belonged to the worker. So, as such, you don't need any advertising. There were no 'gurus.' It was the only car there was and it was the only one you could have even if there had been others...."

Lapine sat back deeper in his armchair. A thread was uncovered.

"Well, there was one 'guru.' And he ordered the car and said it was good for you. The company had no advertising department, and this went on unnoticed for a very long time...."

Lapine smiled widely. The former design chief for Porsche enjoyed equally his new-found role as historical analyst. At the end of the first thread was another. Another revelation. Another thread, far longer.

"VW also didn't have any research department. The research was continually performed by Porsche. Porsche was the developer of the car, the Strength Through Joy car, the KDF-wagen, the Beetle. And even after the war, when the company was operated by the British Military, it still didn't need any advertising. Nor did they need research. Later—much later—it was decided that Porsche would have a formal agreement. To do a set amount of research work. A set amount of time would be devoted to the research for VW...."

Out of the tapestry at this point, Tony Lapine pulled the thread that was the 914. Another thread, called Kurt Lotz, began in black and ended in red. It was a thread cut short. Still another thread, stronger and with a new direction, was called Rudolf Leiding. It was knotted to the 914, and when it was pulled, it came undone.

Leiding was promoted to managing director from within VW on October 1, 1971. His direction was to make Volkswagen's cars front engined and water cooled. His thread veered sharply away from VW history. In the interest of seeing less red ink, Leiding also put Porsche on notice: at the end of the current contract, about two more years, VW would cease needing outside research and begin to do its own.

"'We'll give you something to do,'" Lapine paraphrased Leiding. "'See if you can come up with a sports car, something reasonable in two years time.'"

There was one parameter: use anything that is on the corporate shelf.

"It was fitting," Lapine frowned, intercepting the anticipated protests. "The 356 was nothing more than that. It was a normal approach, where it was possible. The cylinder heads should be different, the brakes should be somewhat healthier, but it was in a typical style of creation for the time. And nobody doubted that the 356 was a genuine Porsche!"

During the summer before Rudolf Leiding's promotion, Dr. Ernst Fuhrmann was

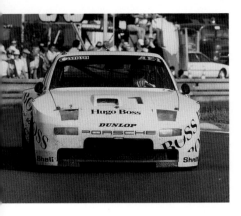

For 1981, Porsche returned to Le Mans again with the 924, but this time, it was the GTP prototype for the 944, using the 2.5 liter, 420hp four-cylinder block derived from half the 928 engine. Jurgen Barth and Walter Rohrl finished 7th overall in an event-free race. Porsche Werke. Right, strictly racing. The last vestiges of Tony Lapine's styling department were removed. Only the fresh air vent remained unmodified. Red line for the 375hp race engine was 7000rpm, both on the tach and on dymo tape on the steering column.

asked to return to Porsche. He had been fired from his previous job and was at home in Teufenbach, Austria, enjoying a long overdue vacation.

Fuhrmann explained. "There are two reasons to fire a manager: one reason is he is not successful. The other reason is he is too successful....

"I was successful. The office manager thought that I did anything I wanted and that I didn't care about him. That was true." Fuhrmann laughed, both at the other manager and about the streak of independence that ironically brought him back to Porsche.

"Well, the position offered at Porsche was very simple and easy to handle. It was no complicated thing....

"But four weeks later...." Fuhrmann's already soft voice went even quieter.

"In 1966, Ferdinand Piëch had gone to Volkswagenwerk with a new car, the middle-engine car, the car to replace the Beetle, the 914. Porsche's success was with that

program. Then Mr. Lotz was fired; he was the man who had collaborated with Porsche on that car. There was a competing program, which was the Golf. Mr. Lotz was succeeded by Mr. Leiding who had developed the competing car....

"So, he chose the Golf with the other engine, not the Porsche design," Fuhrmann recalled. "A new prototype was already in development for VW as a successor to the Golf. It was Mr. Piëch's and Mr. Bott's proposal to build our 911 successor from this new VW prototype....

"Well then, VW-werk decided not to build the Porsche-designed car. And also to cancel the research contract. (In that time, the whole costs of our development center were supported by VW. Weissach was its development center. It meant Weissach cost nothing to us!)

"And within two months of returning to Porsche, I had no successor to the 911, and I had no work after the next year for Weissach. For the time remaining in the contract, Mr. Leiding gave me the order.

"See if you can come up with something reasonable....

"And I said, 'That's what we're here for!'" Fuhrmann explained.

Five hundred kilometers away, at his home in Baden-Baden, Tony Lapine picked up the story: "So this time, Porsche had a freer run of the shelves, and there were more shelves to pick from! Look at the engines available, the transmissions! There was Audi, VW. That was the beginning of the 924...."

But within a year, it was the end of VW project EA425, the code by which Rudolf Leiding and his associates referred to "something reasonable." Leiding had anxiously awaited its delivery. Tony Lapine's stylists had done an outstanding job on the car's interior and exterior and Leiding was plainly excited. He anticipated that it would improve VW's image in the world. There was even a supposition that he could use it to compete with Porsche as an affordable sports car.

Leiding's ambitions began to trip themselves up however, as internal problems and expansion began to cost too much. This was complicated in late 1973 by the creation in the Middle East of the Organization of Petroleum Exporting Countries, OPEC, whose first order of business was to increase the value of its own primary product, oil. Suddenly sports cars were less appealing.

Leiding was relieved of his job a year later, replaced by Toni Schmücker, in early 1975.

"Schmücker saw the car," Lapine recalled, "and said, 'Well, it's a very lovely car, but you know we have some other problems that we have to solve and we will not be building this automobile, at least not right now.'"

But nothing is so simple.

Schmücker's evaluation of Volkswagen concluded that the firm had too much capacity compared to production. Among the sites chosen to be closed was the former NSU plant just 27 miles north of Stuttgart, in Neckarsulm.

"Well, the capacity for building this car was reserved right from the beginning, and it was planned for Neckarsulm, in Baden-Württemberg. And so a labor situation popped up. What was going to happen to this factory, to these workers now that VW does not build this car?

"We suddenly had three parties interested, curious, and effected by the VW decision to not build the car. First, the state of Baden-Württemberg was looking at the labor and unemployment insurance problems. Second, Porsche really wanted to see the car on the road because it knew it was a damned good car—for what it was. And third, VW wouldn't mind if this car did show up, because they would be selling it through their dealers whether it said VW or Porsche."

Lapine smiled. The threads of the story had become a tangled mess. "So the three parties got quickly together and the upshot was that Porsche bought the project back.

"But this doesn't mean we would stay with everything as it was then! As soon as we could we'd install a five speed. The first things were simple, a new steering wheel and a different ignition key...."

The 924 began series assembly in November 1975. Six months later, production was up to sixty cars a day, including a series for the US market. Introduced in Ger-

many at 23,240DM (about $8,900), the US version sold for $9,395.

In order to bring its performance up to match its looks, the 924 was turbocharged for the 1979 model year. While the production turbo version produced 170hp, up from 125hp from the first cars, it was the 1979 Frankfurt Auto show that introduced Porsche's best kept secret, the 924 Carrera GT.

Much of Tony Lapine staff's interior was removed, replaced with spare, black-painted metal and simple cloth racing bucket seats. Overall the 924 Carrera weighed 150kg (330lb) less than the stock turbo.

Under the hood, the 2.0 liter Audi-based engine, turbocharged and intercooled, produced 210hp at 6000rpm. Under the fenders, widened and bulged out, 225/50VR16 tires could be fitted at the rear. Four hundred cars had to be built to meet FIA homologation requirements for Group 4. Within months, they were built and sold out. Fully half remained in Germany.

From there, development tugged at another thread. Under orders from Ernst Fuhrmann, Norbert Singer was asked to prepare the 924 Carrera for Le Mans, running under the newly defined GT Prototype category (GTP). An aluminum roll cage was designed to strengthen the few weaknesses in the body. The result was a car even stiffer than the 935. The 2.0 liter engine was heavily modified. The turbocharger was relocated slightly left to allow for cleaner exhaust flow. The brakes were already superb in the homologation versions; for Le Mans, the

The interior was gutted in the Carrera GTS, fitted instead with simply upholstered racing bucket seats. In all, 170kg (375lb) was removed. GTS top speed was 248km/h (155mph). Instrumentation was more like the future 944. The tachometer was redlined at 6800rpm. Below, strictly Norbert Singer race preparation. The engine was inclined and relocated further to driver's left, to accommodate cleaner exhaust flow. The inline four, of 86.5 x 84.4mm bore and stroke displaced 1984cc.

The 2.0 liter Audi four-cylinder engine was fed by the high-output fuel distributor similar to the 928. With turbo and intercooler, the engine produced 245hp at 6250rpm, at 1.0bar boost. The slightly more common Carrera GT rated 210hp at 6000rpm, and sold for 50,000DM.

rotors came from the 917/10 Can-Am cars and the calipers came out of the 936. Singer enjoyed the same freedom of interpretation as he had in his other Le-Mans efforts.

In all, four cars were constructed for 1980. In keeping with the experimental department's tradition of special chassis numbers, these four were 924-001 through 924-004. The first car, -001, was strictly a test mule built for the Le Mans effort. Where the US specification production 924 Turbo had weighed in at 1,280kg (2,816lb) and the Carrera weighed 1,180kg (2,596lb), the Le Mans versions were stripped to 930kg (2,046lb) dry. With 310hp available, the cars topped out at 288km/h (180mph) along Mulsanne in practice.

Three cars were prepared and entered: 924-004, wearing the flag of Germany, 924-002 for Great Britain, and 924-003 for the United States. Jürgen Barth and Manfred Schurti drove the German-flagged entry, Al Holbert and Peter Gregg were to drive the US car, and Tony Dron, Andy Rouse, and Derek Bell were chosen for the British car. A road accident kept Gregg from driving so Bell joined Holbert.

Nothing miraculous was expected from the cars that could only lap Le Mans in 4:08 in practice, that could not exceed 290km/h (181mph) in calculations. However, when the race began in the rain, hopes were raised and Bell and Dron anticipated some surprises they could deliver to the rest of the field.

However, a problem that had been experienced in 924-001 in the Paul Ricard tests reappeared. Valve overheating crippled first the American and then the British car. The first cylinder on each engine lost nearly all compression. With the engines running on three cylinders, both returned to the race, but near the end of the 24 hours, they lapped the circuit at 4:30 to 4:45. Singer recognized the long flat-out runs along Mulsanne had defeated his efforts at improvements after Ricard and ordered the German entry to slow to 4:15 laps.

At 4pm, surpassing all expectations, all three cars were still running with Barth finishing in 6th, and Bell in 13th. In what could only present an accurate representation of

the complexity of the Index of Performance category, the Dron/Rouse three-cylinder 924, finishing 12th overall and 5th in class, took 2nd in the Index!

For 1981, Porsche tried again with two 924s. One, 924-004, had run the year before. The second car, 924-006, was new. It looked nearly identical outside; Lapine's styling was largely respected. It was typical Porsche design studio work, but careful examination suggested something was different and only careful examination would reveal what it was.

During the winter months, Singer constructed another new prototype, 924-005, which underwent extensive testing at Paul Ricard. The prototype and the Le Mans car had modified bodywork to cope with the demands of a new engine. More air was needed for the engine and fatter tires ran in back so the rear quarters were widened.

Only under the hood was the difference apparent: it was the prototype of Porsche's successor 944.

The engine was half a 928 block, with a bore and stroke of 100 x 78.9mm, displacing 2.5 liters. Placed in the compartment at a 45 degree angle, the engine used Porsche's new belt-driven overhead camshafts and four valves per cylinder. The crankshaft was also new, a counter-balanced piece capable of high engine speeds with virtually no vibration. The engine also utilized a computerized fuel injection and electronic ignition system, allowing extraordinary sensitivity to air and throttle input. With boost set at 1.1 bar for the race, the 998kg (2,196lb) Le Mans GTP produced 420bhp at 6800rpm.

Profiting from the 1980 experience, Singer installed a fifth-gear ratio that made it impossible to exceed 6200rpm. When the checkered flag fell on Sunday, Jürgen Barth and World Rally champion Walter Röhrl finished 7th overall. They had spent no more time in the pits than what was necessary to refuel.

Tony Lapine returned the story to series production: "The 924 was done for a client. We prepared two sides, in keeping with Porsche design. One side, the complex, organic, traditional shape, like the 928. No creases. The other side, that was done with some creases. They looked at it, Mr. Leiding and his associates. 'Well, thank you very much, but we prefer the other side with the creases.' And that's how it went into production."

Lapine smiled. The look on his face suggested there was one more thread to pull, one that would unravel the entire history, or bundle it all back up in a tight ball.

"Butzi Porsche was my first supervisor. I worked directly for him. My contract draft read, 'Assistant to F. A.Porsche.'

"I'd barely gotten there, been there one month, and we were sitting in a development meeting with Dr. Porsche presiding. Mr. Piëch, Bott, Peter Porsche (the production manager), Butzi, Richard Hettman (head of passenger-car development), Wolfgang Eyb (chief engineer), and myself.

"Dr. Porsche said, 'VW has all of the sudden shown not so much interest in continuing this project here and what they would like is to see another proposal for the body.'

"So, I got my first assignment. And what was it? I was to do the next Golf. VW's front-engine water-cooled Beetle replacement."

Porsche's best kept secret started life as another Volkswagen, though this version was certainly no Vopo. When Porsche bought the project back and met with success, it improved the breed. First came 400 Carrera GTs and then the GTS in series of about fifty. Family resemblance to the 924 Turbo was obvious.

CHAPTER 28

1980 Interscope Indianapolis

Rules Are Meant To Be Changed

In those days, the Indy 500 was still entered, attempted, and contested by some marginal teams, rugged individuals who measured the mortgage payment against the cost of new pistons. Others, organizations, showed up with transporters, teams of drivers and support personnel, and armies of mechanics. Ted Field readily grasped the potential of a Porsche Champ Car effort. It would take some development work but he believed, with Danny Ongais to drive and a Porsche engine to drive Danny, that his Interscope team could eventually dominate.

Indy was the Holy Grail. Jo Hoppen, competition director for Porsche+Audi Division of Volkswagen of America, understood what the Midwest on Memorial Day meant to the American racing enthusiast.

Hoppen already had accomplished two successful open-wheel-car racing series, the Super Vee program with the SCCA and his Mini-Indy series with USAC. Both were recognized as a part of the unofficial USAC/Indy 500 "undergraduate program." The best drivers from Super Vee series advanced in the next season to the Mini-Indy where they hoped to be noticed by team owners and sponsors for the big show.

Hoppen understood selling racing: "The American public liked to see it fast, furious, close, exciting, and still heavily populated at the checkered flag." He also understood what it took to sell a racing program to management. It took lots of someone else's money.

In California, Jo Hoppen's close friend Vasek Polak had a solid relationship and good friendship with Ted Field whose Interscope Racing Panasonic-sponsored 935s were doing well in IMSA. (Field, with Danny Ongais and Hurley Haywood, would win the Daytona 24 Hours in January 1979 in an Interscope 935.) Now, Field had ventured into Champ Car racing, as it was known at the time.

Danny Ongais drove Field's Cosworth-engined Parnelli. In 1977, Ongais, driving for Field, had been named Rookie of the Year, and in 1978, at Indy, Ongias qualified 2nd and led the race for 145 laps until his engine failed.

Ted Field, young and savvy, readily grasped the potential of a Porsche Champ Car effort: with the firm's dominance in sports car and endurance races, it would take some development work, of course, but his Interscope team could eventually dominate the Indy car series.

Having sold an entrant and a sponsor, all that remained was for Hoppen to go to Germany and sell Porsche on the idea.

"But that was an uphill battle," Hoppen explained. "Open-wheel racing was not something highly regarded at the factory. Its past involvement had been more as a result of momentum rather than any clearly planned strategy. It began in 1957 with RSKs at the Nürburgring. Jean Behra requested a center-steering RSK in 1958. The entries evolved into the cigar-shaped 718s and 787s with Bonnier, Hill, and Gurney in '59, '60, and '61. And all the way up to the full factory effort in Formula 1 in 1962, again with Bonnier and Gurney.

"Ferry Porsche had been a reluctant leader. Plainly, he was not really sure why his firm was spending the money on something that bore no resemblance to anything he sold to the public."

But Hoppen was prepared. He was bringing in a sponsor and an entrant, with its own chassis—initially the Parnelli—although Hoppen did imagine an eventual Porsche chassis. The entrant/sponsor was capable of paying the costs of the project. All Porsche had to do was an engine program to fit into Field's chassis.

The obvious choice was the engine with the water-cooled cylinder head from Le Mans in 1978, as it fit USAC's displacement regulations and its development was already at an advanced level.

"Ferry Porsche reluctantly agreed. His

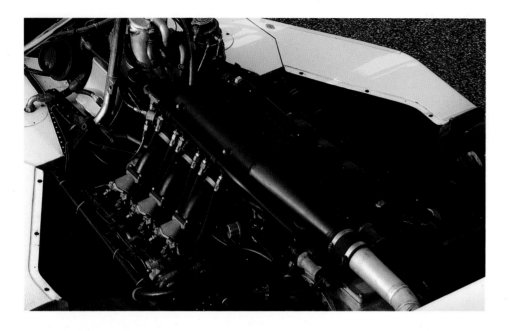

hesitation stemmed from the fact that this had all indications of being Porsche's premier racing program. And it was not in Europe."

Yet Hoppen argued effectively. The United States was already a primary Porsche customer base. The company sought to sell more cars—needed to sell more cars. Racing every other Sunday in an IMSA event drawing a crowd of 60,000 or even 100,000 spectators was nothing compared to the Indianapolis 500, which, even in 1979, was drawing 400,000 in the gate and another 60 million television viewers.

For all the negatives, there were more reasons to agree. Hoppen was not asking Ferry Porsche to do a new engine. He was only asking the firm to revise an engine that it had basically already done. The engine would work and the costs would essentially be borne by someone else.

The easiest sell at Weissach was Ernst Fuhrmann, an engineer, an "engine" engineer. And Fuhrmann agreed. Porsche would go to Indianapolis.

This was early in the fall of 1978. Coincidentally, it was also early in the fall of USAC.

In those days, the Indy 500 was still entered, attempted, and contested by some marginal teams—clusters really, not organizations—of rugged individuals who

measured the mortgage payment throughout the year against the cost of a set of new pistons while building its Champ Car in the garage. Some did the entire USAC oval season with Offenhauser-powered specials. But some just came to Indy, and they were pretty well financially strained.

However, Indy was also being entered and attempted and contested by Roger Penske, Pat Patrick, Ted Field, Jim Hall and his Chaparrals, and Dan Gurney and his Eagles. These organizations showed up with their transporters, teams of drivers, support personnel, and armies of mechanics to tend to their Cosworth-powered cars. These were organizations worth money far beyond the resources of the traditional Champ Car owner/racer.

But USAC was a "democracy." Its president, Richard King, was elected by the majority. And the majority ruled. The majority could thwart the efforts, topple the ideas, frustrate the ambitions of the few, the rich, the organized.

Which is why, in late summer of 1978, Championship Auto Racing Teams, CART, was founded. CART then approached USAC and expressed the members' concerns. CART represented the teams with substantial investments. CART understood "where USAC was coming from." But CART hoped USAC understood the team owners with valuable sponsorships who were spending vast amounts of money, who had specific needs that they wanted satisfied. This was where CART was coming from.

USAC understood. The democracy turned its back on the elite. CART warned USAC that a split was eminent. USAC believed a split was impossible. With USAC controlling the tracks, where would they race? Parking lots? City streets?

But USAC made a mistake. A small mistake, done years before. For some reason, USAC had never convinced Indianapolis to take its 500 mile race date off the FIA calendar. It was always listed as a fully sanctioned FIA event. Which meant if you had an FIA license, you could run it.

And of course, as soon as CART was formed, its members went straight over, joined and got SCCA-issued FIA licenses.

Indianapolis denied the entries of the

CART teams in spring 1979. John Frasco represented CART in court, reminding the court that Indiana was a right-to-work state, that Indy had the date and his clients had the licenses.

When the verdict came in, it was as near a death sentence as could be. In a court sympathetic only to the rule of law and the right to work, USAC had lost.

Jo Hoppen, Vasek Polak, Ted Field, and Danny Ongais watched this closely. The Porsche engines had begun testing, with massive oiling problems as a result. For some reason, oil was not getting to the number one cylinder and several blocks were destroyed as connecting rods separated from crankshafts and punctured crankcases.

In his dealings with USAC, Hoppen had negotiated a turbo boost allowance of 54in of mercury (1.8 bar). The four-cylinder Offy's were allowed 60in (2.0 bar), the eight-cylinder Cosworths were allowed 48 (1.6 bar). Porsche's six straddled the middle. But Hoppen, not a lawyer, never got it in writing.

In December 1979, at Manhattan's Tavern on the Green, USAC President Richard King, Jo Hoppen, and the Interscope Indy team unveiled the new car to the press and invited guests. During the conference, a writer asked Hoppen about the boost and, with Dick King standing right behind him, Hoppen explained the 54in limit.

USAC was struggling at this point to keep its part of the Champ Car series alive. CART was proving a formidable force. While Hoppen had actually made appearance promises to both USAC and CART, it was USAC which were present at the Porsche's public unveiling.

With Porsche, USAC now had two jewels. The other was A. J. Foyt.

Foyt was curious about Porsche's efforts. A wise and wily competitor, he had the same grasp of Porsche's potential as Ted Field. When Foyt won at Le Mans in 1967 with Dan Gurney in a 7.0 liter Ford Mk IV, he beat two 330P4 Ferraris and another Mk IV. But it was 2.0 liter Porsches that finished 5th, 6th, 7th, and 8th.

Foyt knew what Porsche could do, given an even chance. And that was something that he preferred not to have happen. Foyt

had set his sights on the Champ Car title for 1980.

"Which is why," Hoppen continued, "I took USAC technical director Jack Beckley to Stuttgart to see the engines on the dynamometer. Accompanying Beckley was Howard Gilbert, the man who built engines for A. J. Foyt."

Foyt was running a four-cylinder Offy at the time. He had expressed his concern to Beckley and to King that the boost rules allowed too much leeway. Simplifying the rules, Foyt suggested 60in boost for four-cylinder engines, 48in for engines with more than four cylinders.

Hoppen's visit with Beckley and Gilbert was to reassure Foyt that the Porsche was not yet a serious threat. What the two Americans saw on the dyno that day was another steaming, broken engine, another punctured case.

When the engine had run, nearly 630hp had been achieved...as long as the engine had run.

The blown engine was not what Hoppen wanted to show off. And insufficient power was not the message Foyt got when Gilbert and Beckley returned home. Rumors circulated that Foyt threatened to join CART if the boost rule wasn't "simplified."

"Interscope had begun chassis tests," Hoppen explained, "running on the Ontario Motor Speedway oval east of Los Angeles. Engines still blew. But enough laps were done to indicate the car had serious competitive potential. In tests observed by helicopters high above the oval, the car ran faster than Field's Cosworth-powered Parnellis. And in the end, duplicating the Indy 500 four-lap qualifying series, the Interscope Porsche lapped with an average speed of 192mph (307km/h)."

With Porsche having pledged public allegiance to USAC in Manhattan, USAC was less concerned with losing the German manufacturer. The loss of Foyt would be the last nail in their coffin. And after the public show, where would Porsche go? To CART? They still had to run the lower boost at Indy anyway. And Porsche had come to the series to run Indy.

With one month till the track opened, USAC "simplified" the rule. Porsche's six-

The Garrett AiResearch "regulator," scratched with the initials VP2—from Vasek Polak's intense testing—is now rusted into place below the turbo. At 54in of boost, the Porsche was simply too much of a threat to some of USAC's supporters. So USAC simply changed the rule—in mid-April 1980.

cylinder racing engine would be limited to 48in of boost.

Hoppen remembered how Ferry Porsche reacted: "'How can we, at this late date...? We developed the engine for 54in of boost! How can you change the rules with one month to the race? We cannot test and develop a new engine in one month? We cancel the project!'"

But Jo Hoppen was as wily and wise as Foyt. And he had been in racing long enough to know. Rules are meant to be changed. He had advocated testing and developing the engine at 48in of boost as well. His strategy was to huff and puff, bluster and threaten, and then show up at the Brickyard and run.

And in that strategy, he had a natural ally, Ernst Fuhrmann.

And yet, it never happened.

Hoppen: "Porsche management never wanted the program. They saw it taking money and resources away from projects they wanted to do at a time when there wasn't a lot of money or resources available.

"They said, 'Great! We don't know...no one knows what we could do with a 48in boost engine. Therefore, our public excuse is we simply cannot do it at all in the time remaining!'"

And without telling anyone, without informing its "partner," Ted Field, Porsche simply shut the program down.

Four cars were built for 1980. The completed test mule was used for press kit photography. Roman Slobodynskyj had designed a new car, the Interscope Indy 81, an extremely streamlined shape that could likely have taken the Porsche beyond 200mph.

Instead, all the cars went to a warehouse.

In May, Johnny Rutherford qualified CART owner Jim Hall's Pennzoil Chaparral. The 48in-boosted Cosworth V-8 took the pole at 192.256mph (249.93km/h). A. J.Foyt qualified his 60in boosted Offy-engined Maverick as twelfth fastest, at 185.500mph (296.80km/h). On race day, he finished 14th; after 173 laps, his engine let a valve go.

Field and Interscope had been racing with Cosworth engines in a Parnelli chassis. The chassis had been sorted out so it was only a matter of fitting in Porsche water-cooled-head engine from the 935/78. It fit USAC's displacement regulations and its development was as advanced as the Parnelli. With engine, the Interscope Porsche weighed 680kg (1,496lb). Its wheelbase was 2654mm (104.5in), overall it measured 4547mm (179in) from nose to tip of the rear wing. It stood 927mm (36.5in) tall.

Jo Hoppen: "Porsche management never wanted the program. They saw it taking money and resources away from projects they wanted to do."

CHAPTER 29

1982 Typ 956

The New Dynasty Is Born

"Porsche gave us racing that was really racing," Derek Bell reflected, recalling days when a dozen teams raced 956s in the World Endurance Championship. *"You could have eighteen cars going nose to tail. People loved it."*

Group C. The "consumption" group. FISA invented one of those challenges that the engineers loved and the racers hated.

"I must say," Paul Frère admitted, "that I was 80 percent responsible for the introduction of the 1982 Group C regulations that specified completely free engines and restricted the fuel consumption. It was a responsible thing and a good engineering challenge."

"I hated it," Derek Bell said, emphatically. "We are in show business. The public cannot understand that we go round Silverstone in 1:15 to qualify and then in the race go round in 1:24. Just to conserve fuel! I mean, bloody hell, 9 seconds off the pace is a bit of a joke!"

For 1,000km races, the regulations allowed 600 liters (158gal) of fuel; for Le Mans, 2,600 liters (686gal). Conservation.

Porsche engineers looked at their 2.65 liter Indianapolis engine, the Typ 935/76, and saw the possibilities. The engine was first developed for the 935 (as Typ 935/71) with a KKK turbocharger and air-to-air intercooler for each cylinder bank. With compression set low, at 7.2:1 to maintain fuel efficiency, the engine still produced about 620hp at 8200rpm with race boost set at 2.2 bar.

The FISA regulations required "crushable" structures surrounding the driver ahead of the firewall/bulkhead. They had also set a minimum windshield height that eliminated Porsche Group 6 936s and derivatives from consideration. So Norbert Singer, questioning the difficulty of accommodating "crushability" with a tube frame, set out to produce a new chassis.

The result was the racing department's first effort with monocoque structure, where the torsionally stiff body actually is a load-bearing member, absorbing suspension and drive loads without benefit of a separate chassis. In the new 956, this monocoque extended from the firewall/bulkhead immediately behind the driver's head, to the footwell. With the fuel tank behind the monocoque, and allowing room for the engine and transaxle (themselves partially stressed members), the wheelbase was fixed at 2650mm (104in). This set the driver's feet ahead of the front axle.

The Kevlar-reinforced fiberglass bodywork represented another experiment for Porsche: ground effects. The engine and transaxle were actually slightly inclined—about 5 degrees off horizontal—to accommodate air tunnels below the belly pan. The narrow 907/917-style cockpit left room on either side for the various cooling radiators to be located in sponsons. The water, oil, and turbo intercoolers were placed in various controlled airflows.

The cars were still being constructed in the race shop in December 1981 when a number of Porsche Cup drivers visited. Eugen Kolb had designed and fabricated both short- and long-tail and short- and long-nose versions for the car. Based on his experiences beginning with the 906LM and refined more with the 917, the variants for the 956 were the most subtle yet. The nose curve radius of the Le Mans long-tail versions was tighter and drooped slightly lower, while the long tail was less than 500mm (19.68in) longer than the short version and the wide wing was lower.

Jürgen Barth, as factory test driver, was the first to drive the new 956 on Weissach. His first impression was that he was too tall.

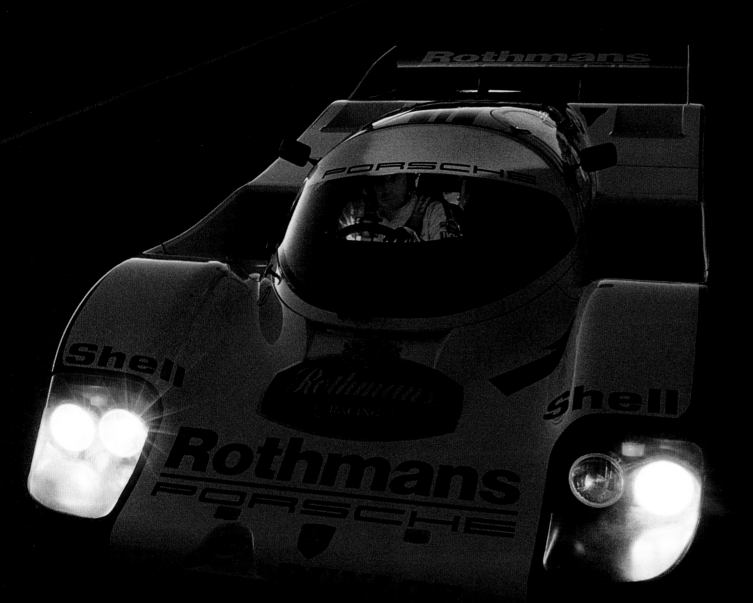

"It was a car built specifically for Jacky Ickx, who is 1 meter 70, where I am 185. So I was jammed inside. And when I first drove it...."

Barth whistled. "You see, no one had driven ground-effects sports cars before. And the cornering forces were simply incredible. I went out and did about five laps and came in to check the fluids. And Professor Bott looked around at the rear of the car and asked me if I had gone off the road?"

Barth laughed. The unexpected discovery surprised everyone. "I said no. He pointed out the dust and we realized the tunnels under the car had *vacuumed* the track!"

For Barth and colleague Roland Kussmaul, their learning experiences were just beginning. Barth drove a 1,000km test session over the rough road, Weissach's cobblestone track, to check chassis durability.

"With my knees smashed up under the cowl, it was brutal. We could only go for a couple hours each and then when we got out, we couldn't walk. With ground effects the suspension is extremely stiff, there is nearly no travel. So the driver absorbs a lot of the shock through his body." And if that wasn't enough, a week later, Barth and Kussmaul were to begin the same tests over the hillclimb circuit, a portion of Weissach with hills and tight turns.

"Well, let us just say the steering effort was very high," Barth laughed again. "We could not do it all at once, the four days, because after your two hours in the cars, you could barely lift your arms. And of course, even with the safety harnesses, my knees took a lot of the effort."

Derek Bell first drove the car at Paul Ricard, the smooth, fast French circuit favored by many teams for testing, in March 1982. Because it was a Porsche, he knew what to expect. The car, however, was better than he could have imagined.

"It had no vices!" Bell recalled ten years later. "Of course, I'd never really driven a ground-effects car before. I'd driven the odd Formula 1 cars. But it was just excellent. It was a typical Porsche, it gave a lot of feedback!

"Porsches always tell you what they're doing. They're so consistent in their performance. If it understeered through a turn at 155km/h (97mph), it understeered through that turn at 155km/h forever!

"Until you came in and changed it. And then it reacted. We needed stiffer sway bars and stiffer shocks. But each, we could feel the change. The car was always very positive in the way it felt. They were stable as hell!"

Their first race was at Silverstone. The race was still called a 6 hour race yet the FISA had imposed its 600 liter/1,000km race fuel allocation on it. For the 820kg (1,804lb) Porsches to last the distance against their prime competition, a turbocharged 1.4 liter 640kg (1,408lb) Lancia spyder, the Porsche's qualified fast but raced slow.

Bell and Ickx finished 2nd, three laps down. The smaller Lancia was more fuel frugal at speed and in order to finish, the Porsche had to conserve. Bell's frustration at racing 9sec off the pace founded his hatred of Group C regulations.

In Le Mans trim the cars weighed 860kg (1,892lb), carrying a toolbox, some spare parts, and extra lights. Wearing Kolb's long tails, the cars hit only 347km/h (216.88mph) along Mulsanne, some 22km/h (13.75mph) slower than the 936/81s had run with a similar engine. The ground effects dragged the cars top speed down yet the lap times were slightly quicker.

Once the race began, Jacky Ickx raced hard against some of the Ford Cosworth-powered cars and eventually the Fords retired from the strain. Teammate Derek Bell took over and soldiered on, overtaken by teammates Al Holbert and Hurley Haywood around midnight. But within an hour Bell and Ickx were back in the lead, and for the remaining 16 hours, their car, race numbered 1, ruled the race. At the end, they had covered 4,899.7km (3,062.3 miles) and

averaged 204.12km/h (127.58mph) to win. It was Ickx's sixth and Bell's third Le Mans victory. Colleagues Jochen Mass and Vern Schuppan (race numbered 2) and Haywood and Holbert (number 3) finished in that order. They were the only three Group C finishers out of twenty-nine entries in the new category.

Consumption category indeed. The 1981 winning 936 had used 52 liters per 100km (4.54mpg). The Ickx/Bell 956 used 48 liters per 100km (4.95mpg).

The heaviest consumption was the competition. For privateers like Reinhold Jöst and Erwin Kremer, Porsche had good news at season end as it announced the 1983 cars. A run of twelve cars—built to 1982 specifications—would be available for the 1983 season. Group C was about to get more interesting.

The principal factory improvement for the 1983 cars was the adoption of Bosch's Motronic MP engine management system. Compression for the 935/82 engine eventually rose to 8.5:1, increasing horsepower to 650hp. Better fuel consumption was expected as well.

Porsche went to Le Mans in 1983 with the intention of entering four 956s, running 7.5:1 compression to stretch the fuel and last the distance. But when the light turned green at 4pm Peter Falk had scratched one of his entries. Car number 4, for Jürgen Barth and Vern Schuppan, was withdrawn because Falk felt no need to run the extra entry. Confidence was high at Sarthe.

Eight private 956s had entered: Kremer Racing, sponsored by Kenwood; SORGA, with two cars sponsored by NewMan and by Marlboro; John Fitzpatrick, with three cars sponsored by Skoal, BP, and JDavid; Obermaier, sponsored by Hugo Boss; and Richard Lloyd, sponsored by Canon.

Ickx again took the pole, lapping at 3:16.56 for 210.18km/h (131.36mph). It gave him the advantage until his second lap on Mulsanne when, in hard braking at the end, he bumped Jan Lammers in a private 956. Both spun spectacularly at more than 200km/h and each lost time in the pits repairing the damage. Teammates Jochen Mass in car 2 and Holbert in car 3 sped away. But Porsche's factory problems were

The culmination of Norbert Singer's engineering and Eugen Kolb's long-tail designs appeared in the 956. Despite a frontal area larger than the 936 and ground effects dragging speed off the car, Kolb's tail cleaned up the airflow enough to aid Holbert, Haywood, and Schuppan in a dramatic Le Mans win in 1983. Porsche Werke

Derek Bell:
"It had no vices."

The Kevlar-reinforced bodywork with its narrow 907/917-style cockpit left room on either side for water, oil, and turbo intercoolers to be located in the sponsons. Eugen Kolb designed both short- and long-tail versions. Yet his experience beginning with the 906LM and refined with the 917 produced the most subtle variants. The long tail was barely 500mm (19.69in) longer than the short tail, and about 50mm (1.96in) lower.

not over.

As Bell and Ickx sought to regain the lead they routinely touched 394km/h (246.25mph) along Mulsanne as they reeled in Barth (2) and Holbert (3). The Barth/Mass/Stefan Bellof car suffered ignition problems and then starter problems that made every fuel stop a heart stopper as well. It ground them down to 11th place through the night.

As Ickx and Bell pressed the other Porsches, fuel stops took on additional drama. Group C consumption regulations also limited refuelling speed to 1 liter per second. A full tank meant nearly a 2 minute stop.

Sunday morning, howling out of Mulsanne corner, Bell's electronics failed. Pulling to the side in 250km/h (155mph) traf-

fic, he frantically hefted up the huge rear compartment and replaced the Motronic black box himself. With Barth transferred, replacing Haywood who had taken ill during the night, Holbert/Barth/Schuppan had the lead.

Sunday afternoon, another pit stop, another driver change. With Schuppan back at the wheel of number 3, not quite 25 minutes into his shift, he radioed to Falk that the door flew off on Mulsanne. This drastically upset airflow over Kolb's long-tail body and through the water radiator on that side. Falk radioed back that it would take them several minutes to prepare a new door. Schuppan was to stay out another four or five laps before coming in. Schuppan returned to the pits, a new door was slapped in place and the car took off, now with Holbert behind the wheel. But within several laps, he returned to finally have the door secured properly.

By that time, Falk was questioning his earlier confidence. At about 2pm, car 2 retired with a cylinder-head failure. Bell climbed in to car 1 for the final hour, alerted by Ickx that a brake rotor had cracked. Holbert got into car 3. With each lap, Bell heard Holbert report to Falk on the engine temperature.

"Temperature is 200," Holbert reported.

"There is no water temperature," Holbert radioed on the next lap. There was no water.

"Bring him in, bring him in!" cried Bell into the radio.

"The engine in Holbert's car momentarily seized," Bell recalled. "Then it released. Holbert was told to continue. On the previous lap, I had been nearly a minute down. And I did the last lap actually balls out. Blitzing the course."

Bell sighed loudly. "And the silly marshals were out there with their flags, waving congratulations.... We were still trying to win!"

On Holbert's last lap, an oil leak complicated an already serious situation. When he crossed the finish line, steam poured from the exhausts on the left side. The car managed another 20 meters.

Although it was never officially recorded, Derek Bell came across the finish for 2nd place less than 30sec later. As the crowd flooded the finish line, surrounding Holbert's car and blocking the track, timing and scoring officials simply gave up, feeling frustration like Bell's.

For 1984, the privateers were offered the 8.5:1 compression 956 with the Motronic that had been run everywhere but Le Mans. These were fitted into B Series cars, with a lighter monocoque that reduced running weight right to the 800kg (1,760lb) limit. The factory was concerned with a new FISA regulation.

While FISA had given lip service to the idea of blending its regulations more closely with IMSA, the Americans gave little care to fuel efficiency. Curiously, the FISA rules for the 1984 World Sports Car Championship called for 15 percent further reduction in fuel consumption.

Porsche invested heavily with Bosch in a variety of experimental engine management systems to achieve FISA's difficult goal. Work continued through the winter. But six weeks before the season opener, FISA postponed the fuel economy regulation but invoked IMSA's construction regulations: overall performance was tied to a formula relating engine displacement to vehicle weight. And driver's feet must be behind the front wheel centerline.

Porsche's 956 (and Lancia's Group C car as well) were immediately illegal. And obsolete.

It forced Porsche to withdraw the factory team from Le Mans in protest. An action contemplated in years past—threatened as a result of other mercurial regulations from the ruling body—came to pass with this new ruling. Le Mans was left to privateers, fourteen Typ 956s in all. And two in Typ 962s.

IMSA's regulations for 1984 allowed two variations, the 2.65 liter engine bored out to 2.86 liters, to race in the 850kg (1,870lb) category, while the 3.2 liter would race in the 900kg (1,980lb) category. These were basically 935/77 engines but for IMSA, they ran single turbos and intercoolers with the Motronic management system. To accommodate the driver's footwell, the wheel-

The cockpit bore family resemblance to the previous fifteen years' developments. The climb over the bodywork to enter the car was far greater than either the 907 or 917, however. The tight fit badly bruised the knees of the development drivers.

base was stretched 125mm (4.92in).

Designated the Typ 962, the prototype had appeared at Daytona for the 1984 IMSA season opener. The car didn't finish. But it did repeat a common Porsche warning: these cars will be campaigned by the factory until there are enough to go around, usually at season end. Afterward, they will be available to privateers. If you cannot afford to play or pay, you may as well sit in the stands and watch.

The planned merge of regulations between FISA and IMSA never happened. It kept IMSA entries in the United States except only for annual June visits to France. The World Endurance Championships, WEC—successor to the Sports Car Championships—did visit the United States for one or two events a year but otherwise the Atlantic remained a wide, wide ocean. Through 1985 and 1986, the ranks of privateers on both sides grew and grew. Crashes that destroyed 956s brought 962s as replacements to nearly every team. By the time June 1987 arrived, the date when FISA had outlawed the forward-pedal box, only 962s were allowed at Le Mans. And FISA had mandated use of commercial fuel. Twelve 962s—eight of them privateers—appeared for inspection.

The factory intended to enter four cars but lost one in testing at Weissach. Once more in Rothmans livery, Bell, Holbert, and Hans Stuck drove car 17; Mass and Bob Wollek drove 18, and number 19 was driven by Schuppan and Price Cobb.

But at Wednesday night practice, Cobb hit a patch of oil in, ironically, Porsche Curve, and destroyed car 19 along the ARMCO. And then the factory cars were two.

At 4pm the race started. Thirteen minutes later, Reinhold Jöst's first car lost an engine. Five minutes after that, Jöst's second engine expired. At 4:30, the first Kremer was out. At 5:01, the number 18 Rothmans factory car entered the pits, its engine blown. And then there was only Hans and Al and Derek.

In the next eight hours, the three drivers pulled out a cautious lead over the threatening Jaguars. To stave off challengers, they used too much fuel but Peter Falk rea-

soned it was something that could be adjusted later. And fate cooperated.

At around 2:45am, the 4th place Jaguar crashed heavily on Mulsanne. It took course officials two hours to remove the debris and repair the ARMCO—two hours in which Porsche followed the pace car. Shortly after the pace car went out, Stuck dove into the pits. Falk, recognizing that the cool night air and slower speeds would affect several engine functions as well as fuel economy, had an engineer hastily cut a new chip for the Motronic on a computer in the pits. For the next two hours, Porsche took advantage of Jaguar's hardship. When the pace returned to normal, the factory car was sixteen laps ahead—of another 962. Eight hours later, it was four laps further ahead and the Rothmans car led three other Porsche-engined cars across the line.

Porsche withdrew from the World Endurance Championship after the 1987 Le Mans. The 956/962 was five years old and Weissach sought to concentrate on a new single seater for racing in America.

"But in hindsight," Derek Bell suggested, "the biggest mistake they ever made was pulling out. At the time we thought so, but we saw it from the driver's point of view without a ride."

Bell's laugh was dry, with more irony than humor.

"If Porsche had kept developing the 962 from '85 on, kept racing after '87, people would be buying its cars, and the World Championship would have been full of cars!

"You know, that's really it." Bell's voice picked up. "Porsche gave everybody the option to buy a racing car. And be competitive. *You know* the number of teams that won races!

"Porsche did a lot more for motor racing than people ever really give them credit for. People just talk about results. They don't talk about the fact that Porsches filled fields. Maybe it was Jöst, maybe it was Kremer. Or Rothmans or Brun or Richard Lloyd. You can go on and on.

"They were all Porsches but people didn't mind. They were all different colors. Different shapes even, slight aerodynamic differences. People loved it. It was thanks to Porsche that we had sports-car racing for so

Jürgen Barth:
"You see, no one had driven ground-effects sports cars before. And the cornering forces were simply incredible."

"But that's the point, really. That Porsche supplied all these cars. Take the eighteen customer Porsches out, leave the two factory Porsches in there, it leaves you what there is now.... Two French, three Japanese, two British, good night!

"Now nobody is selling cars. And it's been the downfall of IMSA and of the World Championship and...."

And Bell went silent again.

long."

Bell stopped. He remembered another effect of Porsche's stopping, a seriously personal effect. "You know, when Porsche withdrew, it left Hans Stuck and me without a ride. We already had a lead built up in World Driver's Championship points. So we had to go shopping around to rent rides—to win for ourselves, to win for Porsche. Incredible." This was not sour grapes talking. It was the recognition of all the ramifications.

"Porsche gave us racing that was really racing. You could have eighteen cars going nose to tail. People talked about it with affection! About the dices. It was something everybody followed.

The Typ 935/76 engine (92.3 x 66mm) of 2.65 liters was an adaptive reuse of the 935 Indy project. With Kugelfischer mechanical fuel injection and twin KKK turbochargers through air-to-water intercoolers, the water-cooled-head engines produced 620hp at 8200rpm.

189

CHAPTER 30

1983 930 Turbo Flat Nose

Mass Production Special Wish

Porsche engineer Rolf Sprenger initiated Sonderwunsch in 1979 after watching too many good Porsche customers go elsewhere for custom work. His first proposal was to replicate the Typ 935 race car looks for the street. The rear remained stock; engine cooling problems could not be solved. Three Special Wishes versions of the Flat Nose were produced by Rolf Sprenger's department from designs from the Styling Department. The first mounted the headlights into the front bumper. The second introduced the pop-up lights together with the Group B oil cooler mounted in the nose. The third, for the United States, deleted the cooler.

"All my life—all my *automobile* life—I was of the opinion that racing *must* have a connection to the normal automobile." Ernst Fuhrmann laughed as he made the distinction between his life at Porsche and his life outside. "And when I returned to Porsche, we were just beginning the Can-Am with turbocharged cars.

"And when this car came, this race car was noiseless!" Fuhrmann could see and hear the connection between the turbocharger and the series-production cars Porsche was offering. The 911 was threatened. Marketing and sales people were lobbying strongly for a successor. A Volkswagen project, a much smaller car with a four-cylinder engine, was occupying much of Weissach's time. "Mr. Piëch and Mr. Bott proposed to build the successor for the 911 from the new Porsche prototype for the VW-werk. Plans were to end the 911 in 1973. The new car would come then.

"But then, in the VW-werk, Kurt Lotz, the general manager, had to leave the firm. They decided not to build the Porsche car; this was quite a different car from what you ever saw. And now Porsche had no successor for its 911."

For Ernst Fuhrmann, after only six months back at Porsche, his crisis was just beginning.

"And then, the whole family left the company! Ferdinand Piëch left; Ferdinand Porsche left; Peter Porsche, the production manager, left.

"So there was just Ernst Fuhrmann there together with company president Heinz Branitzki. Without any agreement with the Volkswagenwerk. Without work for Weissach. Without any possibility of a new car.

"I looked again at this turbocharged race car. Our engineering was so far ahead.

"Why don't we put this success into our car?"

Fuhrmann, the small-framed man with the quick sense of humor and a strong sense of irony, sat in his living room in Teufenbach, Austria, only 50km from Gmünd. He stared out the window a long time, remembering the challenges he put to his engineers.

"They said, 'Oh, this was tried already.'

"'But not in a car that was done right,' I said.

"'It was refused by management,' they said. 'It was impossible,' they said, 'not enough room.'

"This was my contribution," Fuhrmann explained, clarifying history. His eyes lit up. "I looked in the engine compartment and said, 'There must be room! It's not impossible!'"

With that, Ernst Fuhrmann dismissed his contribution to the Porsche Turbo. In those days, challenges to Weissach brought out the best in everyone. And, in all days, a challenge from Dr. Fuhrmann was easily interpreted as an order.

Fuhrmann had left Porsche in 1956 as an engineer to go to Goetze, a maker of piston rings. He returned to Porsche in September 1971, as an engineer who had become the technical director, experienced in all phases of management. His "style" in those days was to go to Weissach every evening, "to see if they were a step ahead. I did push a little bit on this project."

Insufficient room was not the real problem. Three years earlier, experimental 2.0

Engineer Ernst Fuhrmann was the father of the 930 Turbo. He believed racing must have a connection to production automobiles. Impressed with the "noiseless" turbocharged Can-Am cars, he pressed his development engineers to turbocharge the production automobiles. Hans Mezger and Valentin Schaeffer extracted 300hp at 5500rpm from the 3.3 liter Typ 930/60 engine. Within the small engine compartment, they buried the turbo beneath the left rear corner of the engine and fitted an air-to-air intercooler, which dropped fuel temperature.

liter Typ 901 engines had been turbocharged and one had been fitted into a 911 and another into a 914/6. But testing pointed out problems with heat dissipation, detonation, and, of course, lag as the turbo wound up to speed.

In the course of their experiments, Hans Mezger and Valentine Schäffer worked out a viable compromise to produce the power they sought: keep the boost pressure high and the engine speed low. This combination worked and the first production 3.0 liter engines, designated Typ 930/50, produced 260hp at only 5500rpm. Complicated plumbing adapted from racing applications diminished the lag to something they believed was acceptable to production customers.

Introduced at the Paris Auto Show in October 1974, the project had taken slightly more than eighteen months from the engineers protests of "no room." They found room; the turbo fit beneath the left rear corner of the engine, above the muffler. Its ducting rose across the front of the engine, past the vertical air fan. Once installed, however, there was no more room.

It was a guarded success. A Swiss magazine achieved 0-160km/h (0-100mph) times of 12.6sec, and Belgian journalist Paul Frère topped out a test car at 249.3km/h (155.8mph). But its handling scared many owners. Arriving at the boost in the middle of the turn introduced many inexperienced drivers to the laws of physics. And to trees.

In 1977, Porsche introduced the new 930/60 engine. This 3.3 liter version developed 300hp, still at 5500rpm. But much of the additional power came through the use of an intercooler that dropped the intake air temperature by more than 120 degrees Fahrenheit. Numerous internal changes accompanied and resulted from the increased engine displacement. And subtle improvements continued into the 1980s when a significant modification became available for the Turbos.

At the end of 1982, the FIA published new racing regulations, including those for Group B cars. Two hundred of the two-seater GTs had to be produced each year and few modifications were permitted from stock. Its weight limitation, a minimum

1,235kg (2,717lb), meant the car had to be raced with virtually the stock interior intact, including the air conditioning and even the electric window lifts. These were removed and lead ballast placed where the weight would be more useful—down low.

Only wider wheels and a larger oil cooler could be fitted. This was placed in the nose spoiler and replaced the small fender-mounted unit. But at year end, the protoypes Group C split in two and Porsche's 930 Turbo Group B was removed from the Weissach racing catalog.

It was relocated to Zuffenhausen as a 330hp "Special Wish" option. Turbocharger boost was increased from the stock level of 0.8 to 1.0 bar; a larger intercooler was used along with an exhaust system with less restriction. The oil cooler from the Group B cars was retained.

Sonderwunsch, the Special Wishes program, was started in 1979 as an element of Porsche engineer Rolf Sprenger's customer service department. He was tired of watching outside "tuners" modify Porsches and frustrated by turning away his own good customers who asked for special modifications. Sprenger approached his bosses. His proposal was approved and one of his first ideas was to offer, primarily for the turbo customers, a body modification, EXC 010. For slightly less than 40,000DM, Sprenger's technicians remodelled the nose of the car to resemble the 935.

"We also wanted very much at that time to change the rear spoiler. Because we thought, for the whole car, it would be good to have a different rear look." Sprenger described the problem from his office in Werk I. "But there was no technical adjustment for the thermodynamics. The Weissach people couldn't give us another rear spoiler that would not cause overheating problems in traffic. This is the reason we stopped. We had many more ideas how to change the car in back."

It was the front modification customers came to know: the *Flachtbau*, the Flat Nose. There were three versions, the first only featuring flat fenders and headlights mounted in the bumper. In production only a very short time, it evolved into the second version. This nose utilized the pop-up headlights

and the 930 Group B oil cooler mounted in the nose. A low spoiler finished the treatment. Owing to US crash standards, a third version was made available for American customers, without an oil cooler, which could rupture in a front impact.

Customer Service and the *Sonderwunsch* program could go far beyond the packaged versions however, if the right customer appeared, with the right imagination, the right style, and the right pocketbook. In April 1975, Count Gregorio Rossi di Montelera took delivery of a 917 K—for the street. It had formerly been raced by Gerard Larrousse in Martini & Rossi colors. In July 1983, Mansur Ojjeh took delivery of a 935, also for the street. His car had never raced in his firm's colors. Those appeared only on Formula 1 McLarens, sponsored by TAG, Techniques d'Avant Garde. Ojjeh's 935, like all of

the 935s, was based on a production 911 Turbo, with heavy modification.

After a life spanning fifteen years, the 930 was replaced by the 911 Turbo for 1990. The Flat Nose was no longer available because of substantial front-end structural and suspension redesign. But the 930 breathed life into Porsche and, through FIA regulations, provided the platform, basis, and inspiration for nearly a decade of race cars.

Ernst Fuhrmann recalled the first Turbo and its impact on the fifteen years of production cars that followed. He was proud.

"We never stopped the 911, of course. It came through all this better than the sales people expected.

"And with this Turbo, we really *did* something for the 911."

In 1982, the FIA regulations for Group B set minimum weight at 1,235kg (2,717lb). This limitation meant the car could be raced with stock interior intact. Normally, these were removed and lead ballast—relocated to lower the center of gravity— replaced the weight of air conditioning and electric windows.

CHAPTER 31

1984 928S Coupe

The Replacement Is No Pretender

Introduced in the fall of 1977, the 928 was powered by a 4.5 liter water-cooled V-8 with 240hp. In 1980, the 928S was brought out with a 4.7 liter. Until the 1985 introduction of the 5.0 liter four-valve, US buyers received substantially less power and performance than European buyers.

Psychologist Leon Festinger's research produced a work called *The True Believer,* dealing with a concept now familiar to clinical psychologists that is called "cognitive dissonance." It works this way: the practitioners acquire an item of markedly inferior quality or performance. But since they have paid a goodly sum for this item—and because they do not want to be embarrassed admitting its failure or their possible bad judgment—the owners claim its performance is entirely satisfactory. If not downright terrific. The behavior is dissonant from the facts as known.

The opposite of this condition is one that many manufacturers are familiar with. It is called "mass hysteria." This results from nearly opposite conditions. The product acquired meets or exceeds expectations. But because some of the purchasers are incapable of using the product up to the degree of performance possible, they blame some design or manufacturing flaw rather than embarrass themselves by admitting their own failure.

In the earliest days of the 356, it might be said that some Porsche customers could also have been cognitive dissonants. But by the late 1970s, the screaming hysterics had

taken over. And they outnumbered the merely dissonant by a not-so-silent majority. The US Government was about to get involved to protect drivers from themselves. The "handling," the driving characteristics of automobiles was to be legislated and anything "different" was suspect.

"We all know that part of the 911 success was its uniqueness," Helmut Flegl explained. "What is unique? Rear engine, air cooling. Its sound.

"Maybe you like the 'child' a little more who has a few problems...?" Flegl shrugged. It was nearly twenty years since the company had talked about doing away with the "child." Yet, it still amazed him.

"The customers were complaining all the time. 'You have to improve this and that, fix more and other things.' From time to time, there was the issue of so many problems, questions of people not liking this 911 any more. They seemed to kind of want to get away from it...."

Coincidentally, at just about this time in the United States discussions were becoming strident on the subject of "handling."

"They wanted to control the handling! What the handling had to be like going down the road!" Flegl was mildly amused years after the fact by the "they." However, no one at Porsche was at all amused at the time.

"You have the rules as they were in people's minds. These were, for certain, 'rules' for the American car. But the 911 was absolutely not an American car.

"There was talk of 'tests,' of 'procedures.' There was quite a bit of nervousness here. Whatever 'rule' they wrote, we could not guess what the 'handling' was to be. They would define it, but they surely would not forbid American cars! They can make all the rules as they want, but somehow, American cars would meet their rules....

"By then we clearly knew rear-engine, air-cooled cars already did not meet their rules.... A rear-engine car just has different handling. We knew if these new rules came to life, we would have no car we could sell in the United States!"

"It was then we knew we must make a

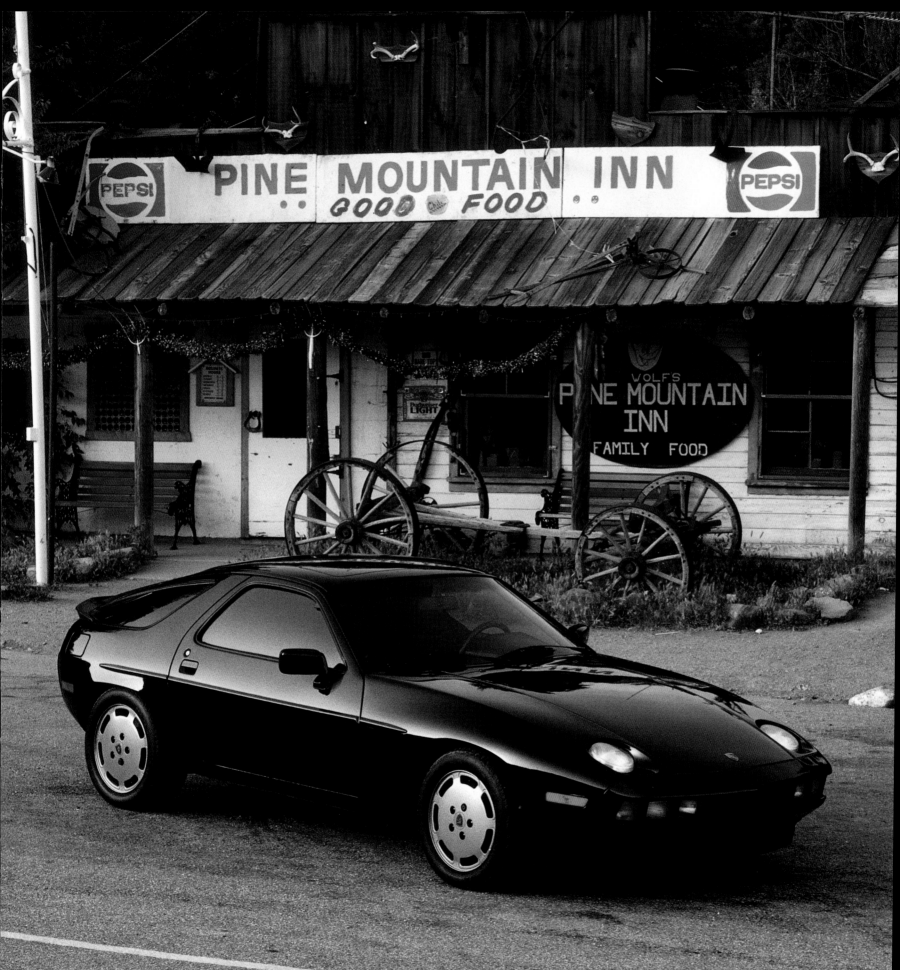

"We all know," Helmut Flegl reasoned, "that part of the 911 success was its uniqueness. Maybe you like the 'child' a little more who has problems? But there was talk of 'tests,' rules. It was then we knew we must make a front-engine car...."

front-engine car...."

Engineer Helmut Flegl, Porsche's Director for Research and Sport, became manager of the front-engine car project in early 1974 for the nearly three years of prototype testing that preceded manufacture. He took over from Wolfhelm Gorrissen, who had been design director through the drawing board stages right up to running prototypes. It was engineer Gorrissen who worked closely from the first days in 1971 with the 928 design studio chief, Tony Lapine.

"The type of designer who works at Porsche," Lapine explained, "has a big admiration for the talents of the engineers." Lapine was an unabashed fan. "We did the 928 the way any intelligent development team should do. We did engineering and design simultaneously."

When he arrived at Porsche in 1969, Lapine went to work immediately for F. A. Porsche as his assistant. He quickly understood his role: he was being trained to guard the tradition, to maintain the Porsche identity.

At GM, he had worked in body development, doing what he called "human engineering." "It was where I learned to make intelligent compromises," Lapine explained. He began to put into perspective the difference between a multinational conglomerate and the still-family-owned firm he had just joined.

"You had a living legend presiding at a meeting. If you wanted to know what a Porsche was all about, you could ask the source. This was unheard of at GM. No family, it was corporate law. That made everything simple. And so god-damned unromantic.

"At Porsche you had romance. Butzi was a critical and cool thinker in lines of design. At the same time, you had Mr. Piëch who was a brilliant engineer who didn't know any such thing as second place....

"At Porsche, you have a team effort. Two, maybe three design studios. Each had twelve designers, each had as many modelers. Maybe more. The designer created on paper. The modeler was the designer who continued from there, who may anxiously have thought, 'Hey, give me that thing! You'll be amazed what I can make of

it!' The professional modeler brought out the nuances the designer could not get on paper." Lapine's son Hans worked for his father, as a modeler.

"And each studio had at least two engineers."

Lapine smiled as he reconsidered the concept of aliens in an alien land. Yet the engineers in Lapine's studios were integral.

"They are my lawyers!" he said, laughing. "They take our work into the meetings....

"I could not go up to Dr. Porsche or Professor Fuhrmann and talk 'designer lingo' to them like at GM styling: 'this things needs more oomph here, we have an idea for a little more pizazz along there....'

"You better come up with very sound, well-footed arguments. There should be a dominance in logic. Especially at Porsche, where there are forty-three designers surrounded by 2,000 engineers...."

With the legacy, the heritage of Porsche's 356 and 911 to live up to and to absorb from, Lapine and his designers began to work on the front-engine car. Water cooling was part of its specification. A broad-angle V-8 engine was to be used. New engineering technologies had to fit into a car immediately recognizable as a Porsche—or at least as being *from* Porsche.

"Compromises? There were hundreds. But they only pained me at the beginning. Once I understood, I had no pain. The compromise of suspension or engine placement or where the seats fit relative to the transmission....

"You have a car that is so wide that it causes too great a frontal area...or it is too long to fit into a garage!

"Someone asks about brakes. We have a legacy of large wheels filling the wells. So, it offers possibilities. We can use 16 inch wheels and fit in larger brake calipers. But 16 inch wheels mean more height to accommodate suspension travel. Suspension travel is good—long, long suspension travel. Softly sprung, tightly dampened. Allows for jounce. So the fender goes a little bit higher.

"If I understand that a water-cooled engine of a designated displacement producing a specific horsepower needs to have a radiator of a certain size, then I can compromise. I can incline it. Someone will

research airflow and they'll discover a mathematical ratio of radiator area to distance from air intake ducts. Together we learn we can use intakes about one-third the area of the radiator. We can place them below the bumper centerline so the Porsche front-engine, water-cooled car has a flat hood. The traditional elements. It follows the legacy.

"And *that's* tradition with Porsche."

Lapine quickly went off in search of his photos of the oldest 356s. Returning, he smiled. "The 356 had bumpers," he pointed out. "They were always body color. They had chrome overrides, bumper guards, but the 356 had its bumper in the body color.

"And it was even underlined by the fact it was sheet metal. OK, 1 millimeter sheet

steel! As a bumper in the classical sense, say, parking by ear, worthless!

"But what was done? The bumper, as such, was not a thing of beauty. When you finish a body outline as a designer, you finally have to say, 'Ohhh, and now the bumper. What's it look like? How does it attach?'

"And then you ruin the silhouette of whatever you had drawn.

"But Porsche, very early in the game, through an aesthetic sense from Mr. Komenda, Mr. Rabe, Mr. F. A. Porsche, decided to continue the 'illusion' that the bumper was part of the body—because the bumper was the same color as the body."

Lapine sat back. For him, explaining the

"I admired the lads who came up with the 'folded paper' styling first," Tony Lapine decided. *"But our tradition was not folds. A shark does not have creases. A dolphin does not have creases."*

"The type of designer who works at Porsche," Tony Lapine explained, *"has a big admiration for the talents of the engineers. We did the 928 the way any intelligent development team should—engineering and design simultaneously."*

philosophy, the practice, and the aesthetic of design was to welcome someone to a new religion.

"With the 928, we had a clean sheet. This time we said, 'The body is the bumper. Our engineering friends said, 'What? We didn't hear right!' So we repeated. And once more. 'What?' they asked. 'Do you want us to make it in rubber?'

"We really depended greatly on the engineers. We knew there was a more intelligent way of making the body absorb the abuse of traffic. They still were not sure. They said it would be expensive. They asked if anyone else did it? Who else did it?

"I said, 'Thank God! No one! We'll be the first. And when we have it, everybody will be forced to copy us!'"

The engineering was difficult. GM had experienced problems integrating a deformable bumper into the front of the 1968 Pontiac GTO. The Detroit version, however, was still a separate bumper. There was a noticeable seam between pieces.

But even more difficult was finally controlling the problem of paint discoloration. The same color painted on steel and then sprayed onto something that was not steel, not aluminum—not metal!

The elasticity of the bodywork was another concern. How could they dissipate the energy of a collision over large enough an area so as not to crack the material? Or permanently deform it?

"At the rear, that big round back end spreads the energy across the entire width. Ernst Fuhrmann, who championed the car, was rear ended in his 928. He suffered practically no damage. The car behind was a big Mercedes, now badly damaged, and spilling all the juices on the roadway.

"Dr. Fuhrmann joked with the man. In Germany it is not allowed to drive a car with crash damage. It must be repaired immediately. Dr. Fuhrmann inspected his car and laughed. He told the other man, 'Look, it could be your word against mine. I could say nothing happened at all and you should be fined for driving such a car....'"

Beneath Lapine's clean sheet of paper was the legacy. Once the parameters for the car—wheelbase, track, height, width, weight—were set, the legacy returned. The

Organic Shape.

"The shape of the 356. It was something we 'found.' We didn't invent it. Very complex shape. The 911, traditional shape. Very beautiful shape, beautiful elements. So what the hell can you do with the 928?

"I admired the lads who came up with the 'folded paper' styling first. It was innovative, exciting. But our tradition was not folds. A shark does not have creases. A dolphin doesn't have creases. When 'folded paper' was en vogue, we had but one crease on the 928. At the Geneva introduction, we were surrounded."

Helmuth Bott was Porsche's Chief Engineer as the 928 was conceived and developed. Years later, he spoke with Betty Jo Turner in *Porsche Panorama*, and he explained compromise.

"If you have a lot of people with the best knowledge in theoretical things," Bott began, "and you bring all the best components together, it will not be the best car. A car always is a compromise and to decide the right compromise, you should have the feeling in the seat of your pants. And you should know how the compromise should be. You cannot get the best handling if you can't compromise the comfort. You cannot get the best surface for the car if you can't, perhaps, compromise the ease of entry into the car.

"To make that decision is very important, especially for Porsche. One should see in a car the handwriting of the man who decides the compromise."

The 928 was conceived before the Volkswagen project 924. But VW's contract with Weissach helped pay many of Porsche's bills. Its desire for a new, prestigious, evolutionary sports car put Porsche's own new prestigious, evolutionary sports car in abeyance for several years.

As Ernst Fuhrmann returned to Porsche, Volkswagen prepared to cancel the 924 project. The income was lost and that project was to be compromised one step further. Designed by Porsche as a Volkswagen, it was now to become a Porsche. When Fuhrmann looked around Weissach, he also saw the stillborn 928.

Cognitive dissonance met the first 924 in 1975. Buyers disappointed by its too-many compromises still claimed love. It was the right car for the early 1970s; it was just not yet the right car.

Mass hysteria met the 928 in 1977. Powerful, luxurious, zaftig, it was a courageous product. The screamers decried it as irresponsible to a world rocked by Mideast oil economics. They labelled it under their breath as Ernst Fuhrmann's shopping car, Porsche's Mercedes-Benz's 450SLC. But that does the SLC, Fuhrmann, and the 928 a gross disservice.

Fuhrmann recently asked a visitor, "Who has the right to define a Porsche *only* as a rear-engine, air-cooled car? Just because the first two cars were this, can we not grow? Do we not evolve?"

And then the screaming hysterics drove the 928. Sweeping through the proper turn at speed, they could see the signatures of Wolfhelm Gorrissen and Helmut Flegl. In the last glow of daylight, they could see the signature of Tony Lapine, of Helmuth Bott, of Ernst Fuhrmann.

The US regulations never materialized to the extent that led to the 928. Now, as the car reaches its twentieth year, the minimum life span Lapine imagined for a Porsche, the screaming hysterics themselves have had twenty years of high speed therapy. The front-engined, water-cooled sports car quieted the *compromise* dissonance.

"A car is always a compromise," Helmuth Bott confessed, "and to decide the right compromise, you should have the feeling in the seat of your pants.... One should see in a car the handwriting of the man who decides the compromise...."

CHAPTER 32

1986 Typ 959 Paris-Dakar Rally

Grown Men Gone Playing In The Desert Sand

The Africa Safari Rallye was still a jewel missing from for Porsche's crown. The 26th running in 1978, over 5000km (3,125 miles) saw rain turn Africa from dust to mud. Two 911SCs started, Vic Preston finished 2nd, driving number 14, and previous Monte Carlo winner Bjorn Waldegaard, driving number 5, finished 4th.

Hypothetical question: Do automotive engineers learn more if they start from a clean sheet of paper?

Even with a fresh page, there are still notes from the management, conditions and stipulations of what the new car must be, how it must perform, what it must cost. Even with a mandate to reinvent the automobile, with carte blanche to imagine new ideas, is it as much of a creative reach as it is to adapt from history?

Would the same engineers be more challenged if they were forced to stretch the present product into the future, to see fifteen years, twenty-five years beyond? Some costs would be saved: design of the overall package, development of its chassis, conception and development of its powerplant. And the ideas from the past, those shunted to the side, those with great potential, could be developed to completion.

For Porsche, the idea of four-wheel-drive preceded even the Cisitalia Grand Prix car. An unnumbered design study by Karl Rabe in 1934 suggested the adaptability of four-wheel-drive to a Volkswagen project. It was adapted, adopted, produced, and proven during World War II. It came first as the Kom-

mandeurwagen, then as the Kübelwagen, and then with an amphibious version, as the Schwimmwagen. And after the war, its first peacetime application came with the Porsche Typ 360, Piero Dusio's Cisitalia GP car.

In the early 1960s, Porsche bought an English Jensen Interceptor with Harry Ferguson's Project FF four-wheel-drive. The concept of unequal torque split between the front and rear axles further inspired Helmuth Bott. But Jensen's execution disappointed him. The handling was not what he desired from a sports car, despite the Ferguson surefootedness.

Shortly after Peter Schutz arrived at Porsche AG in January 1981, Weissach's engineers recognized a new champion in the new President at Stuttgart.

Schutz was born in Berlin on April 20, 1930. In 1952, he graduated in mechanical engineering from the Illinois Institute of Technology. After four years in the US Army, he spent most of the next eleven years in engine development, first at Caterpillar Tractor Company, then at Cummins Engine Company as Director of Corporate Planning. Just before his 48th birthday, he moved back to Germany as head of the Deutz Engine Division of KHD. As he turned 51, he was beginning to develop his reputation at Weissach.

One of the first who recognized Schutz's sincere support was Helmuth Bott. One day, engineer chief Bott pulled open his desk drawer and showed engineer president Schutz the ideas that had been there for a while.

Bott was curious about the future of the 911. How far could it be advanced. What were the limits to its chassis? Schutz listened. All-wheel-drive? Schutz did not protest.

When he received approval from Porsche President Peter Schutz to proceed with development of a 911 for the future, Bott knew the path to follow. His long experience with the company had involved many racing programs as the way to accelerate development of a new product. The FIA's Group B category regulations came closest to fitting what Bott had in mind.

This 911SC started life as a regular production car, then was heavily reinforced by the competition department. The 3.0 liter mechanical-fuel injection engine produced 250hp at 6800rpm. Top speed was 210km/h (131mph), more than fast enough for the tortuous ruts and deep mud.

The original engine for this project came out of Porsche history whereas the final engine for this project was not quite shunted to the side. More accurately, it was a fully developed engine waiting to find its true mission, a project looking for a home.

The four-valve flat six, originally created for the 935/78 Moby Dick, was further developed for the 1980 Indy car series for Interscope. When the Indy project was shelved, the development work was not wasted. The engine, with its air-cooled block, watercooled heads, and four valves per cylinder, had proved itself in testing. Converted back to gasoline, the engine powered the 936 win at Le Mans in 1981.

It was then enlarged to 2.85 liters for Group C regulations for the 956 race cars and was capable of 650hp. Its record there was formidable.

But when the homologation requirements for Group B could not be met, another avenue of competition opened up. Well, not quite avenue. More like course. Or trail.

Jacky Ickx had won the 5th Paris-Dakar Rally in 1983 driving a Mercedes 280GE Gelandewagen, essentially a specialty four-wheel-drive vehicle. This race, unlike the rallies that Ferdinand Piëch's Audi Quattro was winning, had been a specialty-vehicle event since its beginning. However Ickx, with plenty of seat-time in the durable 956, wondered if the race could be won in a four-wheel-drive sports car.

In international rallying, Piëch's Quattro was redefining what the modern rally car should be. With full-time four-wheel-drive, the Audi coupes had begun life as front-engine, front-wheel-driven cars. They pulled and pushed the way for Porsche and others to follow.

"You see," Helmuth Bott explained, "our concept with the 911 has always been that it's an all-around car. With very few changes, you can drive a rally, and then go to the racetrack at Le Mans.

"The idea was not only to show the people that this car could win Paris-Dakar. But doing that would also show that it's a good long-distance car."

And 14,000km (8,750miles) of dust and heat for three weeks was certainly long distance. Bott, the father of Porsche's four-wheel-drive efforts, had seriously understated.

"We learned a lot. Of course we learned that four-wheel-drive is much better in sand and conditions like this than two-wheel-driven cars....

"I have had a four-wheel-drive car, the development 911 car known as C-20, since 1981. And every year it was a better car, improved. I had to send my car to Africa for the practice. Because now it was the oldest.

"We were in the Sahara together with Jacky Ickx. After the second day, one of the front axles broke. So what to do? The only thing to do is take out these two front axles and to drive as a rear-wheel car to the next stop. And that was really a key thing.

"Because, with four-wheel-drive, the car handling was perfect. You could exactly drive between the dunes. Left and right, allowing only 15 centimeters clearance. And then, when it became the rear-driven car, we had to allow 2 meters left and right. The center of gravity moved around all the

time on the sand; to correct the car was very difficult. A good driver could do it but....

"So the next day, we got by aircraft the front axles and again the car ran perfectly. Jacky Ickx could position the car very much more precisely, very much faster. We discussed it there.

"We thought, if a car is so much better under such bad conditions, then you must feel it on the dry road!"

Bott looked around. At home, in retirement in the Swabischer Alps in southeastern Germany, he was a long way from the Sahara. But his Alps got snow. And rain. And mud.

"And you do feel it. Your slip is the same on four wheels. Your tire friction is less if you have four wheels driving. Your tire wear is better if you have the differential or intelligent clutch in the middle. So many advantages. The only disadvantage is more

weight." Bott shrugged and smiled. The weight was a compromise, a trade-off easily made for the increased traction and safety.

"We went to the desert because it was the only race at the time where all the regulations were free, unlimited. You could do anything. And what we had to test.... Not only was it mechanical, but so much electronics...."

"That was the problem," Bott recalled. "To show the people, without changing the concept, this car, this 911, is capable of completely different things."

The year 1984 brought the development project known as the 911 four-wheel drive, Typ 953. Production 911 Carrera bodies were used as the starting point for assembly, complete with the big flat Carrera wing. In keeping with the philosophy of the racing department, steel panels—front and rear deck lids and doors—were replaced with

Twenty 911 SC/RS cars were built to Group B regulations for the European Rally series. Rothmans had six team cars, rebuilt at Silverstone, England, by David Richards. Homologation weight was 960kg (2,112lb). The 2994cc Typ 930/18 produced 255hp at 7000rpm. Bosch mechanical injection, redesigned cylinder heads, forged pistons, and a new cam contributed. Turbo 930 brakes were used, front calipers used all around with adjustable balance. Porsche's next step was already conceived and running, the Typ 953 four-wheel-drive.

Porsche assembled cars to stay together, David Richards rebuilt them to come apart. And after each rally, cars were taken apart, thoroughly refreshed and reassembled. Richards refabricated factory pieces for quick release. Below, the non-adjustable racing seats were bolted in place. In the mid-1980s, the competition was Peugeot's 205 Turbo 16, Ford's RS200 turbo, Audi Quattro Sport turbo, and Toyota's Turbo Celica. The Porsche benefitted from no turbo lag and, as a rear-engine car, it had a cooler interior.

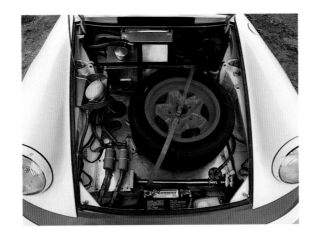

aluminum, fiberglass, or Kevlar. Side windows were plexiglass. Even a thick under-chassis skid plate was made of Kevlar and drilled to reduce weight.

Bott continued with the unequal torque split. Through a center differential, 60 percent was sent rearward, the rest to the front axles. The front limited-slip differential and the center transfer case were variable and locked manually, while the rear was full-time.

The 6th Paris-Dakar running, in 1984, was nearly 12,000km (7,500 miles), and in the end, after wrecks, rolls, and even electrical system fires, Rene Metge won it outright with Dominique Lemoyne in one of Bott's new 953s. Jacky Ickx and Claude Brasseur came 6th and Roland Kussmaul—despite status as a support vehicle, and the fact that most nights he worked all night on the other two cars while the others slept—finished 17th!

"Never before have such high technology cars been taken out into the burning desert," Roland Kussmaul commented to a magazine writer afterwards. "In such coun-

try, it would lead a normal car to total destruction. In the desert, it was our daily bread!"

For 1985, the Metge and Ickx teams competed in non-turbo Typ 959s and the third car, the support vehicle was turned over to Jochen Mass and Ekkehard Kiefer. Kussmaul, team manager that year, did not compete. For Porsche, it was a race fraught with frustration and failures: of bolts and parts and navigation. The three cars retired before the end of the 13,000km.

For 1986, Kussmaul went to the rally start as Piëch had gone to Le Mans in 1970:

equipped and supported. Porsche had three Rothmans cars, a Mercedes Gelandewagen as advance support (same as Ickx's old winner—but fitted with a 928 engine), two giant MAN team support trucks, and an airplane.

These new 959 Paris-Dakar turbos were specifically built for one purpose: to win Paris-Dakar. They made use of the electronic multi-disc viscous clutches. Under normal circumstances, these varied oil pressure between 4.75 and 19 bar, depending on the percent of engagement. These were modified to permit complete disengage-

Full-fledged 959s were entered in 1985 as Paris-Dakar was recognized as an extraordinary testing ground for a Porsche for the future. With full-time all-wheel-drive and countless computer systems aboard, the cars were more electronic than mechanical. But mechanicals failed and none of the three finished in 1985.

ment of front-drive for the high-speed stages. A marvelous program in the electronics removed oil pressure in the front-drive clutches completely during rear-drive mode. But touching the brakes would instantly boost pressure back to 19 bar to allow for the advantages of engine braking through the front axles. Kussmaul's experiences in testing dictated that braking capacities were more important even than acceleration or top speed.

Jacky Ickx, 1986 team manager, and Peter Falk adopted a new strategy based on the success in 1984 and the failure in 1985: "Go slowly where there is risk; go flat out where there is not." Flat out meant nearly 225km/h (140.6mph). The 1986 cars were virtually race-specification 959s. The engine was twin-turbocharged but single-intercooled and was detuned to 370hp.

Jacky Ickx had once said, "Give me three cars and I will win Paris-Dakar." This

was a remarkable offer. Ickx loved long-distance drives. He won Le Mans six times. But it was known he does not love the heat.

On January 1, 1986, when Porsche departed from Versailles for the start (it had been moved from Paris the previous year due to large entry and spectator numbers),

For 1986, Porsche—and Ickx—tried again with three entries, left page The modified 959s were lifted 290mm (11.4 in) above the ground and ran on special Michelin 205 x 18 tires. Between the seats, controls adjusted boost and brake balance, and shifted power between front and rear differentials. Left, Jacky Ickx's desert attack was led by fellow Belgian-René Metge to the finish in 1984 in a 911-based four-wheel-drive prototype, the Typ 953. Again, in 1986, Metge won. Below, Metge streaked to his second overall victory in this car.

Great attention was given to combatting dust. Beneath massive vents and filters, the 2.85 liter engine operated with water cooled heads. For the special stages, 449hp was on tap at 6500rpm. Top speed was geared to only 210km/h (131mph), providing startling acceleration: 0-100km/h (62.5mph) in 3.9 seconds. Right, the next time Porsche returned to Africa, it was by way of Paris. Three 911-based four-wheel-drive Typ 953s entered the 6th annual Paris-Dakar Rally in 1984, a 12,000km (7,500 miles)run to the beach in West Africa. Belgian endurance champion Jacky Ickx had promoted Porsche interest, fellow Belgian René Metge won it.

Rene Metge was again teamed with Dominique Lemoyne and Ickx codrove with Claude Brasseur. The third car was once again Ickx's secret weapon. Roland Kussmaul and Kendrick Unger, the two development engineers from Weissach, were Ickx's support personnel and were entered in the third car.

The late Thierry Sabine's diabolical rules had always required any support personnel to accompany the desert racers. Sabine was the brilliant originator of the desert march. Each night he delivered something like an evening prayer: "You'll never forget tomorrow. You'll hate me by the time the sun sets."

A huge entourage of entrants and their support vehicles left Paris for Sète, in the Camargue region of southern France, to catch a ferry to Algeria and into Africa.

Oargla, El Golea, Ain Salah, Amguid, Tamanrasset, Herouane, Agades, Bilma, Chirfa, Adrar Bous, Tahoua, Goa, Timbuktu, Nema, Tidjikdja, Kayes, Kedongou, Tambacounda, and finally to the beach at Sali Portudal, Dakar.

Helmuth Bott's goal of proving the Porsche was a good long-distance car was a challenge. He came to see the desert as the ideal test track for the next generation car. If, with all its technology and all its electronics and all its sophistication, the Rallye 959 could also win, it would mean much more than yet another Porsche Le Mans victory. And many more competitors started the 22 days of Paris-Dakar than start the 24 hours of Le Mans.

At the end of the 8th running, after ferocious storms and numerous serious injuries to competitors, the Gelandewagen had lost its gearbox on day one, and one of the two giant MAN transporters rolled, taking with it half the team spare parts. Most days, the airplane could not land anywhere close to the racers. And rally founder Thierry Sabine had died in a helicopter crash.

On January 22, when 14,000km (8,750 miles) of sand and silt, rock, mud and sun had settled, Metge fulfilled again Ickx's prediction. Out of 500 starters, out of only eighty finishers, Metge took 1st. Ickx himself came 2nd. And Kussmaul and Unger, definitely Porsche's secret weapon, finished 6th.

CHAPTER 33

1988 Typ 959 US Sport

Helmuth Bott's Jewel: The Most Capable 911

"They wanted a special show car for Frankfurt," Tony Lapine explained, *"to exhibit right alongside the winning Dakar Rally car. The car was virtually done in three months. This was definitely a design studio effort."*

Manfred Jantke was driving. He and passenger Peter Schutz, President of Porsche AG, had business in Switzerland. It was their first drive in an early prototype of the 959.

The autobahn from Weissach to Zurich goes north, then turns south from Karlsruhe. The E4 follows the Rhine river. Even that early in the morning, traffic is substantial. This is the main avenue from Frankfurt to Switzerland or eastern France. Germany's autobahn system covers 440,000km, with posted speed limits from 80 to 120km/h. In the 1990s, there remain only 7,000km of unlimited-speed road, enjoyed best in powerful, fast cars.

"On the autobahn near Freiburg, Herr Schutz said to me, 'Now, Manfred, let's see what it does. They say it exceeds 320km/h, so....'"

"Well," Jantke explained several years later, "when the President of the company says, 'Let's go!.'" Jantke's face was expressive, and wrinkled deeply telling the story.

"So I took it up to 330 kilometers on the speedometer. Very, very fast. A little bit over 200mph. At that speed we were passing trucks on only two-lane autobahns!"

At that speed, there is little time to look over to see how the passenger is feeling. Or reacting. Jantke's own reaction came quickly.

"This was one of the early cars. A very few existed only, from Mr. Bott."

Jantke lifted off the gas sharply and the car slowed hard.

"'Manfred!' Herr Schutz asked me, very nervous. 'What's wrong?'

"'Herr Schutz,' I said, 'I am driving with the President of the company. We are driving 330km/h. We are in one of Mr. Bott's jewels. Imagine my responsibility if something happens....

"'We can always get another President. But what would I tell Mr. Bott?'"

These days, Professor Dr. Ing. Helmuth Bott and Anatole Lapine both look like mature versions of earlier photographs. Bott has, if anything, slimmed in his retirement, and his hair has silvered. Lapine in his retirement has foresworn the beard of his youth.

Their 959 is a mature version of their earlier cars, too. Both speak of their brightest offspring with parental pride. Bott's "jewel" was also Lapine's. Yet, Bott, the professor, discusses the 959 more as one parent to another. Lapine, the designer, has become Socrates, probing visitors in an intellectual give-and-take to exact from the questioner the answers to his own questions.

"I am really very close to this car," Helmuth Bott said. "My racing engineers wanted to do a mid-engine car, a car on the 914 base, and make a race car, as a Group B car." He shook his head. "And I was fighting against them. We do so many mid-engine cars. We cannot learn anything."

Bott, as Porsche board member for Research and Development, was also uncertain there would even be serious competition in Group B. To homologate, there must be 200 examples, which would generate a considerable expense even if Porsche could sell them. But could it sell a car for which there was no racing competition?

"If we have to build a car 200 times, we can also build it 1,000 times. It would actually be expedient to build this and have customer feedback!" Bott recalled this concept with excitement and with fondness.

On January 21, 1983, Helmuth Bott gave birth to the Typ 959, deciding to follow as engineering parameters the FIA specifications for Group B: the new car had to follow the silhouette of the production car but there was virtually no restriction to mechanical modification. "Do you know," Lapine asked, "what the assignment was? It was to 'improve' the 911. What does that allow us to do? Do we remember tradition? Or can we step beyond?"

"Let's take," Helmuth Bott began, "all the knowledge from today into the car...to see what happens. In my mind, I would take this car into the future. Let's see if there is anything against our building this car for the next ten, fifteen years...."

"There is really a very big love from our customers for this 911. If we do a Group B car, let's look at what's the future of the 911? Let's see if there's anything *against* our building this car for the next ten, fifteen years."

Bott smiled and paused. Surrounding him on the sun porch of his summer home in the Swabischer Alps were all the mementoes of his years at Porsche. Wind-tunnel models of the 917 long tail hung alongside scale models of 956. Photos of him mounting test equipment on Dan Gurney's Formula 1 car hung alongside photos of Bott testing the 959 in northern Canada's frozen wilderness.

"Let's take," he began again, "all the knowledge from today into the car to see what happens. Let's take a very powerful engine to see the limits of the chassis and roadholding and the four-wheel drive system.... You see, it was a goal, a task much greater than to build a race car.

"In my mind, I would take *this* car into the future. We had an engine with nearly 700hp in the 961 race version, at Le Mans. We could try the two-clutches gearbox to test its capability into the future...to take everything we could learn from electronics...."

Bott stopped and looked out the window, remembering a glimpse of the future from a long time ago.

"There are so many possibilities with electronics. I am sorry not to be ten or fifteen years younger." He smiled and turned back. "I knew a Mr. Fubilli, the head of IBM technic in the sixties. He wanted to bring the

computer into the car. He knew it could do so many possibilities. We came together, did a lot of planning. But in the end, after he heard how much money we had, he said 'Stop! Stop this project! That is not enough money for IBM!'" Bott laughed.

"But this was because, at the time, the computer had to stay at 22 to 25 degrees Celsius, with so many other considerations." He laughed again. "And we, of course, had a car. Bumping and jumping. Minus 40 degrees. Plus 50 degrees. And this computer wouldn't even *fit* in the car....

"So, now, with all the new inventions from outside, it is possible to take all the new things we could learn to make this car better—as an experimental car.

"With Porsche, we cannot walk above the ground, always looking twenty, thirty years ahead. Things change so quickly, so completely. We are small, we must keep our feet on the ground, thinking over things that we *can* fulfill. Instead, we look ten years ahead. What's possible in ten years we fulfill in two years and end up eight years ahead of the others."

Helmuth Bott had joined Porsche in 1952, the same year Tony Lapine joined General Motors. But it was in 1969 that Lapine, after 13 1/2 years in Detroit and four with GM's Opel in Russelsheim, joined Porsche. Years before, seeing his first 356 in Hamburg, he was struck by what he saw and what he couldn't believe.

"The engine was where it couldn't possibly be," Lapine said. His tone of voice was reverential. He could have been as easily discussing his first kiss. "Especially with two jump seats in the back and the fastback coming down. An engine, 1300cc, sufficient to hurl the car along at 185km/h. There it was, a lovely solution, a beautiful answer to a question.... 'What should a car be *if* I do not have to carry an excess amount of people, luggage?'"

Joining Porsche, Lapine inherited luggage: a design legacy. "From Komenda, from Butzi? Certainly. Definitely. Absolutely. I understood my job as being the custodian of the tradition. I may improve on it but I may not change it. Changing is easy. Improving on it is harder, much harder.

"The elements, too, I inherited. The tradi-

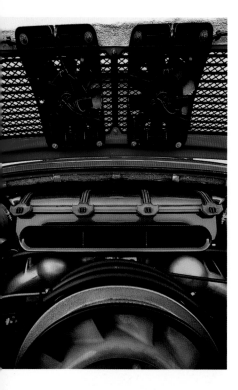

From his earliest days with Porsche, Bott had followed his interest in tire technology. Tires which could be run safely while flat, wheels that monitored tire pressure—and perhaps even carried reservoirs to reinflate low-pressure tires—were Bott's goals for his car of the future. To meet Group B regulations, the engine could be no more than 4.0 liters displacement with the turbo multiplier. The 935/77 and 935/78 at 2.85 liters conformed. For racing purposes, 600+hp could be relied on, but for street tractability, 450hp was deemed more practical, reached at 6500rpm.

tional design characteristics. Porsche cars are expected to last in the marketplace for a model run of at least twenty years." Lapine laughed as he thought of contrasts.

"In America, I could do every three years a new car. If I make a mistake this time, I can correct it quickly. And yet, for Porsche, it was reasonably easy. You had the main characteristics from your tradition."

Lapine smiled. As chief of the Design Studio, the elements of the Porsche tradition had become so much a part of his aesthetic life, it was like looking at an old family reunion photograph and recognizing everyone. "All Porsches had smooth hoods. We have always had large wheels. It fills that space, gives it purpose. It finishes that side profile. That organic shape. It was something we found. We didn't invent it.

"Now, it's all in a 'book,' you know? When you start a project, you get an assignment book. 'This car, when finished, will weigh x-amount of kilograms, will have this power-to-weight ratio, these aerodynamic qualities, cornering speeds, the following braking values.'

"And then the compromises begin. Hundreds! To make it all work." Lapine, relaxed now, sat in his living room in Baden-Baden, on the far side of the Black Forest from Weissach. The room, spare of furniture, was filled with fine art and audio equipment. The distance through the forest to his old office elongated, clarified the perspective. Reassessed the compromises.

"They wanted a special show car for

Frankfurt to exhibit right along side the winning Dakar rally car. The car was virtually done in three months. Literally burning the midnight oil....

"That was definitely a Design Studio effort. And when the car came back, they said 'Now we build 200 cars!' We said, 'Wait, if you build 200, give us more reasonable time to do the car! I mean, the two sides of the car weren't even the same!" Lapine laughed.

"But since you can't see both sides at the same time....

"The cars for production were redone. The uninitiated couldn't tell. But we knew. *Every* surface was different.

"Do you know what that assignment was?" Lapine asked rhetorically. "It was to 'improve the 911.'" Lapine paused, the next question forming in his mind. "What does that allow us to do? Can we change every surface? Or only refine? Do we remember tradition? Or can we step beyond?

"If I could have complete freedom? Without limits? A whole new car! But again, it would have appeared 'in the tradition.' What does that allow different from what was done?

"OK: outside sheet metal costs money. But we could have new front fenders. Hood could stay what it was—flat, the 'tradition'—but it got raised! Same hinge point, but raised. To accommodate a better line into the bumper. Not so severe! And of course, rear bumpers and the integrated spoiler...."

He looked away, let his voice trail off. He came back. "Had they allowed us to go into the roof...." He smiled again, forcing thought, imagination. "You maybe can have a little bit less departure angle for the top that would give a little bit more headroom for the occasional rear passenger. And you can improve aero and you can improve...."

"These are gentle departures. You look and you still know exactly what it is. Yet it is better. And if you look carefully you also know *that* too." Lapine edged forward.

"Naturally, we would like to have done more. Something completely original. But you have to deliver something within a very short time. The assignment reads that way, too."

Back at Weissach, Manfred Jantke turned in his seat. He looked out the window, then turned back, his face a broad smile of memory. "We took two of the 959s down to Switzerland for a demonstration. It was wintertime, and we had pure ice.

"But the 959 has its own tire size. The tire people had no snow tire in 17 inch size, and no mold. But they said they could make the same tire with different compounds, for the cold.

"These tires were incredible! Identical looking! But we could drive on ice. Well, you couldn't believe we could drive so fast!

His eyes squinted tightly. "We had rented an airfield. The whole thing was surrounded by snow walls. In a way, this was a safe arena, about 2 kilometers long. So we could play around.

"We drove on the airfield ice all morning. One after another. Journalists, owners, passengers. We did the same thing. Accelerate fast up to 220km/h (137.5mph). On pure ice. Then we go down, get hard on the brakes, and turn around. It was in the shade, it was *so* cold. In a deep valley. We stopped for lunch.

"After lunch, with the next passenger, we accelerated. Up to 220. Hit the brakes. It didn't slow down at all. The car was flying, really fast.

"This passenger did some rallying. As a driver. He knew. 'We're not going to make it, are we?'

"These snow walls were just very high. Very high. This snow can be as hard as ice. I didn't know. What was behind it? Or under it? A building? An airplane?"

Jantke's face relaxed. Then, as now, there was a moment of philosophical awareness, a realization and categorization of possibilities. "I could make my choice. How would I like to hit? The car still seemed to steer. The car could turn but it wouldn't slow....

"We went right in with the nose.... Sideways, how hard would we have hit? I made the right decision.

"What had happened, it was a valley. At lunchtime, the sun came. At the little part where we braked down, it was in the sun. It became wet, slippery.

"And when you expect braking, decel-

eration, and it doesn't happen, you have the feeling the thing is picking up speed even.

"The 959 has a covered undercarriage. We went straight into the snow. And the 959 went up!"

Jantke gestured like a ski jumper.

"And it came down." Jantke gestured the worst nightmare of a ski jumper.

"And we just sat there. Pure luck. If it was ice, we would have crashed tremendously. If there was a building...tremendous crash. But nearly nothing happened. Only, we couldn't get out of the car!

"We landed, sunk to the doors. It took a huge truck, with three axles, a plow, and chains to pulls us out. And the car was OK. We continued for the rest of the day."

The words of Helmuth Bott came back again.

"That was the problem. To show the people, without changing the concept, this car, this 911, is capable of completely different things."

The body was Kevlar, the suspension was active, the transmission was six speeds, the production was 229 (including prototypes), the price was 430,000DM. The objective was Helmuth Bott's: "To show the people, without changing the concept, this car, the 911, is capable of completely different things...."

CHAPTER 34

1989 911 Speedster

Classic Redux Thirty Years On

It took thirty years, a generation, from the end of the classic Speedster to the debut of its revival. Porsche President Peter Schutz met development chief Helmuth Bott and together they approached Tony Lapine, head of design. It was not a hard sell.

"The original plan was to provoke corporate management. Harley Earl always wanted to provoke them. It was something I learned from him. To provoke management."

Tony Lapine was dead serious. He didn't laugh. But he didn't mean "provoke" in a confrontation sense. Well, slightly confrontational.

Harley Earl wanted to make GM management think about what was possible. If he had to confront them with someone else's idea, show them something else already done by competition, well, as long as it forced them to think....

"We," Lapine brought the conversation back to more recent times, "were allowed to *think* of maybe a slight rework, of maybe a minor modification of the panel...to think of maybe a new windshield....

"Because anything more will cost money...."

For Lapine and his forty-three Porsche designers, the 356 Speedster was an object of reverence, not a matter for confrontation. Pictures of the early Speedster outnumbered Porsche's other production models on the wall space in the design studios. It was a source of inspiration.

"On the 356, they were better off," Lapine suggested. "They had greater freedom. They could come in on the length. They could change major structural pieces.

"We would like to have done more. Done something completely original. New." Lapine's voice trailed off. Memories.

Shortly after Peter Schutz arrived at Porsche AG in January 1981, he quickly befriended development chief Helmuth Bott. Bott routinely pulled open his desk drawer and showed Schutz the ideas that had been there for a while.

Bott had been curious about the future of the 911. Schutz listened. All-wheel-drive? A true cabriolet? These were ideas that had shifted around in Bott's desk.

Bott continued. He admired Porsche's Speedster, he explained. Promoted as a automotive marketing project in the late 1950s by Max Hoffmann and John von Neumann, Bott thought the timing and the circumstances were right for another look.

Back in 1965, at the same time Peter Schutz had been assigned to the development of Caterpillar's diesel truck engine for use by Ford, F. A. Porsche had begun working to develop an open version of his new 911.

Butzi Porsche had preferred to begin from a fresh lump of clay. He believed convertibles looked best when born of notchback coupe styling rather than from modifying a sliced off fastback. But as the company's open cars had not yet accounted for much more than a quarter of total sales, Porsche's concept for a new car was overruled.

The first results with a cutting torch yielded disaster. Styling and appearance were fine. The amount of support that came from the fixed roof was underestimated. Even doubling the floorpan was barely sufficient to eliminate a dangerous amount of torsional flex. While the car had visual appeal, it could not go around a corner.

F. A. Porsche's solution to the flex problem was hailed as a brilliant idea. For Porsche, it was also supremely logical: form follows function. While a rollbar offered protection in race cars, it also enhanced their

Lapine's designers produced two prototypes, named after the instigators, and from each one came elements of the final version: the Bott Speedster developed the rear covering, the "camel humps", the Schutz Speedster lowered the windshield and adopted the 930 Turbo flared wheel arches. Left, the times change but tachometer redlines and speedometer maximums carry on. From four cylinders and four speeds to six cylinders and five speeds, the differences are vast, but the similarities numerous. Below left, faithful to John von Neumann's original concept, the electric luxuries were deleted from standard equipment. But faithful to the original, anything and everything was optional.

chassis stiffness. The public's perception would enhance the sports-car identity of Porsche's new open car.

Reaction was mixed. Porsche had fitted a brushed-steel covering over the integrated rollbar. The bar and its function were too obvious for some. There was animated discussion about camouflaging the "compromise" by painting it in body color—like the bumpers, another functional, structural piece—rather than highlighting it as was its function.

Butzi Porsche prevailed. As he knew, people listened to him, and accepted what he said. He attributed it to being the boss' son. As likely was a reluctant recognition that he was right.

The solution not only provided chassis stiffness. It took a large step to eliminating the designer's other concern with open cars—the billowing of the soft top at high speed. By reducing its length and supporting it in the middle with the rigid rollbar

For 1956: four cylinders, 1582cc, 75hp at 5000rpm, 835kg (1,837lb), 168km/h (105mph) top speed, $3,495. Total production: 3,820 (approximately).
Far right, for 1989: six cylinders, 3164cc, 214hp at 5900rpm, 1,259kg (2,769.8lb), 238km/h (148.75mph) top speed, $65,480. Total production: 2,100 (approximately).

Tony Lapine:
"You had a living legend presiding at a meeting. If you wanted to know what a Porsche was all about, you could ask the source."

bodywork, there was less of an expanse subject to the wind.

The car was introduced at the Frankfurt Auto Show in October 1965. It had been named in a meeting with its critics and its advocates. Evi Butz, Huschke von Hanstein's capable assistant in press operations, was by then press chief. The Baron was devoting his full attentions to the racing operations. Butz reminded the group of the firm's homage to the Mexican race, Carrera , when it named the 356 models with Ernst Fuhrmann's special engine. She suggested similar attention to another region of Porsche's success, in Sicily.

In Italian, "Targa" means "trophy," and the Targa Florio was named for the race originator, Vincenzo Florio. The races had been clear Porsche successes.... Porsche's new open 911 was named.

The Targa took Porsche open-car sales to new levels. Calling it successful would not be quite adequate.

But calling its success complete would not be quite accurate. Always, in the background, the interest in a true open Porsche simmered. It would sell well but it would need expensive development work. Porsche's economy—the costly racing ventures in the late 1960s, followed by the changes in managements, and the world's economy—all kept the true open Porsche on a back burner, simmering only.

Sixteen years later, the stew pot was served. It was as startling a concoction as F. A. Porsche's Targa had been.

With a blessing from Ferry Porsche, the vehicle that would introduce this new inno-

vation to the public was begun.

Ferry Porsche once explained his father's belief: the birth of any new car should take no longer than the birth of a new child. With the blessing came the obligation. During a hasty seven-month gestation, Schutz and Bott conceived and gave birth to Porsche's first all-wheel-drive show car—which appeared under the skin of Porsche's first completely open car in eighteen years.

Viewers at the Frankfurt Show in October 1981 clustered six and eight deep. They stared, took pictures, stared, peeked under it, examined the reflection in the mirror tiles showing its all-wheel-drive mechanical parts, and stared again.

Where sales of the Targa eventually had become brisk, the show reaction to the Cabrio—with or without its all-wheel-drive—made it clear that production was necessary. Chassis modifications that let Fuhrmann's turbos handle the power and torque were most of what was needed to handle a 911 Carrera's power in an open car. A few additional points were stiffened and during the summer of 1982, the first production 911 Cabriolets were delivered. And soon after, Peter Schutz returned to Weissach to visit Helmuth Bott.

"Do you remember, Herr Schutz, the Speedster?"

It was time to visit Tony Lapine again.

By then, a styling study already existed in Lapine's studios. In 1:5 scale, it showed a 911 Carrera Speedster that strongly resembled the 356. But the same cost constraints that had stopped Butzi Porsche from making a new notchback body for the 1966 cabrio-

let caught Lapine. Budgets could be stretched to experiment in small ways.

"But, you have to remember," Lapine chastised the listener, "we had to deliver something original in a very short time. This assignment read that way!"

The birth of a new car should take no longer than the birth of a new child.

Design parameters were specific. They paralleled the first speedster: Low weight by omission of luxury features. Open above the doorsill. Handling comparable to the coupe. Driving output comparable to the coupe. Bodywork modifications or adaptations possible. Competition suitability.

Eliminating the "luxury features" took out electric window lifts, electric seat recliners, and an electrically operated convertible top. It saved nearly 70kg (154lb) beyond what removing the top took away.

Two prototypes were built, nicknamed after the two proponents. The Schutz Speedster was a more rounded cabriolet with a low windscreen. It incorporated the

Turbo's swollen rear fenders. The Bott prototype introduced the rear covering with a "camel hump" but retained the 911 Carrera fenderlines. The windscreen wrapped all the way around to the hump. A philosophy emerged. It suggested this car, like the original Speedster, was cut from purist cloth. Did it even need a top?

By the time of its introduction in 1987, again at Frankfurt, the Bott and the Schutz Speedster had been homogenized. An edition of 2,100 was allowed. And then, as quickly as it came, it was gone. Introduced at 110,000DM, it sold out.

During assembly, secrecy had prevailed. To some in Weissach, this new project resembled the commando team mentality that Ernst Fuhrmann had initiated with the 936. No one was to know.

Speedster "teams" were assembled. Whenever possible, these teams included the older craftsmen, mechanics, body men, and upholsterers who had produced the first 356 Speedster more than 30 years ago.

This project was conceived and executed in secrecy. Yet the factory, still filled with master craftsmen from Reutter Karrosserie, which built the first generation Speedsters, gathered them together again to build the new cars.

Technical Notes

By Kerry Morse

Sharp-eyed enthusiasts will notice that this data differs from listings in other books. It became obvious while researching and checking this area that there were discrepancies that had to be resolved. I put this question to the person whose books are accepted—and rightly so—as the definitive works on the history of Porsche: Paul Frère.

In describing to him the variations I had found over the years in press releases, magazine articles, automotive books, and the factory files, I expressed a frustration in trying to get correct and accurate information. He listened and stated that when writing such a book, you have to work with what they will give you and where you are allowed access.

The following technical specifications are a result of much work. They are, simply, the latest ones available.

There have been many people who have been of great help and have provided much inspiration that I would like to thank in this space:

At Porsche AG (past and present): Jurgen Barth, rally driver, LeMans winner, golfer, the guy with the beard. Norbert Singer, perhaps the greatest racing sports car engineer of his time—to understand his story is to understand what Le Mans is all about. Eugen Kolb, from the 906LM Wagen to the 962C—wanna fly down Mulsanne? Also Tony Lapine, GM's loss was Porsche's gain, automotive culture would never be the same. Gaby Sturm, former press secretary to Manfred Jantke and the late Klaus Reichert—a true company loyalist. Bernd Mueller and Dagmar Rechkemmer, the backbone of Kundensport for many years.

There are others: Bill Oursler (drinking buddy and writer); John Dinkel (editor and baseball coach); Len Frank (storyteller and opinion deliverer); Steve Earle, (driver, historian, and benevolent dictator); Leah J. G. Moya (a lot of race cars are here because of her); Chris Parsons (founder of OSCAR and responsible for the great races of Group C); Mark Cole (also of OSCAR—remember all the WSPC races on ESPN?); Maggie Logan (race photographer and connoisseuse of all things visual); John Wyer (was and always will be the greatest even while gone but not forgotten); Carl Thompson (who knows more about racing parts than anyone on the planet); Betty Jo Turner (the best editor a "club rag" could possibly have); John Frankenheimer (who explained to me what can be done with a camera); Robert Palmer (who taught me about words and their effect); Gerry Sutterfield (who has owned everything we all want); and Vic Elford (who is my choice for greatest driver, ever).

And fortunately, still others: Steve Sailors, Hans Lapine, Debbie Donovan, Gary Emory, Hal Thoms, Dave Minkler, Heather Adams, Arnold Getty, Mark Bartosh, Simon Leach, Jim Tidwell, Jan Lapine, Simone Barth. David Seibert, William Overgard, Gustav Nitsche, Helmut Greiner, Francois Duret, Richard Reventlow, Gerard Larrousse, Vern Schuppan, Bob Siedemann, Susann Miller, and Arnold Wagner.

Last but certainly not least: my wife Nicki who never complains about the weird hours I keep, and my two sons Bryan and Robin. I will always remember the start of the 1988 24 Hours of Le Mans, which was broadcast live on television. Bryan, six years old at the time, said, "Aw Dad, it's just another race."

Specifications

Model:	**1949 Gmünd coupe** Seventeenth coupe produced	**1951 356 Cabriolet RHD** First right-hand-drive cabriolet	**1952 Typ 540** **America Roadster** First instance of outside market dictating product	**1955 Continental Coupe** Coupe model designated for US market. Available with 1500 Normal or 1500 Super engine
Engine:	Typ VW 369	Typ 506	Typ 528	Typ 528/2
Configuration & displacement:	Flat four, 1131cc	Flat four, 1286cc	Flat four, 1488cc	Flat four, 1488cc
Bore & stroke:	75 x 64mm	80 x 64mm	80 x 74mm	80 x 74mm
Fuel delivery system:	2 Solex 26 VFI	2 Solex 32PBI	2 Solex 40 PBIC	Solex 40PBIC
Horsepower @ rpm:	40 @ 4000rpm	44 @ 4200rpm	70 @ 5000rpm	70 @ 5000rpm
Torque @ rpm:	52 @ 3300rpm	52 @ 2800rpm	80 @ 3600rpm	80 @ 3600rpm
Compression ratio:	6.5:1	8.2:1	NA	8.2:1
Transmission:	Typ VW	Typ VW	Typ 519/2	Typ 519
Type & gears:	4 + Reverse	4 + Reverse	4 + Reverse	4 + Reverse
Final drive; limited slip:	NA	4.43:1	NA	NA
Chassis:				
Material:	Steel	Steel	Steel	Steel
Wheelbase:	2100mm	2100mm	2100mm	2100mm
Length overall:	3860mm	3880mm	3880mm	3950mm
Width:	1665mm	1666mm	1640mm	1671mm
Height:	1300mm	1300mm	1100mm	1311mm
Weight:	780kg	810kg	705kg road; 605kg competition	873kg
Body:	Porsche		Glaser (Heuer); 1 by Drauz	Reutter
Configuration:	2 door, 2 seat coupe	2 door, 2+2 seating, cabriolet	2 seat, 2 door roadster	2 door, 2 seat coupe
Material:	Aluminum	Steel	Aluminum	Steel
Performance:				
0-100km/h (0-62.5mph):	NA	NA	9.3sec	12.7sec
Top speed:	140km/h (87.5mph)	150km/h (94mph)	170km/h (106.3mph)	162km/h (101mph
Production:	Approx. 58	NA	17 in two styles	NA
Original price:	15,000 Swiss francs ($3,750)	Approx: 12,200 DM; £2,300 at the show ($3,935)	14,260 DM ($4,600)	$4,782 with options, including $500 for S engine

Model:	1956 356A Carrera GS Right-hand drive	1959 356A Carrera GS-GT	1955 550/1500RS Spyder This example, 550-0090, was the last produced	1957 Sauter Bergspyder
Engine:	Typ 547/1	Typ 692/3	Typ 547/1	Typ 547/1
Configuration & displacement:	Flat four, 1498cc	Flat four, 1587cc	Flat four, 1498cc	Flat four, 1498cc
Bore & stroke:	85 x 66mm	87.5 x 66mm	85 x 66mm	85 x 66mm
Fuel delivery system:	Solex 40 P11-4	Weber DCM3	2 2V Solex 40 P11-4	2 Solex 40 P11
Horsepower @ rpm:	100 @ 6200rpm	115 @ 6500rpm	110 @ 6200rpm	100 @ 6200rpm
Torque @ rpm:	87 @ 5200rpm	NA	96 @ 5300rpm	87 @ 5200rpm
Compression ratio:	9.0:1	9.8:1	9.5:1	9.0:1
Transmission:	Typ 644	Typ 716/4	Typ 718	Typ 741/1
Type & gears:	4 + Reverse	4 + Reverse	5 + Reverse	4 + Reverse
Final drive; limited slip:	4.428:1	NA	4.857	NA
Chassis:	Platform chassis and floorpan	Platform chassis and floorpan	Welded tube	Tubular space frame
Material:	Steel	Steel	Steel	Aluminum
Wheelbase:	2100mm	2100mm	2100mm	2140mm
Length overall:	3950mm	3950mm	3600mm	3700mm
Width:	1671mm	1671mm	1552mm	1500mm
Height:	1311mm	1311mm	1016mm	920mm (top of windscreen)
Weight:	NA	835kg	590kg	550kg
Body:	Reutter	Reutter	Wendler	Sauter
Configuration:	2 door, 2 seat	2 door, 2 seat	2 seat race car	2 seat, 2 door hillclimb spyder
Material:	Steel	Steel	Aluminum	Aluminum
Performance:				
0-100km/h (0-62.5mph):	11.3sec	9.8sec	7.2sec (4.85:1 final)	NA
Top speed:	200km/h (125mph)	225km/h (140mph)	205-255kmh (128-159mph)	200km/h (125.0mph)
Production:	Approx. 12 rhd 1956-1959	NA	90	1 w/ Carrera engine, 1 w/ 1100
Original price:	18,500 DM	NA	24,600 DM ($6,150)	20,000 Swiss francs ($6,100)

Model:	1957 356A 1500 GS Carrera Speedster	1958 Typ 718 RSK One of six built as customer cars with optional center seating and steering	1959 Beutler Cabriolet Custom body built for German royalty	1961 718 RS60 Factory team car, chassis 718-044; only car to run with 2.0 liter engine
Engine:	Typ 547/1	Typ 547/3	Typ 616/1	Typ 587/3
Configuration & displacement:	Flat four; 1498cc	Flat four, 1498cc	Flat four, 1582cc	Flat four, 1966cc
Bore & stroke:	85.0 x 66.0mm	85 x 66mm	82.5 x 74mm	NA
Fuel delivery system:	2 2V Solex 40 P11	Weber 46 IDM	2 2V Zenith NDIX 32	2 Weber 46 IDM
Horsepower @ rpm:	110 @ 6400rpm	148 @ 8000rpm	60 @ 4500rpm	185 @ 7200rpm
Torque @ rpm:	91 @ 5200rpm	108 @ 6300rpm	81 @ 2800rpm	156 @ 5000rpm
Compression ratio:	9.0:1	10.0:1	7.5:1	9.8:1
Transmission:	Typ 741/1	Typ 718	Typ 716	Typ 718
Type & gears:	4 + Reverse	5 + Reverse	4 + Reverse	5 + Reverse
Final drive; limited slip:	4.428	4.428	4.43	4.428
Chassis:				
Material:	Steel	Steel	Steel	Steel
Wheelbase:	2100mm	2100mm	2350mm (stretched 250mm)	2100mm
Length overall:	3950mm	3600mm	4300mm	3600mm
Width:	1670mm	1511mm	1651mm	1511mm
Height:	1220mm	889mm	1396mm (top up)	980mm
Weight:	815kg	530kg	920kg	590kg
Body:	Reutter	Wendler	Beutler	Wendler
Configuration:	"Speedster"	2 seat open	Special 4 seat cabriolet	2 seat spyder
Material:	Aluminum doors, front head, and rear deck lid	Aluminum	Aluminum	Aluminum
Performance:				
0-100km/h (0-62.5mph):	11.1sec	NA	14.9sec	NA
Top speed:	200km/h (125mph)	NA	158km/h (99mph)	269km/h (168.1mph)
Production:	NA	6	1	NA
Original price:	$5,266 (Carrera GS) FOB New York	Werks racing car	26,000 Swiss Francs ($8,390)	Werks race car

Model:	1960 356B 1600 Abarth Carrera GTL	1962 Typ 804	1965 904 Carrera GTS Final development stage of first fiberglass race car; development car for 906	1965 Typ 904/8 Bergspyder 2nd 1965 Targa Florio; one of first *Kanguruhs*, #906-007
Engine:	Typ 692/3A	Typ 753	Typ 901/20	Typ 771
Configuration & displacement:	Flat four, 1587cc	Flat eight, 1494cc	Flat six, 1991cc	Flat eight; 1991cc
Bore & stroke:	87.5 x 66mm	66 x 54.6mm	80 x 66mm	76 x 54.6mm
Fuel delivery system:	Weber 40 DCM 2	4 Weber 38IDF	2 Weber 46 IDA 3 C	4 Weber 48 IDF
Horsepower @ rpm:	135 @ 7300rpm	180 @ 9200rpm	210 @ 8000rpm	240 @ 8500rpm
Torque @ rpm:	93 @ 5500rpm	113 @ 7200rpm	144 @ 6000rpm	152 @ 7500rpm
Compression ratio:	9.8:1	10.0:1	10.3:1	10.4:1
Transmission:	Typ 741/5	Typ 718	Typ 904/01	Typ 822
Type & gears:	4 + Reverse	6 + Reverse	5 + Reverse	5 + Reverse
Final drive; limited slip:	4.428	NA	4.428	4.40:1
Chassis:	Platform unit body	Tubular space frame	Welded box members	Sheet, 904-based
Material:	Steel	Steel	Steel	Steel
Wheelbase:	2100mm	2300mm	2300mm	2300mm
Length overall:	3980mm	3600mm	4090mm	3302mm
Width:	1671mm	840mm	1542mm	1499mm
Height:	1221mm	800mm	1067mm	915mm
Weight:	778kg	455kg	640kg	570kg
Body:	Abarth/Zagato	Porsche	Heinkel	Porsche
Configuration:	2 seat, 2 door racing coupe	1 seat	2 door, 2 seat race car	2 seat open hillclimb car
Material:	Aluminum	Aluminum, with some fiberglass panels	Fiberglass. Body weighed 149.7kg; frame 53.9kg	Fiberglass
Performance:				
0-100km/h (0-62.5mph):	NA	NA	5.5sec	4.8sec
Top speed:	225km/h (140mph)	270km/h (168.75mph)	252km/h (157.5mph)	240km/h as fitted (150mph)
Production:	21	4	Uncertain number of Werks 904s were built for 6- and 8-cylinder competition	5 in various body styles
Original price:	Approx. $6,000	Werks racing car		Werks racing car

Model:	1967 911R	1966 911 Bertone Roadster	1967 Typ 907 Porsche's first right-hand-drive racing car	1969 908LH
Engine:	Typ 901/22	Typ 901/01	Typ 771/1	Typ 908
Configuration & displacement:	Flat six, 1991cc	Flat six, 1911cc	Flat eight, 2195cc	Flat eight, 2921cc
Bore & stroke:	80 x 66mm	80 x 66mm	80 x 54.6mm	85 x 66mm
Fuel delivery system:	2 Weber 46IDA3C	Weber	Bosch mechanical injection	Bosch mechanical injection
Horsepower @ rpm:	210 @ 9000rpm	130 @ 6100rpm	270 @ 8600rpm	350 @ 8400rpm
Torque @ rpm:	152 @ 6800rpm	130 @ 4200rpm	170 A 7000rpm	235 @ 6600rpm
Compression ratio:	10.3:1	NA	10.2:1	10.4:1
Transmission:	Typ 901/53	Typ 901	Typ 907	Typ 916
Type & gears:	5 + Reverse	5 + Reverse	5 + Reverse	5 + Reverse
Final drive; limited slip:	NA	NA	NA	NA
Chassis:	Standard 911	Unitary		Tube space frame
Material:	Steel	Steel	Aluminum	Aluminum
Wheelbase:	2211mm	2159mm	2300mm	2300mm
Length overall:	4163mm	3734mm	4020mm	4839mm
Width:	1610mm	1600mm	1830mm	1830mm
Height:	1280mm	1118mm	938mm	938mm
Weight:	810kg	1050kg	575kg	680kg
Body:	Porsche	Bertone	Porsche	Porsche
Configuration:	2 seat, 2 door coupe	2 door, 2 seat Roadster	2 seat, 2 place coupe	2 seat long-tail coupe
Material:	Steel, fiberglass, and aluminum	Steel	Steel	Fiberglass
Performance:				
0-100km/h (0-62.5mph):	NA	NA	NA	NA
Top speed:	250km/h (156.3mph)	NA	295km/h (184.4mph)	320km/h (200mph)
Production:	4 prototypes, production run of 20	1	NA	NA
Original price:	45,000 DM	$20,000 to build prototype plus 911 chassis	65,000 DM	Werks racing car

Model:	**1970 911ST/GT** 1970 Monte Carlo winner	**1971 Typ 916** *Sonderwunsch*	**1972 917/30** Car designed with variable wheelbase to test handling	**1973 Carrera RS** RS 2.7 liter lightweight
Engine:	Typ 911/20	Typ 911/86	Typ 912/51	Typ 911/83
Configuration & displacement:	Flat six, 2195cc	Flat six, 2341cc	Flat twelve, 4999cc	Flat six, 2687cc
Bore & stroke:	84 x 66mm	84 x 70.4mm	86.8 x 70.4mm	90 x 70.4mm
Fuel delivery system:	Bosch mechanical injection	2 Weber 46 IDA carburetors	Mech. injection/twin turbos	Bosch mechanical injection
Horsepower @ rpm:	180 @ 6500rpm	190 @ 6500rpm	1000 at 7000rpm	210 @ 6300rpm
Torque @ rpm:	148 @ 5200rpm	159 @ 5200rpm	723 at 6400rpm	188 @ 5100rpm
Compression ratio:	9.8:1	8.5:1	6.5:1	8.5:1
Transmission:	Typ 911/81	Typ 923/01	Typ 920/50	Typ 915/08
Type & gears:	5 + Reverse	5 + Reverse	4 + Reverse	5 + Reverse
Final drive; limited slip:	40% lock	4.429:1 @ 40%	NA	4.43:1
Chassis:	Reinforced 911	Reinforced standard 914	Tubular space frame	Unitary
Material:	Steel	Steel	Magnesium	Steel
Wheelbase:	2268mm	2450mm	Variable: 2316mm to 2500mm	2271mm
Length overall:	4163mm	3985mm	Variable: 3950mm to 4562mm	4102mm
Width:	1750mm	1740mm	2087mm	1652mm
Height:	1310mm	1230mm	1156mm (w/ wing and rollbar)	1320mm
Weight:	960kg	1,000kg	802kg	960kg
Body:	Porsche	Porsche	Porsche	Porsche
Configuration:	2 seat, 2 door coupe	2 seat, 2 door Targa-type	2 seat, 2 door racing spyder	2 door, 2 seat coupe
Material:	Steel, fiberglass panels, and bumpers	Steel	Fiberglass	Steel and fiberglass
Performance:				
0-100km/h (0-62.5mph):	NA	6.9sec	2.3sec	5.8sec
Top speed:	180km/h (112.5mph)	235km/h (146mph)	332km/h (207mph)	245km/h (153.1mph)
Production:	4	11 in 1971	1 with variable wheelbase	NA
Original price:	43,000 DM	40,000 DM ($12,000)	450,000 DM for standard, non-variable wheelbase	33,000 DM with M471; M472 Touring add 2,500 DM ($10,300)

Model:	**1973 Carrera RSR** RSR 2.8 liter competition car	**1976 Typ 934** Group 4 and SCCA Trans-Am specifications	**1978 935/78** Nicknamed Moby Dick	**1976 936-001** Ernst Fuhrmann's Black Widow
Engine:	Typ 911/72	Typ 930/75	Typ 935/71	Typ 911/78
Configuration & displacement:	Flat six, 2806cc	Flat six, 2993cc	Flat six, 3211cc	Flat eight, 2142cc
Bore & stroke:	92 x 70.4mm	95 x 70.4mm	95.7 x 74.4mm	83 x 66mm
Fuel delivery system:	Bosch mechanical injection	Bosch K-Jetronic w/ turbo	Bosch mech. w/ two turbos	Bosch mech. w/ turbo
Horsepower @ rpm:	308 @ 8000rpm	485 @ 7000rpm @ 1.3 bar boost	750 at 8200rpm	520 @ 8000rpm
Torque @ rpm:	217 @ 6200rpm	434 @ 5400rpm	615 at 6500rpm	347 @ 5400rpm
Compression ratio:	10.3:1	6.5:1	7.0:1	6.5:1
Transmission:	Typ 915/	Typ 930/25	Typ 930/60	Typ 917
Type & gears:	5 + Reverse	4 + Reverse	4 + Reverse	5 + Reverse
Final drive; limited slip:	4.43:1 80%	4:1 @ 80% lock	NA	NA
Chassis:	Unitary		Tubular space frame	Tubular space frame
Material:	Steel	Steel	Aluminum	Aluminum
Wheelbase:	2271mm	2269mm	2279mm	2400mm
Length overall:	4147mm	4630mm	4890mm	4250mm
Width:	1610mm	1800mm front; 1986mm rear	1990mm	1981mm
Height:	1300mm	1304mm	1200mm	1021mm with rollbar
Weight:	917kg	1,120kg	1,025kg	700kg
Body:	Porsche	Porsche	Porsche	Porsche
Configuration:	2 door, 2 seat coupe	2 seat, 2 door coupe	2 door, 2 seat long-tail coupe	2 door, 2 seat racing spyder
Material:	Steel and fiberglass	Steel, some fiberglass	Fiberglass; ultimate interpretation of FIA regulations regarding bodywork	Fiberglass
Performance:				
0-100km/h (0-62.5mph):	4.0sec	NA	2.8sec	NA
Top speed:	280km/h (175mph)	305km/h (190.6mph)	365km/h (228.1mph)	350km/h (218.75mph)
Production:	49 competition lightweights	31 (plus 10 in 1977 for IMSA)	2	3
Original price:	59,000 DM ($22,500) for M491 competition package	Introduced at 97,000 DM; sold at 108,000 DM	Werks race car	Werks race cars

Model:	1980 924 Carrera GTP	1981 924 Carrera GTS	1980 Typ 935 Indy	1982 930 Turbo Flat Nose *Sonderwunsch*
Engine:	Typ 924GTP	Typ M31/60	Typ 935/75	Typ 930/60
Configuration & displacement:	Inline four, 1984cc	Inline four, 1984cc	Flat six, 2650cc	Flat six, 3299cc
Bore & stroke:	86.5 x 84.4mm	86.5 x 84.4mm	92.3 x 66mm	97 x 74.4mm
Fuel delivery system:	Mechanical injection w/ turbo & intercooler	Mechanical injection w/ turbo & intercooler	Mechanical injection w/ single turbocharger	Bosch electronic fuel injection with turbo
Horsepower @ rpm:	375 @ 7000rpm @ 2.1 bar	245 @ 6250rpm @ 1.0 bar	630 @ 9000rpm @ 54 in. boost.	300 @ 5500rpm
Torque @ rpm:	282@ 4500rpm	247 @ 3000rpm	412 @ 6400rpm	412 @ 4000rpm
Compression ratio:	6.8:1	8.5:1	9.0:1	7.0:1
Transmission:	Typ 937/50	Typ G31/30	Typ Weismann	Typ 930/34
Type & gears:	5 + Reverse	5 + Reverse	4 + Reverse	4 + Reverse
Final drive; limited slip:	NA	4.125:1 @ 40 %	Locked	3.44:1
Chassis:	Unitized	Unitized	Parnelli monocoque	Reinforced 911, unitary
Material:	Steel	Steel	Aluminum	Steel
Wheelbase:	NA	2400mm	2654mm	2272mm
Length overall:	4254mm	4320mm	4547mm	4291mm
Width:	1849mm	1745mm	2019mm	1775mm
Height:	1198mm	1275mm	927mm	1328mm
Weight:	930kg	1,121kg	680kg	1,300kg
Body:	Porsche	Porsche	Porsche	Porsche
Configuration:	2 seat	2 seat, 2 door racing coupe	1 seat open cockpit	2 seat, 2 door coupe
Material:	NA	Steel/fiberglass/GFK plastic	Fiberglass	Steel
Performance:				
0-100km/h (0-62.5mph):	4.9sec	6.2sec	NA	5.2sec
Top speed:	288km/h (179mph)	250km/h (155mph)	347km/h (216.9mph)	260km/h (162.5mph)
Production:	6	50	4	NA
Original price:	180,000 DM	110,000 DM	Werks racing cars	930 Turbo Coupe with Flat Nose option: $59,000

Model:	1984 928 S	1986 Typ 959 Rally Car Final version, winner of 1986 Paris-Dakar Rally	1989 959 US Sport	1989 911 Carrera Speedster
Engine:	Typ M19/20	Typ 959/50	Typ 959/50	Typ 930/25
Configuration & displacement:	V-8, water-cooled, 4664cc	Flat six, 2847cc	Flat six, 2850cc	Flat six, 3164cc
Bore & stroke:	97 x 78.9mm	95 x 67mm	95 x 67mm	95 x 74.4mm
Fuel delivery system:	Bosch LH-Jetronic electronic injection	Bosch electronic injection & 2 KKK turbos w/ intercooler	Electronic injection, twin water-cooled turbochargers	Bosch LE-Jetronic injection
Horsepower @ rpm:	234 @ 5250rpm	449 @ 6500rpm	450 @ 6500rpm	214 @ 5900rpm
Torque @ rpm:	263 @ 4000rpm	372 @ 5500rpm	350 @ 5500rpm	195 @ 4800rpm
Compression ratio:	10.0:1	8.3:1	8.3:1	10.3:1
Transmission:	Typ G28/08 Manual	Typ 959/01	Typ 959/01	Typ G50.01
Type & gears:	5 + Reverse	6 + R	6 + R	5 + R
Final drive; limited slip:	2.26:1	4.125:1 w/ Variable electronic transfer case & front/rear differentials	4.125:1 into electronically controlled front/rear differentials	3.44:1
Chassis:	Unitary	Reinforced 911 chassis	Reinforced 911	Reinforced 911 unitary
Material:	Steel	NA	Steel and kevlar	Steel
Wheelbase:	2500mm	2300mm	2272mm	2273mm
Length overall:	4462mm	4320mm	4260mm	4290mm
Width:	1836mm	1780mm	1840mm	1650mm
Height:	1282mm	1490mm	1280mm	1219mm
Weight:	1,520kg	1,260kg	1,350kg	1,259kg
Body:	Porsche	Porsche	Porsche	Porsche
Configuration:	4 seat, 2 door coupe	Modified Typ 959, 2 seat coupe	2 seat, 2 door coupe	2 seat, 2 door "Speedster"
Material:	Sheet steel, aluminum fenders and hood	Kevlar-reinforced fiberglass	Steel, fiberglass, and kevlar	Steel
Performance:				
0-100km/h (0-62.5mph):	6.8sec	3.9sec	3.9sec	6.1sec
Top speed:	235km/h (147mph)	210km/h (130mph)	315km/h (195mph)	238km/h (148mph)
Production:	NA	3	200 plus 29 prototypes	2,106
Original price:	$46,000	275,000 DM	430,000 DM	$65,480

Index